Mister Moffat's Road

Stan Moore

This is a work of fiction. Any resemblance to persons living or dead is entirely coincidental. Some of the towns and establishments described do in fact exist. However, I have taken liberties with their descriptions and of locations and geographical features.

Many people have given input and criticism which has been invaluable. Particular credit goes to the final editor and cover artist, my long-patient wife, Kiki. Her opinions and judgment have helped me over many a tough stretch. Any errors are mine alone.

Design by Jack Lenzo

This book is dedicated to the people who built the railroads of the American west.

Anonymous and far from home were many men and women. They felled trees, scraped grade, laid rail, bored tunnels, cooked for others, fed and cared for animals. Their efforts were loyal, varied, and tenacious, and an unknown number gave their lives. These nameless, common people made possible the settling and industrial growth of the nation.

Contents

I

Prologue

THE HIKER SCANNED OVER SLICK ROCK, RED DOMES AND CLIFFS. She could see ancient beds of sand, once sand dunes. The layers were originally laid down a little at a time, on ancient seafloors. Nature turned those layers on their sides, bent them by pressure, and stacked one on another. Time and geological forces made them into stone. Those layers were visible everywhere. Now they were huge cliffs of sandstone hundreds of feet high. A dash of green leafs and grass told of water, an oasis. As she savored the view, she thought that this was a fine remote desert campsite.

It had been a long hard hike in. First they had driven miles off the paved highway. Then, after several tries to find it, they headed down a dirt road they wanted. It got gradually rockier and steeper, and at some point it became a four wheel drive route. You couldn't call it a road any longer. The drive down to the end of that was slow and jarring. Then the good part, the fun, started. It was time to walk. To go out, beyond the back country.

The band of friends donned their backpacks. These weren't day packs with a canteen, lunch and a jacket. Rather each was loaded with a sleeping bag and seven or eight night's worth of food, and perhaps a shared tent or stove. There was no trail, no wide and level path to walk on. This was to be a cross country journey. The car was parked at the end, or start, depending on how you look at it, of a canyon. Up the gulch the group went, picking their way, finding a route, as they went.

It was not difficult in the sense of getting lost. They simply could not leave the gorge since its sides were pretty much vertical and hundreds of feet high. There was no straight path. They had to pick their route around and through obstacles, small cliffs, big boulders, sometimes a huge cottonwood tree which had gathered debris for many decades. They had to work around waterfalls or pouroffs. About half the time that meant backtracking or climbing up into a side canyon first. Several times they had to pass packs. When too big or difficult a barrier presented itself they had to stop and find a way past it. Packs would be taken off because the cliff or gully was steep. Not impassably steep, just too steep to safely climb with a forty or fifty pound pack trying to pull the climber down. One person would work his or her way up, sometimes with ease and sometimes not. Then the packs had to be passed up. In real steep conditions they would be hauled by rope. It was a time consuming process. No one minded. After all, they had all week.

By late afternoon they had had enough fun for the day. Camp was set. As much as any night in the desert, the setting was spectacular. It was a typical dry country canyon, like so many in the slickrock country of Colorado, Utah, Arizona, and Nevada. What is now called the southwestern US. It boasted high cliffs all around and, since it was early in the season, the creek was still flowing. No one took the luxury of running water for granted. They were in a flat spot, mostly fairly level slickrock with small dunes. The space was about eighty yards long and thirty or forty yards wide. Up and downstream, the canyon narrowed to twenty five or thirty feet at both ends, with big cliffs. One side of the clearing was brushy, thorny. The other had sand banks and level rock shelves. There was room aplenty and a good campsite for all. Some opted to pitch a tent. The purists, those traveling light, made do with less. They would simply spread a space blanket and throw out a sleeping bag.

Our hiker had her camp set, tent up and her one luxury—a battery powered pump—was running to inflate an air mattress. She had an hour or so before it was time to fix dinner, if you can call noodles, tuna and dried fruit dinner. Some wouldn't call that a meal much less dinner. In any case, she decided to go explore.

Getting to the other side of the creek was not hard. It took only one largish step. There wasn't a lot of water anyway, the deep spots being only six or eight inches. Once over, the cliff wall looked worth examining. Through the brush, she was pushing branches aside and turning her head to avoid scratches. Her hope was the cliff held some kind of treasures. Maybe she would find a ruin or some rock art. Some of her friends had once hit it lucky in a similar canyon. They found shards of pottery, and back by the wall of the cliff they found an entire jug. It was mostly buried and they left it, taking pictures only. These side canyons held many surprises. Some were left by the Ancient Pueblans when they vacated the area around 1200 AD, and some older items were to be found as well.

No luck. She found no relics or other traces of inhabitants. One thing she did find, though, and was surprised by it. At one spot near the cliff she could hear two friends talking. It sounded as if they were right next to her; she heard every word, their tone of voice, inflections, made out the slang, all crystal clear. The conversation was as understandable as if they were only two feet away. But they were not. She looked over at camp and saw that they were about fifty yards away.

This is interesting, she thought. Out of curiosity, she took a step, moving about a foot to her right. The clear sounding words disappeared and all she got was muffled voices to be expected from a distance. Her two steps to the left gave the same results. But when she stepped back to the exact original spot, the talk was again loud and clear. She was curious but not upset or spooked by this.

The structure of the canyon and the nature of the sound waves made this unusual phenomenon possible. What she had here was this: Sound waves affected by the warp and weft, the texture and makeup, of the rock walls. This spot she stood at was in fact a portal to a space time warp.

The term "space time warp" sounds grandiose, technical, nerdy. Kind of dangerous. Some warps are, some are not. This one was small and not broad banded. It delivered just sound and that only a short distance. This particular one simply made cross canyon conversation sound close up. And it did not warp or bend other forms of energy or matter. Time, light, gravity, atomic structure, the universe itself, none of those were affected by this warp. It was just one of the many small, enjoyable quirks one finds in the back country, she thought. Giving it hardly a thought, our hiker headed back to camp for a quick nap before the evening noodles.

She did not know about atomic structure, light or time bending, or other subjects around space time warps. Had she talked with a cosmologist, astronomer, or physicist, she could have learned more. Physical conditions on this planet can cause small one banded (i.e. sound only) warps like the one she found. For that matter, we know that mirages are transitory one banded space time warps involving light and affecting what people see from near and far.

There are suppositions, hypothetical experiments and approaches, indeed a mathematical basis to this area of knowledge. In theory, it is possible to create and manage the bending of matter. What that is, in every day language: On paper, it is possible to make a door into the next state or country. Or the next planet. One could go from Denver to Boise by stepping through a door. The math to support this has been developed but the technology has not yet been invented. For now all that can be done is to observe and experiment. Many are the places on earth where sound or light are bent and redirected. Some of these warps are stationary, some are intermittent, some are transitory and temporary.

Who is to say the same thing doesn't happen with other bands of energy? There may exist many sites that involve more than just sound or light. They may well be on this world and throughout the universe. At these places more than wafting conversations could happen: physical distance, time, gravity, and the very structure of the universe may also be bent and redirected.

Consider. People go missing. Husbands go out for a smoke and never come back. Wives go shopping and do not return. Kids leave to go for a walk in the park and are not seen again. Crew and passengers of ships disappear. The disappearance of the Malaysian Airlines plane, the deserted ship Mary Celeste, the "Bermuda Triangle" and other stories must have some logical explanation.

No doubt some of this activity is explicable. Planes go down, ships sink, people meet foul play, or just want to go away and start a new life. Many disappearances are totally and boringly explainable. Likely, most are simply lost for a time, or are victims of violence or dire circumstance.

But there are cases which may involve something more. Multi banded space time warps may explain some mysterious vanishings. From time to time a person, or a plane or a ship may well come across a space time warp. They enter unknowingly, accidentally, or perhaps sometimes even willingly.

Portals to somewhere or somewhen. The stuff of science fiction and science fact. UFOs here, ships gone missing... Such gateways may well account for some of these unexplained phenomena.

No one knows for sure. We do know that there are mysterious comings and goings.

II

MR. MIKEL MAS, ESQUIRE, HAD HIS DOUBTS. THE CASE DIDN'T make sense to him. An attorney prominent and knowledgeable in water law, he had never seen anything quite like this. Why review the city of Denver's longstanding water claims and rights? Why look at the legality of hard built diversion and distribution works? After all, these water rights and structures dated back over decades. In some cases the age and seniority exceeded one hundred years. The rights were established beyond doubt by time, usage, decree, and general consent.

But he had been hired, or perhaps to be lawyerly, he should say his firm had been retained. A non profit eco-action group had called a week or so back. They wanted his firm to review all water related actions by the City of Denver. "All" was the specific term they repeatedly used. That call brought to mind a number of reactions. First, how on earth could a nonprofit afford the hundreds of hours billed at hundreds of dollars each? And, really, *all* water related actions? The City's water rights had thousands of filings each with hundreds and hundreds of pages supporting or opposing. Some were so old they needed to be handled with special gloves.

And that was just the start. There had to be hundreds of thousands, over a million, more documents. There was a paper trail, or a tangle of many trails, showing how the city got the rights, the disputes settled along the way, how the water was moved to their treatment plants. And from there the water went out to hundreds of thousands, maybe millions, of homes and businesses. The client wanted them all, yes each and every one of them, examined.

Bottom line, Mik thought wryly, is that it acted as a private full employment act for the people of his firm.

Mik wondered what they could possibly stand to gain. Why poke at such sturdy legal and social foundations? Did they know something? There had been no new law enacted, nor old documents unearthed. Not that he was aware of, and if anyone would know, it would be he or someone in his firm.

Of particular interest, apparently, were some of Denver's oldest claims and filings for rights to water. That would be the place to start in any case. Denver's settlers had drawn water from the Platte and Cherry Creek. Soon, they had spread tentacles all over the Territory, then pretty much the entire State. Reading between the lines, Mik felt that the client's interest was more limited. Their general instructions were for "all." But, in fact the contact person was asking specific questions only about one area. He was nosing around Denver's ownership and rights to water in Summit County and Grand County just west of the Divide. This meant water from the Williams Fork Mountains, the Fraser River, and nearby upper Colorado River drainages.

The nonprofit was quietly asking questions about the water amounts and how Denver had won them. Following that was their interest in the infrastructure. That is, they wanted the reasons and justifications Denver used to build tunnels, canals, and other diversion infrastructure through the wilderness.

Mik knew the area in question. He knew the mountains, the valleys, the parks, the aspen and pine groves and the game in that part of Colorado. This was so because most of his life he had hiked, skied, snowshoed, and generally clambered over and all around it. There were few valleys he and his friend Joe Abrams hadn't visited.

The Williams Fork Mountains were a gentle, relatively low range, with summits only in the high twelve thousand feet. They rise some seventy miles from the Front Range, west of the continental divide and north of highway I70. The Fraser River drains the eastern side of the Williams Forks. It too is entirely west of the divide. But it is north of Berthoud Pass, near Winter Park Resort. These areas yielded tremendous amounts of water to Denver. They didn't take it all but they did most of it.

Of course, Mik put his client's interests to the fore. After the call came in, the contract was drafted. The nonprofit signed it and paid the retainer fee promptly. The firm's resources were mobilized and a plan was drawn up. Associates would review the myriad documents and summarize the issues.

Mik would take to the road: From the first water cases he had worked, he had done this. He started every case with a personal, boots on the ground, inspection. The man drove and walked the area in question. He looked at how and where water was being diverted from and to, and looked over the delivery infrastructure as well. It helped to talk to people along the way. Those who were directly affected gave him perspective and background. Sometimes it was like assessing a battlefield, sometimes it was like renewing an old friendship. Either way, when it came to presenting in front of a judge this practice helped. Having made a recent, personal visit to the area being disputed had served him well over the years.

He was semi retired now. For years, Mik had been an attorney first, outdoorsman second. Now the order was reversed. The firm's letterhead listed him as being "Of Counsel," the senior statesman of the outfit. So these days, the default was to get outdoors, not sit in an office and review law and cases.

His priorities were classed kind of whimsically. When business came to a crunch now, he liked to think of it in the "win-place-show" parlance of horse racing. When there was no big contract needing attention and no hearing scheduled, it was prioritized so: being with family and friends would win, going outdoors would place, and practicing law would show.

Life being what it is, sometimes that order was reversed. This day, for Mik, the practice of law and looking to the client's interest took first place. The fact that it involved being outside in an area he knew well made it easy to rearrange the priorities.

The saying is, water flows to money. True. But it also yields to gravity.

When it came to his boots on the ground review, Mik generally started at the bottom of the hill. Figuratively always, and often literally, he did start at the point where water came out of the delivery system. In this case that meant Ralston Reservoir, tucked into the foothills northwest of the city. There water was stored prior to treatment. The water it held was mostly from the Williams Forks and the Fraser valley after its long downhill run. From Ralston it would be easy enough to follow delivery structures up the system.

The review, like many, entailed looking at unglamorous stuff. Pipelines, canals, and siphons ran up the map and up the hill, north across Rocky Flats. Then the carrying canals veered west. Pipelines and tunnels carried the water high along the side of South Boulder canyon, from yet another holding facility, Gross Reservoir. The water came there by running down South Boulder Creek itself. The creek got the water from a small tunnel next to the Moffat railroad tunnel. That tunnel was fed by the collection system on the west side, throughout the Williams Fork Mountains. That system of canals, small tunnels, and diversion ditches on the other side of the divide was a whole different animal. He would tackle that separately, another day.

Doing it this way helped Mik to picture the system. Although he was still a bit mystified why the client wanted this done. All the more reason for him to keep his review objective and factual. That meant concentrating on acre feet, inches, aquifers drained and supplemented, etc. He did things this way for a reason. If he focused on objective facts and numbers it offset the place names. Place names tended to bring up connotations and memories of case law, disputes, disagreements, and struggles. Those elements of the picture didn't belong in this part of the job. They would be thoroughly analyzed when his inspection report was meshed with the work of firm's young associates. They would review documents and adjudications.

Still, dealing with this territory and this client, he knew he couldn't entirely separate facts and figures from historical context. Once the water was collected on the west side of the mountains, its delivery network of canals, pipes, tunnels, and siphons paralleled the railroad, closely or loosely. Mik mused that development came in many forms. Before buildings could be built the materials had to be obtained and brought to the site. Buildings were fine, but before people could live in them and prosper, water had to be available.

He was fascinated that there were two sophisticated systems which allowed the settling of the western US. Railroads and water delivery were intertwined economically and socially. It was fitting that they were also physically knotted and tangled.

By 1900 the industrial revolution had pretty generally worked its wonders and evils. Much of America was connected by rail, telegraph and canals. Widespread electrification, the telephone, radio and movies, aviation, and automobiles were just around the corner. A middle class was struggling to emerge. That group of striving, hard working people were destined to drive the economy with consumption enabled by factory jobs.

The west generally lagged in enjoying these benefits. Colorado itself suffered from less than thorough and widespread facilities for transportation. In 1900, that meant rail infrastructure. True, railroads came in the 1870's to Denver and on to the mining camps around the state. At that time Denver was the largest city between the Missouri River and the west coast. Yet it had no direct rail line to the west coast and only one to the east. To ship from Denver, one had to go north through Cheyenne to catch the Union Pacific, or south through New Mexico to catch the Southern Pacific. Neither of these lines had any desire for a competing line west direct from Denver.

Fortunes had been made in railroads. Harriman, Gould, Morgan, Jay Cooke...These men had accumulated immense fortunes by building, taking over, and managing railroads. And they had made a fine art of exploiting the leverage those roads gave them. As Mark Twain described the Robber Baron's Gospel: "Get money. Get it quickly. Get it in abundance. Get it dishonestly if you can, honestly if you must." This has Twain's edge to it, but it sums up the business practices of those at the top of the food chain in the late 1800s and early 1900s.

Many Coloradans did alright for themselves in this period. One Denver man who did well was David Moffat. No matter how you measure, by money or ruthlessness, he was not in a league with Vanderbilt, Rockefeller or Gould. Nonetheless he amassed millions in Colorado. Banking, real estate, and railroads were his golden geese. He was an astute businessman, and honest. He gave and got loyalty from his people. He was hard and demanding, but not coldblooded.

Mr. Moffat came from the Midwest. In Denver he first became a banker. For a time he was also a director of the Denver & Rio Grande Railroad. He left the D&RG. There was a dispute over whether to build a spur line to the southern Colorado mining camp of Creede. His instincts said it would be profitable but the rest of the Board didn't see it that way. He resigned. Moffat built his own railroad to the town and added to his fortune. This was typical of the man—he saw an opportunity and grabbed it firmly, making it pay off.

David Moffat had other dreams. He wanted to pierce the Rocky Mountains. He had in mind a steam railroad, not a narrow gauge side spur project like Creede, but a real main line road. He wanted to build a railroad to compete with the Union Pacific and the other big boys. He envisioned his road going from Denver through northwestern Colorado and on to Salt Lake City. Such a railroad would give him access to the west coast via connections in Salt Lake City. Also, importantly, the stretch from Denver to Salt Lake offered many prospects. There were coal deposits to be mined, resorts to build and haul to, ranchers whose cattle needed taking to market, even

Indian Reservations which would need annuity supplies delivered. The opportunities for the owner of a substantial railroad were many and most would be quite lucrative.

All that said, there was a reason such a road hadn't been built. Several decades previous, in 1869, the Golden Spike had been driven in Utah. This spike ceremonially joined transcontinental railroad lines coming from east (The Central Pacific) and west (The Union Pacific). At that point the nation was joined coast to coast by rail. But that route sidestepped Colorado's mountains by going to the north. The original builders avoided the Rocky Mountain's deep steep canyons, rock ribbed crags, avalanches, long distances, high altitudes, and other factors. Those conditions challenged anyone daring to try. David Moffat accepted the dare.

Getting a standard gauge railroad from Denver to the west side of the continental divide would prove expensive and difficult. Even at its lowest, the divide is over 11,000 feet. That is six thousand feet, more than a mile, above the city. And the grade for a mainline road generally couldn't exceed 2%. It wouldn't be easy to keep the grade mild. Climbing not more than two feet up for every hundred feet forward would require ingenious access and skillful engineering. The road would have to snake around ravines, over creeks, through rock cliffs and mountains. And all this was just to reach the base of the continental divide.

Once there, the choice of route became simple, but not easy. Should it go over the mountain or through it? Going over was cheaper to start. It meant building a road up and across the spine of the Rockies. The cost of building the road wouldn't be onerous but the cost and effort to maintain might well be. A tunnel, on the other hand, would be very expensive to build. Once done, it would be relatively cheap to maintain. Its length would be two to ten miles, depending on where the bore was punched through.

There were technical problems to be addressed. Ventilation would be a problem whatever the length. Coal fired steam engines put out a lot of exhaust. Suffocating passengers or even live cargo like cattle or sheep stock would not do. The saying "there is no such thing as bad publicity" goes only so far! But other long railroad tunnels were in use and the problems were fairly well understood and solved. Giant fans at each end of the tunnel would expel the exhaust out and pull clean air in.

Once through the tunnel the worst of the railroad building would be done. From there the run to Salt Lake was expected to be relatively easy to build. It was more or less downhill and the highest and steepest of the mountains would bested. All of these difficulties would submit to proper financing, competent engineering, thoughtful planning, and well managed and supplied artisans.

Other difficulties would not be so readily tamed.

All across the country, indeed around the globe, railroad owners did not look kindly on new competitors. The arena of iron rails and rolling stock was Darwinian in its most brutal and straightforward form. As an example, Mr. E. H. Harriman did not come to control the Union Pacific Railroad by being friendly and accommodating. He and those who controlled other lines did all they could to throttle or make problems for the competition. The preferred method was to kill the baby in the crib rather than let it grow big enough to offer competition.

Moffat knew this. He had done his share of infighting, sometimes losing sometimes winning the battles with competitors. Nonetheless, he was a man who saw opportunities where others saw problems. Despite the obstacles, he was determined to build a standard gauge steam railroad through the Rockies. He was intent on going from Denver all the way to Salt Lake City.

Things got kicked off July 18, 1902. On that date, the Denver, Northwestern & Pacific Railway Company was organized and capitalized. Work started at once. Rights of way were obtained, surveyors were sent out, cars and engines purchased, grade scraped and track laid. Things got off to a fast start.

A century later, Mik stood and looked at the work done. Trains ran regularly up from Denver into the mountains, through a long tunnel under the divide, to the western slope of Colorado. And a parallel set of structures had been built as well. From the tunnel east, Denver installed water pipes and canals to bring the stuff of life to the Front Range. In fact, water from the Williams Fork and Fraser drainages came to Denver courtesy of the efforts of the Denver Northwestern and Pacific. There is a pipeline in the pioneer bore for the railroad tunnel. Too small to be of use as a railroad tunnel, it was leased to Denver Water. The pipeline carries the water harvested on the west side of the divide and dumps it into South Boulder Creek. From there the water goes into pipelines, canals, and siphons, ultimately to end up in Ralston Reservoir.

Those conduits, the pipelines with canals and siphons, were built and run to this day through territory familiar to Mik. As a student at the University he had hiked and climbed around much of north central Colorado. He had hoofed it all over the foothills and cliffs west of Boulder and south past Rocky Flats. The hills were marked with traces of the railroad grades that preceded Moffat's Denver and Northwestern efforts. Also, trails and roads, many of them built to give access for Moffat's crews, abounded.

The country between Boulder and the continental divide was a hiker's smorgasboard. The land offered most any type of human powered recreation one would want. The menu included easy trail walks, exploration of old homesteads, mines, and ruins of hotels. For those who eschew trails there was cross country timberbashing. Cliffs, boulders, and crags offered mild scrambles and serious roped climbing. During the short days of winter, the terrain was good for skiing or snowshoeing. And almost every spot offered views, of either Denver and the plains, Eldorado Canyon's crags, or the continental divide.

In the morning before his "boots on the ground" inspection, Mik mentioned his day of waterworks checkup to wife Sula. She was his sea anchor, his source of sound advice for most any situation. Her day would be busy too. An art appraiser, she had connected with several auction houses. Often she consulted for them. Her specialty was fine arts, appraising actual values and setting minimum bids. Today she had an estate sale to work.

When she heard what her husband was going to do, she stopped thinking bids and values and looked him over. He stood, cup of coffee in hand, dressed in khaki zip pants, poly pro shirt and vest, goretex shoes, and a baseball cap from a big box outdoors store. His brightly colored, hooded windshell jacket hung on a chair. All of his clothes came from an oil well: Everything he wore was synthetic.

"Mik, you look like you are going to Boulder, sit on Pearl Street Mall and sip on a machiatto latte with soy. You know, one of those guys who nurses a four dollar coffee while moaning how bad the economy is. And also discussing how the Endangered Species Act is, thank God, saving the Preble's Jumping Mouse. You could be sitting with fellow world savers, other oh so hip outdoor wannabes. Dressed like that, you would fit right in."

She arched her eyebrows and looked at him. He kind of nodded, sheepishly.

"But you aren't spending the day in the Peoples' Republic of Boulder, are you? You'll be out in the country talking with ranchers, railroad men, Denver Water engineers, and other real world folks, no? If you show up dressed this way, they will shut you off like a faucet." She kept a straight face. "No pun intended, Mr. water lawyer."

Sula grinned. "Seriously, there is no reason to rub people the wrong way. Make it easy on yourself, Mik. Go put on levis and a work shirt."

As usual, she nailed it. Mik hadn't really thought about that angle. It did make good sense to fit in with people whose help he would need today. He went to his closet and changed. His canvas duster coat and an old Stetson went well with his jeans, stout boots and flannel shirt.

"Bye, Sula. I may be late or even over night, depending on what I find. I'll try to call if the day runs long or I have to stay over somewhere. But don't worry if you don't hear from me. You know how cell service is hit or miss out there."

"Okay. My auction may run long too, not sure just how that will work out. Talk to you later. Are you sure you need to go look again at Denver's water canals and pipes?"

"Yeah, no stone unturned and all that. Besides, these are billable hours. And in an area I love to visit anyway. Love you."

"Okay, be safe. Love you too."

Mik got in his car and headed west then north. As he neared the high, windblown plain called Rocky Flats he pulled over. He was at an overpass, looking down on the railroad grade in a cut below him. This was just where the Moffat Road headed west. From where he stopped he could see it make a big loop, an S curve, around to the left then right climbing as it headed north. The S curve was needed to gain altitude before the road went into the mountains.

The water delivery system, Denver's canals and pipes, were here. They stayed pretty much parallel to the tracks, just a mile or two east of them. Of course the pipes needed no S curve. The water in them was running with gravity and didn't need to fishtail for altitude like the road did. The conduits ran essentially due south to Ralston Reservoir. Here, the water was encased in pipelines, big steel pipes eight or ten feet in diameter. The entire system had been built as open canals. As the city growth approached, Denver Water started to enclose them. Now what had been canals across Rocky Flats were no more. They were replaced by buried pipelines.

Mik supposed originally they had been closed up to keep kids and cattle from falling in and drowning. Now there was a security aspect as well—some crackpot horse's ass might try to dump poison in the water supply. He made a mental note on that. He'd have a junior partner look at precedents for providers being held liable in the event of such an occurrence.

There wasn't much to see in this stretch, just old canals now filled over. A few miles north and west it would be different. That was far from town and well off the main roads. It was isolated and access was controlled enough that the canals remained open. Mik knew that the water flowed in canals and pipelines, east out of the South Boulder Creek valley. They ran high above the creek, above the town of Eldorado Springs. From there they went south across Rocky Flats to where he sat. He saw nothing of note, so put the car in gear and moved on.

Eldorado Springs was an interesting little burg. The town is five or eight miles southwest of Boulder. It straddles South Boulder Creek where it comes out of the mountains, literally at junction of mountain and plain. Originally it was a farm town like most along the Front Range. The site boasted a mineral springs spa. People came from far to swim and soak. The waters had attracted Native Americans in their day. Mik had seen teepee rings all along the mesas to the south and east of town. People had been coming to the site for "the treatment" for hundreds if not thousands of years. The springs were just below the mouth of the canyon, where it exits the mountains.

This locale, where the creek exits the mountains, is spectacularly cliffy. The rock climbing in Eldorado Canyon was known the world over. It had good, solid granite with all levels of challenge. A climber or wannabe could find anything from trails to twelve or fifteen foot boulder problems. For the obsessed there were faces with hundreds of feet of virtually smooth, solid, ninety degree rock. The Red Garden Wall and the Bastille were two well known formations.

Tourism aside, Eldorado Springs was the access point for Denver's canal and pipeline network. Whether a task needed done or an inspection was due, this was the place to gain access. Denver Water's delivery infrastructure was accessible here whether you were going upstream or down. Mik had seen most of the network downstream, having driven along and inspected it across Rocky Flats.

Now he needed to think about the upstream segment. He knew he'd need to turn south off the road to Eldo. About a mile east of town several driveways and a road loomed up. Just before turning he noticed, by one of the driveways, a sign saying "Pruden Ranch, 1882." He thought it looked interesting and decided he would research the place when he got a chance.

Up the hill he drove, to a small turnout. Here Mik met a contact from Denver Water. The man was there to let him through a gate. Behind that gate, there was a network of roads along the delivery system. Having worked water law for years, Mik knew the general manager and many of the rank and file. He knew that Denver Water hired good people. He had always worked well with them, collegially and almost never adversarially. He had proven over time that he did not need a minder. Mik would be free to wander at will.

"Hi Mik. How are you doing? Ready to take a magical mystery tour of canals, pipelines, and siphons? Self guided, of course?"

"Hey, Lionel. We're doing good, thanks. You? What's shaking at the water palace? How are the reservoir levels holding up?

"I'm fine, thanks. Business as usual, bring it in and drink it. Actually, it looks like it will be a pretty good year. Even so, I always hope for spring snow to top things off."

"Anything special going on? Are there any situations or issues I should be aware of in the system?"

They talked on the system and its operation for a few minutes.

"So, Mik, the bottom line is that things are running normal, no unusual problems or hot spots." The water man paused, "Listen, you know the drill. Take only pictures, leave only footsteps and all that. Turns out that I have to go to a meeting." He rolled his eyes as the dreaded "m word" came off his lips. "Here's the key, keep it as long as you need to. Gotta run, catch up with you later."

"Okay, thanks man. I'll get it back to you when I can, OK? See you."

Lionel drove down the road leaving Mik in silence. He savored the view. To the northeast was Boulder. He looked around, and all the other points of the compass showed not city, but scenery. Mesa, mountain, and cliffs defined the landscape. There was an old railroad grade running around the side of the mesa. He recognized it as part of the first serious attempt to push rails across the divide—the old Denver, Utah and Pacific Railroad. In the 1880's the company built some grade from Denver and even started a tunnel under the divide. They had crews surveying for the rails well out into western Colorado. The line ran out of money before even one rail was laid. It was one of many railway ghosts that haunted the west.

The lawyer stopped woolgathering. He needed to get to work if he meant to get back to Denver and Sula any time soon. He opened the gate, drove through, got out to close and lock up behind him. He slowly drove up the road. In about half a mile it actually joined the old DU&P grade. At that point he could have gone left to look at canals out across Rocky Flats. He had pretty much seen them on the drive up, not to mention other times in the past. He went right, staying on the grade for a while. It ran along the hogback and now was quite a way above the valley. There were some small rocks on the road to be carefully driven over or around.

The grade wound north then veered due south. The road ran through a cut, a narrow deep furrow put through the hogback by the 80's railroaders.

Hogback, Mik thought. Strange name for a long, rock spined ridge. Someone had told him that the rock spine looked like the hair standing up on the back of a boar pig. Thus the name.

There at the end of the hogback the road made a U turn. Mik wondered how even a narrow gauge train could make such a tight turn. Maybe having to take on such tough terrain is one reason the company never lasted long enough to haul freight, he mused.

Through the cut, the view opened to the west. The town Eldorado Springs lay there. He could see the spring fed swimming pool on the north side of the creek. It was several hundred feet below. The road continued on west up the valley, hitting the level of the creek in a mile or so. But he wasn't going that way. Access to the water pipes was on up the hill, not along the old grade. Mik turned left here, leaving the old railroad grade and heading up a road maintained by Denver Water.

The road steepened, no longer following the mellow old railroad grade. A ways up the hill, say two hundred yards, was a small shed. It was weathertight and well kept but blended in with the hillside. He pulled in here. A rough road led fifty or seventy yards further, up to a huge pipe sticking out of the hillside. Like down by Rocky Flats, this pipe was eight or ten feet in diameter. It was painted a light, almost fluorescent green. Why someone had picked such a color, Mik couldn't fathom. It certainly didn't blend in, but maybe it was an anticorrosive or something. This section of pipe was not too long where it crossed a small valley. Maybe it was forty or fifty yards in length and was supported every so often by steel legs fastened to concrete footings.

He stepped back mentally, trying to picture the system in its entirety. The water line, the pipe he was looking at, came down from the divide, running in or parallel to the creek. The grade it ran at was not steep. It was in fact almost level, put at just enough downhill grade to keep the product moving. The water ran through tunnels and pipes like this, thrown across draws and valleys. There were no leaks or drips. Any of those were fixed immediately. The system was all sealed up with no wastage or rust, and no apparent way for unauthorized access.

The land here was rugged. Mik could see why the railroad that finally succeeded was so difficult to build. At least when the water people built their parallel pipes they had the rails to bring in supplies and for access. He looked up at the rock ribs that ran from the top of the mountain down to the valley. They were regular, like a marching formation, running down the mountain every quarter mile or so. Each rib was punctured by tunnels, train tunnels high up the mountain and water tunnels down at Mik's level. Denver Water too had put in a lot of time and money to build their delivery system.

It was time to look the system over from the client's point of view. First he reviewed the conversation he had the previous day with an engineer at Denver Water. He had known Elizabeth as an intern years ago. Now she was senior engineer for the northwest sector. As an intern she first went by Leeza. It didn't take her long to see that people considered anyone calling herself Leeza an airhead. Her advanced degrees, abilities, and accomplishments were overshadowed.

To get past this perception problem, she reprinted her business cards and insisted on being called Elizabeth. That helped make others focus on the engineering problem at hand, not her name. The woman started to progress, her merit at last perceived, and she now held a responsible position. It probably was not a rare story.

The assumptions we all make, mused Mik, as he listened to her.

"Sure, go ahead and look over the delivery canals and lines," said Elizabeth. "Drive or walk. Your choice. While you're at it, Mik, keep an eye out for anything off kilter or problems in the making. If you run across something, make a note and let us know. You know that we patrol and have a regular maintenance schedule. But there are hundreds of miles of canals and pipes, and thousands of siphons, grills, headgates, joints, linings, retaining walls, and so on. It is hard to keep up on every foot, every bolt holding pipe sections, every turn in a canal. Anything you notice will be appreciated."

She took a quick phone call, solved the problem, and started again. "Anyway... I'll let the field staff know you are coming, and to help you as they can. You know the history, right?"

"Well, kind of. This stretch above South Boulder Creek and across Rocky Flats is a Depression era project, right?"

"Yes and no. It was built in the 1920's and 30's, yes. But it was not financed or made by a federal government job creation program. It was not CCC or Works Progress Administration. Denver Water has had rights to Williams Fork and Fraser River water since the early 1900's. Getting that liquid gold from there to our side of the mountain was the problem. In 1903 the Railroad came through the South Boulder valley and up to the continental divide. Anyway, the railroad intended to drive a tunnel under the divide. They built a line over the top, thinking they would need it only for a few years. But the tunnel under the mountain took years. It is now known as the Moffat Tunnel."

Mik knew about the tunnel. "So Williams Fork and Fraser water comes through that tunnel, right?" Elizabeth grinned.

"Not exactly. The powers that be negotiated a sweet deal with the railroad. See, the builders put a pilot bore through the mountain before the main tunnel. It is a smaller bore of course, and was made to check the geology, stability, any faults, and so on. Once the main tunnel was well underway there was little use for it."

"Anyway, we—someone in the Denver water department—negotiated the right to put a pipeline through the pilot bore. We use it to move our water from the western slope, at least the product from the northern catchment areas. All the water we harvest from the Williams Forks and the Fraser River drainage, and some other, comes through the pilot bore of the Moffat Tunnel. There we put the water into the headwaters of the creek and gravity does the rest."

"We started moving water through that tunnel in the late 20's. The canals and pipelines you'll see today were started then and completed in the late 30's. We had crews all up and down the area, from Gross Reservoir through to Eldorado Springs and beyond. By the way, the name Eldorado Springs is relatively recent. The town was also known as Hawthorne until sometime in the 20's. I expect Hawthorne had less sizzle than Eldorado Springs. At least when it came to marketing the swimming pool and resort, which was a big deal in the 20's. Anyway ... Enough history."

Mik nodded. "Thanks for the background. I'll be sure to make a note of any problems."

"Okay. One other thing, some of the roads you use for access to our system are old. Some were originally built for railroad, hotel, real estate, and other construction starting around 1900. Some are even older, the Denver Utah and Pacific grade you'll drive up on, for example. Most of them are still in pretty good shape, but same thing, if you see problems or a washout, let me know."

So, Mik thought as he pulled the car over next to the shed, *This road I just drove up was likely a wagon road used for access to the rail line construction.*

He patted a pocket to be sure he had matches. That was something he did every time he left town. He had never had to spend a night or other unexpected time outdoors. For some reason he always felt better if he knew he could build a fire if need be. Then he climbed out of the car.

The attorney in him again mused that Denver's water delivery system paralleled the railroad. It stayed several hundred feet below but did not stray far from the rail lines. Denver Water had followed the railroad's lead, taking advantage of their hard work of route finding and pioneering. He listened as a train came down the road up above him. The rhythmic clack and subdued growl of heavily laden wheels on iron was somehow comforting.

The outdoorsman in him studied the lay of the land, the rock buttresses, the valleys, the view over Eldorado Springs. He did a slow full turn, three hundred sixty degrees. He noted the exact location of trees, big boulders, what he could see over the hogback from this angle, and made reference to other points. It was an old habit and had served him well. Whenever going out he took a few moments to locate himself precisely.

One thing he noted which seemed out of place was an apple tree along the old road. *Hmmm*, he thought, *maybe someone from the railroad crew or some wagon driver tossed an apple core there. Someone sure did—apple trees don't grow here naturally*. Shrugging, he started up the old road towards the ghastly green pipeline which spanned a draw.

III

Mik walked ten or twelve steps and stopped. Part of the fun of doing a full 360 to locate yourself was to enjoy the changing view. This he drank in. He enjoyed yet another slow turn, identifying rocks, angles of view, distant landmarks, and other locators. God it was gorgeous country, with a beautiful unfolding panorama.

Making a sweep like this was not really necessary today. He knew the area well. The weather was not a threat. Conditions looked to be stable and pleasant. Still, old habits don't die easily. Knowing what the terrain looks like looking back down the way you have come was important. Making sure he had done so had gotten him home in whiteouts or after dark. It was too easy to just look up when hiking. The trail looks different coming down even in good conditions. When you needed to find your way out later it helped a lot if on the way up you had looked back every so often. That way you knew the lay of the land. Anyway, he was woolgathering. Enough enjoying the view, remembering scrapes he had gotten into, and pondering routefinding.

It was such a nice day, he thought. It was almost too nice a day to work. He decided to put the billable hour meter on hold and take a few minutes for himself. He walked on up the hill past the big green pipe, and through a meadow. The old access road climbed steeply. Up around a corner it went. He could see the railroad grade well above him and heard a clacking whine. Another coal train came down from the Moffat tunnel, the engineer running slow, gearing down to maintain control. More than one train had gone too fast, run off the rails, and crashed coming down the grade. Mik knew there was a jumbled pile of steel just above him, a train that had once done just that.

Even in the twenty first century, much less the early twentieth, the railroad above him was a remarkable engineering accomplishment. A full gauge steam railroad. Tracks the standard four and a half or so feet apart. Mik knew the standard was some arcane number based on the width of horse drawn wagons and Roman chariots before that, but he couldn't remember the exact dimensions.

Anyway, standard track had been driven through, not around, the Rocky Mountains. Rock ribs tunneled through, unstable slopes crossed, avalanche runs overcome and survived, all stirred Mik's admiration and awe. Mr. Moffat and his company managed to get the railroad pushed from Denver clear to the foot of the divide in less than two years. They had no aerial photographs, no GPS, no laser surveying equipment. They used only a lot of brain power and muscle power. That got them to the continental divide.

Over the divide a temporary railroad went, mostly following the path of previous users, game, Native Americans, and horse drawn wagons. Actually those users all went from South Boulder Creek to the upper Fraser River. Over the summit and down the west side of the divide the rails ran. From there, the rails went down the valley through Granby and Hot Sulphur Springs to Kremmling.

Mik was struck again by the beauty of the day.

He stopped musing on the history of the railroad and waterworks. He decided he had better get to work. There were no evident problems, no leaks or washouts, no illegal diversions or taps here. Having seen enough, he turned around and started back down towards the car. It was time to get behind the wheel and drive on up the canyon.

Returning towards the car, he again noted details of the view. The pipeline was just ahead, coming into view. He couldn't resist. He had to take a moment to stop and enjoy one particularly dramatic scene. Pine boughs framed the cliffs of Eldorado Canyon north across the gorge. Mik started to walk again, looking at climbers visible on the cliffs. From here you couldn't really see people, just brightly colored, slow moving dots. Memories of vertical adventures flooded his mind: the camaraderie, the rush of adrenalin alternating with stabs of fear, and elation of topping out ... He was on autopilot, watching his footing on the road but also enjoying and drawing from the memories.

He took another step. All at once the world shimmered and his vision dimmed. There was a momentary flash of turbulence, almost a personal rushing windstorm that lasted only part of a second. He felt lightheaded and queasy, like a sudden onset of food poisoning. It passed and his vision cleared. *What on earth?* he wondered. For a moment he thought maybe his heart had exploded and he was crossing the river. Concentrating solely on his body's signals, he paid no attention to his greater surroundings. He took a breath, calmed, and centered down. He felt ok, his fingers worked, his toes felt alright. He was still alive!

But something was different. He looked around. There were fewer trees on the hillside around him. The ghastly green pipeline was gone! No climbers over on Eldo. The car was…there was no car! The road wasn't grown over with rounded grassy banks above it. It was not the old beat up rocky dirt road he had just walked up. It was fresh and looked newly scraped. It was narrower and wasn't as smooth or as well graded as the one he had walked up on.

Good God, he thought. *Maybe I did die. Where are the bright light and the love? Or am I having some kind of weird schizo episode?* Images and ideas from science fiction stories ran through his head. Of a sudden, the four note tattoo from *Twilight Zone* ran through his head. *Am I imagining this or is there really a change in my surroundings?*

He consciously froze, moving no part of his body but his eyes. Time to take stock. *Okay*, he thought. *I know I am still alive because I am breathing and thinking. But I also know that this happened when I moved. So, let's see what happens when I move back.*

He closed his eyes and said a short prayer. Then, keeping his right foot in the no pipeline world, he shifted his left foot and his weight back to where it was before this weird transition or hallucination or whatever the heck it was. The rush and momentary unease came and went. Weight on his left foot, he opened his eyes. Whoa! Sure enough the pipeline was there, where it was earlier. Lots of trees, including the apple tree he had noticed earlier, down the hill a little way. The car sat parked exactly where he had left it. And there were the bright dots inching up the cliffs across on Eldo.

What the hell?

He shifted back to his right. This time he kept his eyes open. Sure enough, he got the shimmer, the turbulence, the unease. Even his vision clouded and things danced before him for a moment. He focused on his surroundings not his feelings and sensations. Sure enough. Few trees, no pipeline, no car.

Not moving his feet, he memorized his location. To the inch, to the centimeter, he wanted to fix this spot in memory. He looked at near and distant rocks and other permanent landmarks. It was important to fix in his mind, and on the hillside, exactly where this odd change took place. He didn't try to memorize trees, they came and went. Out came the smartphone and he took a 360 video of the spot. He just hoped that the rocks and hillsides wouldn't change. Whatever was going on, it was all just too strange!

He stepped back to pipeline time and saved a GPS waypoint on his phone. Not that it would do him a heck of a lot of good but he felt better. Then he shut the phone down. And stepped back across into no pipeline wherewhen.

After a minute or two he felt confident he knew the hallmarks of his location. He felt sure that he could re-find the exact point. It was time, he felt, and safe, he hoped, to explore a little. It started with taking small steps. These were baby steps taken just one or two at a time, then returning to his spot. By doing so, he isolated the portal. Or door or psychic bump or bad dream or someone's awful joke slipping him some drug or whatever on God's green earth (he hoped!) this thing was.

On one side, he was in the twenty first century, his regular life and time. Sula time, he decided he'd call it, trying to keep some grip on reality. The other side, he was somewhere/somewhen else. It was not clear just what or where or how or why, or even if it was real, but something was sure as hell going on.

Just then Mik felt a distant sound and rumble. Great God, was he in an earthquake? Were there volcanoes here? What was happening? He calmed and realized it was not a general earth shaking. Maybe he didn't know what it was but did recognize that it wasn't general or overwhelming. Whatever had happened, it was a ways away and localized. Falling tree? Landslide? Plane crash? Multi car pile up? He wasn't sure what if anything had occurred. It sounded like there had been a collision or something had fallen. Did that cause this weird transition? Or was it a result of it? He really didn't know, couldn't tell.

Mik sat down next to the spot, in the no pipeline time, and pondered. Again checking, he bit his cheek. Yup, he felt pain, he was alive and awake. He watched the sun to see how shadows got cast. He wondered if it progressed east to west. Sure looked like it. He even turned on his cell to find that it was busy searching for service. He was not sure if that was significant or not. Standing up, he stepped back to and through the magic spot. Sure enough, that was real too. Same weird sensations. On the other side, he felt the pain when he bit his lip, the pipeline and car were there, and his cell had four bars of service.

He spent about an hour going back and forth. He was still trying to sort out what was happening. Mik reached the conclusion that it was somehow another world. It seemed to be an entirely separate, parallel world and place. It seemed to have plant life like home—pine trees, dandelions, prickly pear cactus, and so on.

At least here where he sat it looked to be identical to what he had left Sula in this morning. It seemed to have the same sun, same topography, same flora. But there were no trappings of his twenty first century life. And so far at least, there seemed to be no people. Was this a different, earlier time? Or did he land in the middle of a preserve of some kind? Was he just plain dreaming, or maybe he had in fact died. Maybe he was on the way to purgatory or the afterlife? Or in it?

In any case, this was just too good an opportunity to miss. An adventure like this came around, well, never to a sane person. But here it was, and here he was. Defying all logic (not that logic was really in play about all of this), Mik made a decision. After taking yet another 360 sweep, he consciously chose to stay and check things out a bit. He stepped firmly into what he would later find to be 1903. He took more pictures of the sweet spot where he hoped he could come and go. Saving them, he turned his cell off and put it in an inside pocket. It was little use now but he would need it later for the pictures if nothing else. Recharging the battery was probably out of the question so he wanted to make sure it didn't get run down.

He was excited but a little dazed, standing on a rough dirt track in what he knew was once Colorado. Still puzzling it out, he heard something approaching. It sounded like a horse or mule, some animal not trying for stealth. The animal, and probably the rider, didn't try to conceal themselves. The pattern, the speed of the footfalls wasn't a gallop or even a trot. It was rather a deliberate walk. Some corner of his brain was surprised that it really did sound like *clip, clop.*

It came from the direction of the railroad. He corrected himself. It came from up the hill where the railroad had been this morning. He listened as the rhythmic, slow repeating rhythm grew louder. Coming down the hill towards him, Mik saw a man on a horse.

It was a big guy. He had a dark complexion, at first glance probably one of the dash Americans. African, Native, Mexican, Iranian, whatever. He was not of northern European descent. It occurred to Mik that maybe that type of groupaholic thinking didn't apply here when/wherever he was. But...As the man neared, Mik did a double take. The man was a dead ringer for Kwame O'Brien! His buddy from back home!

Good God! Mik felt like Alice after she had fallen down the rabbit hole.

Kwame was a friend and colleague, an old army buddy who now ran a private investigation firm. Mik's Denver law firm was one of Kwam's biggest clients. They had shared more than a few adventures. On one of those adventures, Kwam had ended up being shot. Thankfully it was a minor wound. That was easy enough for Mik to say. No wound is minor to the target.

Anyway... Kwame! What on earth?!

Mik's musings and wonder were sidelined for a moment when he suddenly realized maybe this wasn't earth. Anyway, what was Kwam doing here in no pipeline time? Would he know Mik? Speechless, confused, almost paralyzed in mind and body, Mik stood watching as the big man on the horse slowed and stopped.

He had a look of wonder on his face, which was chased by a big grin. He laughed then started talking. His language was English but the rhythm and pattern were stilted, unusual to hear. But Mik recognized it as English and was very glad of it. The man was almost yelling he was so excited.

"If it isn't my friend Myron Mast! Out here on the road! Damn, Mik, we thought you were a goner. Everyone was sure that rockslide got you! The face at tunnel four collapsed, we think because of a premature blast. We were afraid you were dead, crushed, buried. Damn, it is good to see you!"

The man got off his horse, dropping the reins so the animal wouldn't move. He walked to about two feet away and faced Mik, still smiling.

"How the heck did you get clear down here, a mile from the tunnel? I called the search off. Hated to do it, you being a friend and all, but we couldn't find you. Work was stacking up, and Denver was pressing to get drilling and grading started again. We really thought you were dead and gone. No way anyone believed you could have survived that slide."

He paused for breath and really looked at Mik. "Where did you get those clothes? How did you get here? Where are you headed? Why aren't you going back to the tunnel for work?"

Mik was overwhelmed and dazed, afraid to speak. He said nothing.

Cam paused, gathering his thoughts. "Maybe the blast knocked you off balance. Let me fill you in just in case you are not sure. I imagine you remember, but just in case..." He looked at Cam with concern and empathy.

"I'm Cameron Braun, the section foreman. I'm responsible for construction of this part of the Denver Northwestern and Pacific railway line. When the dust settled after the blast, I had to make the decision. We searched but found nothing. I didn't want to give up on you, friend, I really didn't. We were all hoping you survived the slide, but finally we had to give up looking for you. I had to get the crews back to work, to clear the debris, make the tunnel safe and push the road forward."

Mik still said nothing, not sure he believed his eyes and ears. This Cam guy was talking about a blast. Maybe that was the rumble he heard earlier? And he said my name was

Myron. Do I look like him? Mik's head was spinning, almost literally, with all the bizarre experiences of the past hours. Myron, who must be my double, my doppelganger? Cameron, a Kwame O'Brien lookalike? This had to be a parallel world. He was trying to wrap his head around some of this as Cam kept talking.

"Mr. Moffat called on the telephone. He consoled me and the rest. Then he pointed out that we have deadlines. Finance and all that. He didn't really want to give up the search either but felt we had no choice. So we said a quick prayer and went back to work."

Cam was getting a little nervous. Mik was saying nothing. Almost like he wasn't the same person. Hopefully his friend was alright, no telling after a rockslide. The foreman was starting to talk just to fill the quiet. He continued,

"So, now, I have day to day responsibility. I am the one who has to oversee building this stretch of railroad. Who am I kidding? I don't *have* to, I *get* to oversee it! From Coal Creek across Eldorado Mountain up South Boulder Creek to Pinecliffe. That is my bailiwick, my patch. Mr. Moffat contracted the responsibility for that to Mr. Good's company. He has in turn delegated that to me. It is a big job but we are up to it."

He finally stopped talking and intently looked at Mik.

"Well, Mik, I've been doing all the talking. Time for me to shut my trap and listen." He couldn't contain himself. "Don't you have anything to say? God in heaven, I am glad to see you!"

Mik was still trying to come to grips with a strange new world, a parallel world. It seemed that Cam here was a doppelganger for a friend from Sula time. He seemed to have a parallel life. A similar life but here and now, whatever that meant. Wow. It was astonishing, literally incredible. But here his friend was and here he was. He felt alive and was standing on the same topography as he walked over this morning. And here was Kwam. But he wasn't Kwam. What on earth was happening?

The inadvertent and unwilling traveler didn't have to pretend that he was dazed and disoriented. "To tell you the truth I don't remember much. Rock slide? Things are kind of fuzzy in my mind..."

"Yeah, we had a slide at the mouth and the face of Tunnel Four. That tunnel has been nothing but problems for us. You were gang chief, the guy who has to go in and check the charge before it gets blown. Last we knew you were supposed to go in and do that. We thought you had gone in and no one saw you come out. Not sure if the blast was premature or maybe it timed right but hit a weak fault and took more down than we wanted. Either case, I am darn glad I found you."

"Me too, I'm still not sure about things. What do we do now, I forget..."

"I'll give the news to Mr. Moffat and the crew. They'll be glad to know. In the meantime, yeah you seem to be a little addled. Maybe you should take the rest of the day off. Rest up, gather yourself. Come back tomorrow if you feel strong enough."

Cam paused, then said, thinking aloud, "I need to tell Steu Wentz about this. You remember him. He is a Deputy Sheriff. He needs to know you are alright. I say Deputy, but he is really the company detective. What's the expression, company dick, company bull, whatever. But the Sheriff deputized him as well. Wentz is the law on the job and he'll want to let his men know to stop looking for you."

Mik smiled weakly and nodded. He didn't want to say something stupid like "Yeah, and have him copy me with the email reporting the blast."

Cam mounted his horse and turned it to head uphill. "Have to get back. You'll go back to the boarding house, right? Rest up there and get your thoughts put back together." He flicked the reins and the horse started ambling. "I'll see you tonight. We can catch up over Mrs. Pruden's dinner."

As he rode up the trail, he felt uneasy about his friend Mik Mast. *Odd*, he thought. *He looks like Mik but he acts a little different. He acted as if he didnt know who I am. Sure hope he is alright. That slide rang his bell, I'm sure. I'll have to keep an eye on him. He might be gun shy, with everything that has happened. I had better find someone else to go in and check the charge before we blast.*

Mik watched Cam ride back up the hill. *Mrs. Pruden's dinner. She must run the boarding house*, Mik decided. *Now, where is it?*

With all that had happened he kind of forgot about the first part of his day. He had driven by the sign proclaiming "Pruden's Ranch 1882" earlier in the day. Or later in the century, whatever. Whenever it was, he had forgotten about it. Right now he just couldn't deal with such gnarled questions and problems.

After a moment's thought it came to him. If Cam went uphill to get back to work, of course this Pruden's place must be down. It wouldn't be up by the construction site anyway.

Mik's head was about to explode. He wondered if his doppelganger, Myron Mast, was really killed in the rockslide. Or was he alive and wandering around here too? Would Mik meet him sometime soon? That would be…He couldn't even come up with words to describe that encounter!

He was still roiled from wonder about Kwam/Cam and Myron Mast. And still trying to get his head around this very real but different and new reality. Before Cam came down the hill he thought it would be fun and adventurous to slip into this life. At least he thought he might look around for a little while. Now, he wasn't so sure. If there were doppelgangers for him and Kwam, who else might he meet?

Should he try to slip in to this life, to fit in and see where it led? Or should he go now? Go back through the magic spot to his life with Sula, the outdoors and the law? Go back to a time he knew and understood? He was torn, and felt very off balance from everything he had seen. What he felt was almost vertigo, so that he had trouble even considering the options.

This was literally a once in a lifetime experience. He had to admit, he was inclined to stick around and check it out, at least for a little while. This was too good, a chance to peek back at the past or maybe an alternative future, or across at another universe, while being a knowing part of it. He should be alright if he kept his mouth shut but eyes and ears open. He could always fall back on the rockslide erasing his memory.

After all, he knew precisely where the portal was. That is, he knew where it was when he came through it a few hours back. He figured, he hoped, he could use it again. At any time he figured that he could step through it and be back in Sula's world. She wasn't really expecting him home that night anyway. And who was to say that even if he spent a week here, it might work out to an hour there? That thinking started his head spinning again, so he abandoned it.

He figured he had better get used to answering to "Myron" or "Mast." Cam had called him Mik so that must be

Mast's nickname as well. Still, he had to be alert and pay attention to everything.

Decision made, he looked down the road. Time to start walking. He set off and shortly came to a sign. It was clearly a temporary sign. Someone had hand written the distance to Eldorado Springs and to Pruden's. It said they were two and three miles, respectively. It also indicated that the worksite at Tunnel 4 was 1 and 1/2 miles the other way. He guessed he'd be walking another forty five minutes to an hour.

There had been no traffic on the road when he first came into this no pipeline land. Nor did he see anyone else while he and Cam talked. But now there were wagons coming up the hill with a load every quarter hour or so. Some held a few rails, or crossties, or other construction supplies. About half of them carried foodstuffs. All were pulled by teams and driven by teamsters who looked bored, like they had been up and down this route a thousand times.

As he walked, Mik wondered why the builders didn't use an engine and cars to bring supplies as far as rails were laid, then move them forward to the construction site by wagon. Later, he would learn that was exactly how most of the supplies were moved. The project was so big that supplies and food had to be brought forward by any means available.

Whatever the reason, the teamsters guiding their wagons up the hill were mostly so bored that they scarcely acknowledged him. That was fine with him. It was a relief not to pretend he knew where he was or what was going on. He kind of nodded if the teamster looked his way, otherwise kept to himself. A ways down the hill he saw two people on foot, coming towards him. He steeled himself for a conversation, reminding himself to be the Myron Mast who been in a rockslide and was still kind of woozy and disoriented.

It had been astonishing but somehow comforting to meet Kwam. Not Kwam, this wasn't the twenty first century. *Cam*, he reminded himself. Cam seemed as solid and calm and able as Kwam. He kept up the self reminders. *Have to call him Cam, and I have to at least not ignore it if someone calls me Myron.* It seemed to be a different world and he wondered if he would find other friends similar to those back in Sula time. *Sula*, he wondered. Would he see her here? Who would she be with? How would he handle that? This line of thinking was getting him agitated and he tried to stop.

When he looked at the two people coming up the hill, he became all the more agitated. It was a man and a…? The second person was either a kind of chubby, curvy man with long hair, or a woman oddly decked out. Hard to tell. They tried unsuccessfully to act as colleagues or acquaintances, not a couple. He was tall and slender, almost skinny, with a calculating, intelligent face. She was blondish with pleasant features. Oddly enough, she was not wearing a dress.

Mik of course thought nothing of seeing a woman wearing slacks. He saw women all the time wearing jeans, capris, pantsuits, long shorts, short shorts, and so on. Almost all of those clothes were styled and sewn specifically for a woman's body shape. Not so for her. This blond had on a pair of canvas trousers, like a miner or cowhand would wear. Her belt was cinched up tight like they were too big. And she wore a man's long sleeved shirt, again a little big. It was almost like she was making a statement of some sort. What kind of statement was unclear, perhaps a feminist or at least a rebellious one. Or an eccentric declaration of independence.

Even though her clothes were several sizes too large, her feminine figure wasn't totally obscured. Her manner was confident, almost cocky. Her blue eyes shrewdly looked Mik up and down. He could feel them even from twenty or more yards away. It was not a "check out the guy" look, it was a frank "is this person friend or foe" look.

The agitation Mik felt was because he knew these two people too! He stopped, awaiting their approach. He was involuntarily drawn, jarringly, back to an encounter with these very two people. Or their lookalikes. These people were doppelgangers of two who he knew in Sula time. It was back several years ago. They didn't seem antagonistic now, thank God. They certainly had been hostile last time he had seen them.

He thought back. Mik and some friends—Kwam was actually one of them—had gotten wind of a plan to do big damage to a town. They had somehow managed to thwart it, or rather to minimize the damage. In doing so, Kwam had ended up being shot. Just after that, Mik had had a violent encounter with these two characters. Or, rather, with two people who looked a lot like the pair walking up the road. Jeez, his life was getting more bizarre by the second. He hoped they didn't remember everything—anything—that he did.

He knew them at that time and place as Delmar Schmidt and Ulora. They were leaders of a gang of eco-vigilantes. The group was in a Colorado mountain town. They tried to take the law into their hands. Of course they said they were trying to do good, trying to improve the environment and help along social change, make things better.

On the night Mik tried to forget, they had double teamed him. The unpleasant memories flooded back. Mik had left Kwam, wounded, with another friend. The friend had to help Kwam and also guard an accomplice of Ulora's. Mik chased Ulora up a mountain where she had met up with Del. Up there, she had trapped him and tried to break his legs. He had gotten free and drove her off. He then jumped the guy,

Del, and was winning the fight when she tried to smash Mik's head with a big rock. So the last meeting had not been a positive one. He sure hoped this encounter went better!

Mik returned to the present, or at least the present that he thought he was in at the moment. He was not in a fight for his life with two wackos. He was, however feeling wacked out as he stood on a road above Pruden's with horse wagons going by. The man and woman neared him. They walked up and stopped. The woman had clearly decided he was not a foe. She looked him over, up close, and acted surprised.

"I know you. You're Myron Mast, aren't you? What are you doing here on the road?" Her mouth then started to run.

"The rumor was that you were killed. I heard there was a rockslide up at the camp at Tunnel 4. And you were in it. How did you escape? Why aren't you at work? Where did you get those clothes? How do you feel, escaping the slide? How did you get down here? Were any animals hurt or lost in the slide, do you know? You are Myron Mast, aren't you?"

Mik was prepared to play dumb. He didn't have to because the woman gave him no chance to say anything. She prattled on.

"It isn't surprising the mountain slid on you up there. Heck, no one knows the stability of those rocks. Moffat and his banker friends are greedy."

Mik was surprised but encouraged to hear the name "Moffat." Maybe, he thought, he was just in a time warp not another universe. Moffat was a name he recognized from Colorado history in Sula time.

The woman continued. "For a profit, he is making men, honest working folk, risk their lives. He surely doesn't go into tunnels and onto rock ledges himself. He does not handle dynamite or swing a pick. That rich old man is making the poor workers drive tunnels where it isn't stable or safe. And he doesn't have anyone looking out for the animals used on the job."

She took a breath and forged on. "They shouldn't try to build tunnels and a road. Problems will continue if they do. Animals and men, more animals and men, will be injured and killed. Moffat's idea of a steam railroad through the mountains is just a monument to him. It is a harebrained scheme and it will never succeed."

She paused, caught her breath, and slowed down. It was almost like she got started and said more than she wanted to. She continued, "I'm Ella. I think we may have met, not sure."

With that she stopped and waited, not too patiently for Mik to say something. He didn't.

She couldn't stand the silence. "It is good that you weren't killed. You dodged a bullet, so to speak. Aren't you fed up with unsafe work on a hopeless project? How did you manage to escape anyway? And where did you get those clothes? I've not seen clothes like that." Her eyes did the up down but he felt the look was not at him, but at his clothes. He wondered, what if Sula hadn't suggested he get out of his synthetics? Then she'd really be goggling and asking questions.

The slender man watched her closely as she talked on, but said nothing. Mik noted that this woman seemed a bit like Ulora in Sula's world. Both tended to talk more than was needed. Both infused their talk and their view of the world with emotion. Feelings first, facts somewhere down the line. If at all. He warily responded to the question about how he escaped.

"I dunno how I got out. Just lucky I guess. Really, I am not sure what happened. Things are foggy and I don't recollect much." He decided to probe a little.

"What are you doing up here? My mind is kind of hazy and I don't remember. How do you fit in? You work for the road too, right? You heard about the slide and me, how did you hear?"

She chose to ignore the questions. Mik did a mental shrug and continued.

"Did you pass Pruden's? I'm still feeling kind of shaken right now. How far is it? Which way do I go? It is crazy, but I forget all this stuff."

The man with her stared at Mik curiously. He was a dead ringer (so to speak) of the guy Mik had last seen in a very serious, no holds barred struggle, rolling in the mud and throwing punches. The guy spooked him, a way deep and eerie unsettled feeling. It was all Mik could do not to jump on him and start slugging. Caught up in a half dream, half fantasy of fists, he at first didn't hear.

The tall guy was starting to talk. With an insincere smile pasted on his face, he stuck out his hand.

"I'm Dale Smertz. Nice to meet you, Mr. Mast. Congratulations on making it safely out of the tunnel. God knows there is enough hurt and damage to go around. We don't need any more."

Mik saw the sense in that, and nodded. Dale continued.

"Moffat is playing with fire, trying to build a road through these mountains. Tough country, no need for another railroad, hazardous to his workers. Don't you agree?"

Mik didn't respond. Smertz paused, then went on.

"I am fairly new here, not an old hand like you. Ella is showing me around. To answer your question, no she does not work on the road. At least not on Moffat's part of it. Me, I have some locating engineer experience. An interested businessman has hired me to look this project over."

Not that I asked about your background and motivation, thought Mik. It sure seemed like a lot of information for someone to volunteer. He wondered what this guy Dale was about. Just what were he and Ella doing up here? The lawyer started digging through what railroad lore he could dredge up. Or dredging through what he could dig up. Whatever. He kind of remembered what a locating engineer did.

"Locating engineer? You fellows work out ahead of even the surveyors, right? Isn't your job to locate the best line for the grade and tracks? I thought you guys were like architects. You lay out the general outline. Then the pick and shovel work gets done by others? I'm surprised a locating engineer would be caught dead back where people are getting their hands dirty by smoothing a road and laying track."

Mik stopped. This display of knowledge and insight was a surprise. He asked himself, *Where the heck did that come from?* It was astonishing to him.

And he let hang the unasked questions: "Why, Mr. Dale Smertz, if you are a qualified locating engineer, are you down here? Why are you hanging around with a woman below the works instead of way out in front of them? Just what are you trying to find out? For whom? Is there really "an interested businessman"? Just what is that man's motivation? Or do you work for yourself or some other interested person?"

Dale was wrongfooted by the barrage of knowledgeable questions. They weren't questions to be fobbed off, either. They went nearer than he liked to the heart of the matter. He didn't respond. He just gave his questioner the fish eye. Then he turned and walked away. Hostility exuded from his actions and body language.

I hit a nerve there, thought Mik. *I wonder what these two are about?*

Ella looked at Smertz' back anxiously. She turned to Mik and smiled politely. "Good to see you again, Mr. Mast."

She started to edge Dale's direction, with small shuffling steps. Looking over her shoulder, she made a valiant attempt to end on a high note.

"Perhaps now that you have had a close call your heart has changed. Maybe we can meet to discuss worksite safety and animal cruelty. If Mr. Moffat continues this reckless scheme he will cause more rockslides and more injuries. People and animals will be hurt. This is an impossible task he has set for himself."

She glanced again at the retreating Smertz. "I have an associate coming in from the east. Mr. Josephus Eggers is an expert on such matters. You should meet him. May I get in touch to arrange a meeting?"

Mik said nothing. Why, he wondered, would he want to meet one of her cohort?

She didn't seem offended at his silence. She looked him in the face and then turned to walk away. She stopped and turned back to offer directions.

"Oh, and Pruden's is a house with barn and outbuildings. You'll find it is about half an hour's walk from here. It is near the road to Marshall, above the creek a quarter mile or so."

Now the sign he had motored by a few hours before came back to Mik. *Of course, the Pruden Ranch*, he thought. Pieces were starting to fall in place, at least a little bit.

Mik walked on. He paid scant attention to the landscape or the wagons on the road. He was just trying to figure things out. First that spot, that door or portal or whatever. From home and Sula to here, where ever or whenever "here" meant. Then meeting Kwam's doppelganger Cam. That was a real eye opener, learning about his supposed rock slide and all. What the heck? Then meeting these two characters.

Meeting Cam was somehow welcome. Back home,

Kwam was a solid man in charge of himself and of his affairs. Cam seemed to be the same sort of person. But meeting the couple, the man and woman. Wow, very strange. Ella and, what was his name, Dale, hadn't harmed him or even been hostile. They did act a little odd, but what the heck. Still, meeting doppelgangers of people who had tried to kill him. It all creeped him out. And Ella seemed a little unhinged, not unlike Ulora back home. And Dale seemed like a user, smart but kind of oily. They too were kind of like two who assaulted him back home. They were, well, the term plastic came to mind. The front he just saw from Ella and Dale was fake. They were not honest. He was glad they didn't know him, even if they thought they recognized Myron Mast.

The encounter made him wonder if he shouldn't bag it all. Maybe he should just make a run for the portal, the spot which would let him step back into Sula's world. This experience was becoming more bizarre by the minute.

On the other hand, what an opportunity! This was a once in a gazillion lifetimes deal. A chance to explore another world. One which was familiar but unfamiliar. One which didn't seem dangerous, at least not yet. He would keep in mind the portal just in case. And he was armed with some knowledge of people's alternate beings. It was too weird that Cam seemed more or less similar to Kwam, and that this Dale Smertz and Ella seemed akin to Del Schmidt and Ulora. Who else would he meet? What did they know about him? Or did they assume he was in fact Michael Mast?

This was shaping up to be just too good an adventure and experience to ignore.

On to Pruden's, and whatever that brings, he decided. *I wonder who I will meet there...*

IV

It was time to put thoughts of returning to Sula firmly out of mind. Mik let gravity do its work and take him down the road. With the wagon traffic coming up from town he couldn't get terribly lost. There was always the "dazed from surviving a rockslide" excuse if he had to ask where he was. It was simple, he just had to find Pruden's. The name, Pruden's Ranch, was the one he had seen on a sign driving by this morning. The location came back to him. Not a problem, he'd find it. What a difference a few hours could make!

As he trudged along, he looked closely at his path. This part of the road looked to be an old railroad bed. It was relatively smooth and wide, and overall not steep or rolling, but had a gradual slope to it. Wagon roads tend to be steep and rutted, with sharp turns to fit the contour of the land. Railroads differ with their consistent width, solid surface, gentle turns, and shallow grade. So this had to be some kind of old railroad or maybe a new one for all he knew. *Ah yes,* he thought. *The same grade he had driven along before going through the rabbit hole to here.* Hours ago and decades in the future.

After a while the road he was walking on left the old railroad grade. He looked and saw the grade continue on south and east around the side of a mesa, gradual and predictable.

His way dropped off a little more steeply and immediately became more rutted and rocky. It headed almost due north towards the valley bottom and the creek.

He walked a few minutes more, for about half a mile. Buildings appeared below and off to the right. They were, he was glad to find, where he expected, working with his memory of the morning. *I'll bet that is Pruden's. Or if not at least they can direct me,* he thought. As he walked nearer he could make out details. All the elements of a working ranch were there—barn, milk house, shed, blacksmith shop, corral, orchards and garden. He heard chickens although he didn't see the coop. And the centerpiece was a nice substantial two story house. Smoke rose from the chimney and the entire place looked comfortably lived in. There was some traffic on the road running by on the north side of the house. He figured it ran from Eldorado Springs to Marshall, or whatever the towns were called here. From there, if he was right, one could catch a train to Boulder, Denver, and points beyond. Curiosity about the place and its people pulled him.

A horse and wagon approached from Marshall as Mik walked up the drive. There were two people. The driver was a man in his twenties, intent on bringing the team to a halt near the door. The rider a mature woman who looked surprised when she saw Mik.

"Why, Mr Mast! Hello! We heard you were lost in the rockslide. It is very good to see that wasn't true. I guess it was just an unpleasant rumor." She smiled as she climbed down from the wagon.

"How are you feeling? Where did you come up with those clothes? How did you get..." She paused. "I'm sorry. I shouldn't be peppering you with questions. If there was a slide you are no doubt shaken and dazed."

Mik just nodded. Better to do that while trying to figure who was who and what was going on.

She continued. "We were just discussing your personal things—clothes and so on. Trying to decide when we should box them up. And then decide who should take them. It turns out we don't have any information on your family. But thank gracious, we don't need to know that now." She realized she was rambling and paused.

"I am so glad that you are here, and whole! And that we didn't do anything rash with your things. No one has touched or molested them. They are still in your room, left top of the front stairs. Of course Mr. Braun's things are there as well since you two share the space. I was going to interview for other boarders. It is a relief not to have to do that."

The woman realized how that sounded, and smiled apologetically. "I am glad for your sake and mine! Again, welcome!"

She turned to the young driver. "Teddy, you remember Myron Mast. I believe he goes by "Mik" rather than Myron. He works at the tent camp near Tunnel 4. Of course that is where Seth works as well. Mr. Mast, you may remember my son in law Teddy Moore."

She appeared to be thinking of tasks to be done and was edging towards the house. She knew Ted had to look after the horses and wagon. She looked at Mik and gave him a parting dose of information. "Mr. Pruden will be along shortly. Dinner, as always, is at six sharp. Good day, and I repeat, it is a happy thing to see you healthy and whole, Mr. Mast."

"Glad to see you again," said Teddy, as he shook Mik's hand. Grinning, he continued, "I'm sure you remember, but when she says dinner is at six sharp, she means it. Don't be late!"

Smiling in acknowledgment, Mik asked, "I am curious just how big the Pruden ranch is, if I can ask."

"We have about 120 acres in hay and grains here in Eldorado. There are two springs up in the field. There is also a separate homestead plot near Plainview, up above the railroad bed. The tracks have gone past it by now, so we can go from there to Denver easily. They have a cabin up there, not a full fledged house. That place is to raise chickens and alfalfa for the milk cows. It helps us with our contract to provide eggs, meat, milk and butter to the railroad building crews at the camp. That arrangement is working well for them and for us. Also, Mr. Pruden has other business and civic interests."

Ted paused and smiled quietly. "Although I have to say as much as he travels, I help out with some of those duties. He is also a Justice of the Peace and travels a circuit. He has real estate and other business interests as well. All in all a busy man."

He looked at Mik, his expression half skeptical and half sympathetic. "But I'm sure you knew pretty much all of that. Why do you ask?"

"I'm a little foggy on details right now, Ted. Truth be told I don't remember any rockslide. Nor, for that matter, do I recall a lot about the railroad and tunnels or, well, about much of anything. I guess the whole experience upset my system and blanked my memory. Apologies if I repeat myself, or ask about things I should know, or don't recognize someone."

Mik shook his head as if to clear cobwebs. "Things come and go, memories and knowledge are sometimes clear and sometimes just gone. I almost suddenly feel like I am a stranger around here."

He was grateful for a reason to be vague and not to know things that Myron Mast would know.

Ted gave a sympathetic shrug and nodded.

"I can imagine you were thrown around and roughly

handled. No doubt you are still a bit bewildered. Working up there is a big and difficult job on the best of days. If something goes wrong it would be difficult to come to grips."

He paused, and offered a little advice.

"You will see several of the construction crew tonight. They board here like you. Talking with them ought to help you bring things back. My wife Odessa and I live here as well. She was distressed to hear of the slide and the news that you were lost. Like her mother, she will be happy to learn the rumor was unfounded. And you know Seth, Seth Pruden. Odessa's brother, works on the survey crew on the road. He'll be back later as well."

He turned towards the team, still harnessed to the wagon. "I had better tend to the horses. Last thing I want is for them to cool down too fast, and get a chill. And I see a board loose in the bed of the wagon. I need to get that fastened and secure." He walked over, ready to lead the team towards the barn.

"We can talk more at dinner. Good afternoon, Mik. Welcome back to the land of the living!" He grabbed the halter of one of the horses and walked the rig away. The two horses didn't stall or try to go their own way, but happily headed towards the barn. Ted didn't need to say a word or pull hard on the reins. They knew their day was done. A combing and fresh hay with a dessert of oats awaited them.

Mik repeated the facts and names Ted had mentioned. He had to burn them into memory—acting as if he were dazed could keep him out of trouble only so long. He was preoccupied as he entered the house and almost ran into a young woman coming out of the kitchen. He guessed that she was Teddy's wife, the Prudens' daughter Odessa.

"Mr. Mast! Mother said you were here and were alright! It was good news to hear you weren't injured or lost in the rockslide after all. I worry about you workers, and of course about my brother, lots of hazards up there." She paused, a look of worry fleeting across her face.

"Yes, Mrs. Moore, I find that I am safe and sound. I have to tell you, I don't remember a whole lot about the event. Whatever happened was a tremendous mystery but somehow I walked through it." Mik chuckled to himself. How true that was!

Odessa had no idea what was going through Mik's mind. She nodded.

"That railroad is a big and complex job. It is just another of the many big, complicated projects that Mr. Moffat has undertaken. He has worked through and triumphed every time. I hope his successes continue with this one."

She switched topics. "By the way, the other day you said you had a question. It was something about our agreement here to provide supplies to the camp. Did you find out what you needed to know? If you still need information, we can talk about it after dinner. But I must leave you now, I need to get back to the kitchen. Good to see that you are alright!" She hurried away.

Ted was right. Dinner was served at six. Not two minutes before, not two after. Six o'clock. There was a rush among the boarders to get washed up and ready. Mik figured that anyone not clean and sitting at the table would miss the first course. Of course, there was no other practical way for Mrs. Pruden to run a boarding operation.

At the table, the conversation and hubbub was informative but kind of made him nervous. He was glad to have had a little while to rest and gather his thoughts. Mik knew that he would have to pay close attention to people and what they said. Again he reminded himself that he could get by for only so long with acting dazed and in a fog.

The women served the meal. They did so as peers, not silently as servants. They listened and participated. Both were quite willing to join the conversation or offer an opinion. There were usually eight people, sometimes less sometimes a little more. It was both family and road workers. The number varied because often as not a road worker would have to stay out on the job overnight for some reason. Of course then he would miss the meal.

Ted was there. He got the horses and wagon taken care of in short order. There was another young man several people greeted as Seth. Mik realized that was Ted's brother in law, Odessa's brother, the Pruden's son. He seemed an intelligent, able person. A man sat at the head of the table and acted as if the place was his. In fact he was one of the principals. Mik assumed correctly that it was Mr. Pruden, or as he was often known, Charlie.

As Mik came in and took a seat, Charlie smiled and nodded. "Mr. Mast, good to see you. I heard that you were up and about, among us still. Terrible thing, that rockslide. It set progress on the job back by a few days. That is not good but can be overcome. I and many others are glad to see that at least it didn't claim you or anyone else."

He looked at Mik, making a frank appraisal. "You are probably a bit addled, or at loose ends. Having a close call with injury or death will do that to a person. Tell us, just how did you manage to escape? What do you recall?"

Mik was enjoying his meal. A man worked up an appetite by traveling to new worlds! He had last eaten with Sula the morning before he left. The food was not fancy but was well prepared and tasty. The roast beef with potatoes and onions, green beans, bread with butter, washed down by coffee just plain hit the spot. He chewed and swallowed.

He considered his response carefully. He was painfully conscious that he didn't know anything about Myron Mast. The last thing he wanted to do was to raise questions. Then again, he thought, no one but he knew the truth. In fact if he told them, no one would believe. No one at the table could imagine that he wasn't Myron and hadn't a clue about Myron's likes, dislikes, and personality. Mik realized that he just had to skate around the edges.

"I really don't remember much, Mr. Pruden. Things are kind of a blank. What I do recall is that I came out of a cloud, a fog, and found myself. I was standing on the road below the camp. I heard a horse approach and up rode Cam Braun. He greeted me and he told me about the rockslide. To be honest I don't remember much before that. Even of my earlier life."

He paused, smiled, and looked around the table. "So feel free to fill me in on my likes and dislikes!" Several of the diners and all the Prudens chuckled.

Ted said, "Here is a chance to build a man from the ground up. Have at it, ladies!"

Mik himself chuckled. "Seriously, if you say things about me or my past, they will likely jog my memory and help me get back. Whatever you can help me fill in is greatly appreciated. Do not be shy or think that any fact is too small, please."

He looked at Charlie Pruden. "I have no real explanation for my escape. Perhaps the reason is that I am just a very lucky man. I was in precisely the right spot for wondrous things to happen." It occurred to Mik that statement was truer than Pruden would ever know.

Cam Braun had come in late. He listened and got up to speed on the discussion. From the expression on his face it was clear he had something to add.

"We have looked into this incident. Thus far in this tunnel job, the rock in the bore has been solid. It has held up well, doesn't flake or scale, and there are no apparent faults. The team who drilled has a long solid, safe record. Their work has always been more than satisfactory with holes the proper depth and diameter."

Seth asked, "That is Svenson and O'Malley, right? Aren't they the team who drilled for that shot?"

"Yes," Cam responded. "Each has eight or more years of experience drilling in hard rock. They seem to know just what is needed for every blast."

He paused to see if Seth or anyone else had questions or something to add.

"It goes on. The dynamite man is crackerjack. He walked me through what he did on this shot. Neither he nor I would change anything. So that part of the job too was correct. Even with these competent workers, the engineer and I both check and monitor the work on a continuous basis. As yet another check, Mik here went in to check before the actual blast. He surely would have halted the shot if he had seen a problem. So we are still trying to learn what happened, why things went wrong."

Mik nodded. He tried to look as if he remembered at least something about checking a dynamite set and blasting cap and cord placement. It was good to triple check such things before firing the hole.

Cam noted the nod. He was glad to see Mik responding positively to something. Earlier in the day the man had seemed passive, confused, and not himself. It was almost like he was someone else.

He paused for an instant and then went on, "From what we have found so far, nothing should have gone wrong."

The big foreman chewed on a mouthful of beef. "On the other hand, the blast seemed big, too big for the amount of dynamite used. It felt and sounded too powerful, way out of proportion to the number of sticks used. We are checking the dynamite inventory to be sure the job didn't get doubled up somehow."

He held the floor. He had one more fact to add, to throw out for his fellow diners. Whether it was important or not, he was unsure.

"There was one thing, one unusual occurrence. Unknown people were around. A slender, bright eyed man was seen on site before the blast. He acted as if he belonged on the site. We're not sure, but he may in fact have been in the tunnel. If so God knows what mischief he could have done. The man was seen near the tunnel exit but no one definitely saw him inside. Now we find out that no one knew him or what he was doing. Everyone assumed someone else had approved his presence. We want to find and talk to this man."

Cam looked around, from face to face. It was as if he was silently asking each if they knew the man. Plus he wanted to emphasize his last statement. The man knew how to work a crowd and motivate people.

Mik immediately thought of the couple. The tall skinny man and the woman in the odd getup. He had assumed it was a chance meeting there on the trail. Of a sudden he wondered if they had intentionally timed the encounter. If they had something to hide they would have wanted to be sure that Cam was already headed back to the tunnel site. From what he remembered someone well could have stage managed the entire meeting.

An image of Del, or rather Dale Smertz, flashed through Mik's mind. Was he the "slender, bright eyed man" Cam described? Dale had implied he had some railroad construction knowledge and was able to put it to good use. If he had construction knowledge he might have the knowhow to doctor a dynamite set. The man's doppelganger, Del, was sure up to no good back in Sula time. Was this Dale character making trouble here and now too? Why? Was he just a natural born troublemaker? And how did she fit in?

The others were all thinking their private thoughts, pondering what Cam had told them.

Across the table, Ted returned Cam's gaze. He asked what everyone was thinking. "Why talk to this elusive man? Surely you don't suspect tampering or sabotage? Or intent to harm or kill? And if this man did somehow make trouble, how did he get onto the site? More importantly, how on earth did he get into a tunnel where live blasting was in progress?"

Jennie Pruden had been listening. She couldn't help but give her opinion.

"Who would intentionally interfere with a shot? Anyone doing that would have to know people could be hurt. They themselves could be caught in a premature blast. It makes no sense!"

There was silence for a few moments as people considered that. Then Charlie spoke.

"Well, we all know that owners of certain established railroads are hostile to this road. There are men who wouldn't mind seeing this project fail. After all, the reason for building this road is to open up northwestern Colorado and northeast Utah. Northwest Colorado has virtually no service and that part of Utah has been served only poorly by their present roads. That suits the established roads just fine."

He thought for a moment, then went on. "But it could be that the road is progressing faster than anticipated. Maybe the rapid progress has some of Mr. Moffat's enemies and competitors worried. Many naysayers predicted that this was an impossible job, to build across Eldorado Mountain and up to the divide. But so far it is all progressing fairly well, with minimal problems or delays."

Jennie had followed what her husband had said. She observed,

"Look at how Harriman, Gould and others have tried to throttle newcomers wherever they can. They have stopped at nothing in the past, all around the country. Why would this be any different? Accidents slow the pace of road building. They cost time and money. Harriman and company would love to kill this road. No doubt he would also love to bleed Moffat and his allies white in the process."

She looked around the table. "I'm not accusing anyone of causing this rockslide. But it is awfully convenient that it is unexplained, and works to Moffat's harm and to his competitors' benefit."

Mik thought back to the history of the "Gilded Age" of American business. Around the turn of the century—from the nineteenth to the twentieth centuries—power and money were concentrated in a few hands, just several hundred of them. The several score extremely rich industrialists who held the bulk of the wealth were called "the robber barons."

They didn't hold businesses individually, rather they used trusts. This was a form of corporation, and could own and control multiple businesses, even big swaths of an industry. The trust was their favored way to hold wealth and wield power. It was anonymous and could be adapted to any industry or business. Oil, banking, shipping, steel and other industries were so dominated.

By about 1900 railroads, both transcontinental systems and most local short lines, were controlled by a few such trusts. Behind the scenes and the trail of ownership, such men as E.H. Harriman, Jay Gould, and James Hill pulled the strings. The trusts they controlled were ostensibly publicly held. Control and voting rights were almost exclusively in private hands.

American business at large was still in a pretty much unregulated stage. There was virtually no effective federal antitrust regulation, no Securities and Exchange Commission, no Truth in Advertising laws. Stock manipulation was part of the game. Alliances were made and broken among the industrialists to gain advantage or to ruin a rival. Big business at that time was very much a Darwinian struggle.

Most people around the table knew that David Moffat was rich. They didn't realize that while he was quite well off, he did not run in the same circles as Harriman, Vanderbilt and Rockefeller. Moffat came to Denver from the Midwest in the 1860s. He was not a penniless waif but had little. The young man worked hard and became a substantial member of the business and civic community.

Moffat was an honest man who expected the same of others. Unfortunately, that didn't always happen. One of the reasons Moffat intended to push his road through to Salt Lake was to gain independent access to the Pacific cities and ports. He had a commitment in Salt Lake City. There he had an agreement to connect his Denver Northwestern and

Pacific with a road which could allow traffic through to the west coast. Or so he thought. The agreement was to connect with the San Pedro, Los Angeles, and Salt Lake Railroad. This road was controlled by Senator W.A. Clark of Montana. Moffat and Clark had a handshake agreement.

This was as good as a contract to Moffat but was meaningless to Clark. At the same time he shook with Moffat, Clark was negotiating with Harriman. He played both ends against the middle and took what he thought the better deal. He decided, unbeknownst to Moffat, to hook up exclusively with the Union Pacific. Nor did he tell Moffat of that decision. David Moffat seldom misjudged men and their actions as badly as he misjudged Clark and the San Pedro, Los Angeles and Salt Lake.

By his nature and outlook, Moffat needed to build and create. Along side those personal needs, he had a number of good reasons to push the road through. As he planned it, it would run about equidistant from other lines, seventy five to one hundred miles north and south of competing railroads. The road would run between the two main competitors: The Union Pacific ran across southern Wyoming and the Denver & Rio Grande ran south of Colorado's main range of the Rockies.

Also, the area he would be opening up with the road had potential. There were a number of prospective resorts. They were ready to develop, and the train would bring guests and the goods to supply them. The towns of Hot Sulphur Springs and Steamboat Springs both had possibilities for tourism and growth. Further, there were coal deposits near Hayden Colorado, an hour or two past Steamboat. And there was agriculture: Year in and year out, ranchers needed to have supplies brought in and their cattle taken to market. All in all, there were many opportunities to make money with a road such as the Denver Northwestern & Pacific Railway.

The organizers of the D&NW were not naïve. Clark aside, Moffat and his men were aware of Harriman's and other's tricks and mischief. They were constantly on the lookout for problems. These included but weren't limited to sabotage, labor unrest, right of way obstacles, artificial shortage of needed materials, and financial backstabbing. And Harriman was based in New York City, financial capital of the railroad industry. He could and did spike attempts to raise money when Coloradans and other outsiders came to town.

After Jennie Pruden's remarks the conversation quickly subsided. Everyone was suddenly wondering about the rockslide. Was it an accident or an attack? Was this a declaration of war on David Moffat and his railroad?

Mik was surprised by the feelings and opinions this information brought forth in him. He cleared his throat then said, "I do not remember the day. But I have to tell you that if that slide, my mishap, was caused by someone meddling or worse, I will be very angry. And I will do my best to find out what really occurred."

Seth Pruden had followed the conversation. As the youngest at the table he was reluctant to join in. He really hadn't said much. Mik's statement made him join in.

He observed, "The challenges of constructing this road are enough to satisfy most anyone. Half way up a mountain, tunneling through rock ribs every time you turn around, access mainly by horse and wagon, high elevation, lack of water, difficulty seeing far enough for meaningful surveys, all make for difficulty. Even if no one is interfering."

He thought for a moment, then continued, "Adding in opposition by unnamed, faceless men will make it that much harder. I am exhausted just fighting the battles we have. I hope we don't face more..."

Charlie Pruden huffed.

"Mr. Moffat has overcome worse. I am confident that he will win out yet. He has his friend John Evans in New York City working every day on financing the work. He has good crews," and here he looked around the table, "doing the actual building. This is a big project and it will benefit us all."

The conversation turned to local issues. There was talk of a hotel to be located high above Eldorado Springs. There would be a wagon road to it from town. Also there would be a road down from a siding on the railroad. That was the attraction, the stop on the railroad. People would ride the train out from Denver to spend the night. It would be called the Crag Hotel. There were plans to install a funicular, a cable car, from down in the valley up to the hotel as well.

Jennie Pruden heard the hotel mentioned. "The hotel site can be seen from here. You can see where a site is being graded out, flat and on the end of a ridge looking out over the valley towards the cliffs. It is high above Eldorado Springs and the creek. The views will be spectacular. It will be a modern wonder!"

Charlie Pruden mentioned that the place was sure to be lucrative for the owners. He himself was a forward thinker, always looking for new ways to make money. He had seen the opportunity to make money with a contract to supply the construction crews with food. So far it was working well. He and wife Jennie were making a good income from the road as it was being pushed through. He was sure there was more money to be made after the road was built. All those people and goods being moved, coming and going, would need handling and tending.

"Getting the railroad to stop there to bring and pick up guests is a good idea. People may want to spend more than a night or two in this country. For that matter, people might be willing to live out here and take the train in to the city to work. Some enterprising soul will make some money off that idea."

The talking ebbed as people finished their meal. Soon they were getting up from the table, going their own ways for the rest of the evening. Mik needed time to think. He was still reluctant to talk much. He sure didn't want to say something he shouldn't. He decided that the best way to do that was not to be around other people. So he headed for the stairs to go to "his" room.

Cam Braun caught up with him.

"Mik, I want you to work with me tomorrow. I want to be sure you are strong and recovered. Then maybe I can send you back to your duties. Plus you still seem a little dazed and lightheaded. It is almost like you are kind of the same person but not really."

He looked searchingly at the man who he thought had survived a near encounter with death. "How is your memory now? Is it coming back?"

Mik shrugged. Cam took that more or less as a yes.

"You know, even if it is returning, for now I want you to shadow me. You'll stay out of the tunnel and off of working on the grade for now. I need an assistant anyway, and you can fill the bill. At least until we are both satisfied of your strength and health. Meet me at breakfast, seven tomorrow morning." Mik nodded and started up the stairs. Cam turned towards the parlor, ready for an evening of railroad talk over a deck of cards.

Earlier on the mountain, before dinnertime at the Prudens, it was a fine and sunny day. After Ella and Dale left Mik, they started up the road towards Tunnel 4. The altitude and their lack of fitness told. Soon walking up the hill made them short of breath. They stopped to catch their wind and talk.

Ella observed, "There is something almost eerie about that man Mast. I met him briefly once a few weeks back. He doesn't seem to remember me or apparently much of anything. Frankly he doesn't quite act like he is all there. Like he knows where he is but doesn't really, and doesn't really know the people around him. That slide must have addled him more than we know."

Smertz nodded. "I of course didn't know him. I guess you'd expect a catastrophe like that to make you confused. Escaping with your life would certainly make him look at things differently. I know it would make me reconsider my priorities."

He thought for a moment. "If what you say is true, maybe we can recruit him. Maybe he isn't so ready to work for the road now. Maybe he isn't willing to give it his strength and life. If we play things right, maybe we can use him. He would be a good one to sow seeds of doubt and fear in the work crew. Did you see how his eyes got big when he first saw us? It was almost like thought we were ghosts or something."

The woman smiled and nodded. "Yes, perhaps we can swing him over to us. It is worth trying. I'll see if I can arrange another meeting. It may take several tries to bring him over. For that matter, maybe it would be good for him to meet this man coming to town. I mean Josephus Eggers."

She turned and started walking again, this time not up to the tunnel works, but down towards town. "Why do we need to go up to the worksite? Mr. Eggers will help us plan and agitate and slow workers down. Let's get ready to meet him. He is supposed to arrive in Boulder this evening. Let's start down to Eldorado Springs. Maybe I can catch a ride for us in a returning wagon. From Eldorado we can find a ride to Boulder to meet this guy."

V

"HIS" ROOM BECKONED MIK. HE KNEW IT WAS EARLY TO RETIRE, but he was drained. Physically, psychically and emotionally, you name it, he had had it. The entire day had been unsettling and bizarre. He had to get his head around what seemed to be happening.

Maybe he was dead, and this was the next life. Or was he really in a parallel world of some kind? And how about this character Mast? What happened to him? Was he wandering around here or somewhere else, equally befuddled? Was there really such a person?

Mik wondered, was he in a psychotic state, or dreaming, or what? He bit his lip again, and definitely felt it. Much as he doubted and wanted to dispute it, Mik decided he really had somehow come into an alternate universe. He was pretty sure he could get back to his real life. He knew he could find the spot where he stepped into this place.

Maybe he should just leave. He owed no one here any explanation or duty to stick around. He could simply walk out and go up to the where he came in. The portal, he had decided to call it. The portal where he stepped through to this place and time was just up the hill a mile or two. But his wonder and curiosity were too strong. Besides, finding a precise square foot of land would be near impossible in the dark. *May as well stick here at least for now and see what I can learn*, he decided.

Mik continued to think of himself as Mik. He knew he would have to answer to "Myron" and "Mast" as well as the familiar name. It was a good thing people had called Mast "Mik" at least sometimes. And he figured he would sometimes fail to respond when someone called out the other name. If and when that happened, he could rely at least for a while on being the dazed and confused accident survivor. Hopefully he would be gone before that became an issue. Whatever, it all made his head hurt.

He needed alone time. First, he wanted to see what personal possessions there were up in Mast's room. It was critical that he fit in, with appearance and manner. Several people today had asked him about his clothes, so they somehow didn't quite fit in. He wanted to blend in as long as he was here, even though he intended to stay probably for just a short while. Of course, that assumed he could get out when he wanted to....

Although, when he thought about it, there was no guarantee Sula time was the same. He might spend a day here, go back and find it was a year later. Or earlier—good God, if that were the case, he might meet himself or something. How strange would that be? Or he could spend a month here and get back there in the afternoon of the day he left...The possibilities started to overwhelm him. Mik realized he couldn't figure that stuff out. He had to just put one foot forward at a time. Decision made, he calmly went on, figuring he'd go back when it made sense for him to do so. *Let the days fall where they may*, he mused. *I'm here for at least a while and can't wait to see where it all leads!*

That problem finally dealt with, he turned to his here and now. It was time, he decided, to see what every day life was like. He looked at the possessions the typical person (he hoped Mast was typical) had and used for day to day living. Knowing about that would help him blend. He felt like a grave robber going through Mast's effects. The clothes would fit him and there wasn't much in the way of the truly personal. Curiously, there were no letters, diary or the like. There was one photo of himself, that is, Mast, and a nice looking young woman. It was taken in an orchard or forest somewhere. He hoped he didn't meet up with that woman.

Mik had to admit he wasn't looking forward to shaving with a straight razor. Maybe he would grow a beard. After all, he had had a close call, hadn't he? One close call was enough and if a man wanted to grow a beard so be it. He thought of Sula. As he drifted off, his hope was that he could get back and see her again.

Morning came soon enough. Starting a beard didn't appeal. Plus, starting a new beard and looking scruffy was an attention getter. Attention of any kind, he did not want. He went about it carefully and slowly. It turned out that shaving with the straight blade wasn't as bad as he had feared. The shave wasn't as close as he would have liked. Most importantly, he managed it with no blood. A good start to the day!

Breakfast was coffee, bacon, and gravy over biscuits. He could almost feel his arteries clogging up, but when in Rome and all...The biscuits and gravy brought back visions of the SOS the Army fed him. Across the years, the memory brought a smile.

Cam had sat across from him, busily scoffing breakfast. Annoyingly, he slurped his coffee. It was loud. To Mik's ears it sounded like a bathtub draining. Looking over the rim of his fast emptying cup, the foreman noticed Mik's smile.

"You must have had a good restful night. You seem pretty cheery this morning!" He smiled himself and kidded, "Can't wait to get back to the job, huh, Mik?"

Mik lightheartedly responded, "I'm just glad to be here. I truly am. Everything I see is a wonder to me!" His smile slipped.

"Cam, my memory really is spotty. It is good that you aren't sending me out to look at blasting. For now, I'm glad that you want me to work with you. If you don't mind I intend to stick close. Be patient. If I ask questions, it is just me trying to get the pieces put back together. I hope it will help me fill in some of the blanks."

"Yeah, we'll talk up at the tunnel." He tilted his head back and took a final swig of coffee, his cheeks filling for a moment before he gulped it down.

"Rather than have you ride up with me, let's do it this way. Change things up a bit. This morning, Mrs. Pruden is sending up a wagon full of supplies—meat, eggs, milk, butter. You can ride up with the driver. Talk with him, he may be able to help you remember things. When you get to the site, ask around. Someone will know where I am."

He forked in one last mouthful of sopping biscuit, standing as he talked and chewed. "I need to get going now. See you up there."

He walked out, climbed on his already saddled horse, and left. Shortly, Mik went out too. He found the partly loaded wagon. Not one to stand around, he pitched in, helping get the supplies and food stowed. Mrs. Pruden was supervising. She had particular ideas about what went where.

"This food is of good quality, you be careful with it. I want to be sure it arrives at the cooktent safely and in good condition. Don't put those jars of butter on top! Put them under the potatoes, in their own box. The butter needs to stay cool. Putting the jars below protects the butter and keeps the produce from getting bruised."

Once the wagon was loaded, Pruden gave the driver two papers. "Here is a list of what you have in the wagon today. I want you to have the cook sign both and bring one back to me. That way we know what was sent and they know what to pay for."

The wagon pulled away, slowly then at a regular pace just faster than a comfortable walk. Mik had to admit that he was curious. And kind of excited. He couldn't wait to meet others, and to see the tunnel excavation and the work camp.

North about four or five miles the morning sun was shining on the city of Boulder as well. Sitting in the restaurant of the James Hotel, Mr. Josephus Eggers savored his morning meal. The choice and preparation of food was very good. He mused that he had traveled a lot on business, even once to Canada. But this was his first trip to the Rocky Mountains. He was impressed with the people and the country. It was beautiful and held a lot of growth potential.

Eggers was a businessman. As a rule he didn't go for stuffy correctness. Joe is what he answered to, not Josephus. He used the full name only when he wanted to impress or overawe someone. Joe felt he was doing well in life, but was always on the lookout to do better. As a youngster, he could have just gone along with what life offered. Had he done that, he likely would have ended up a laborer somewhere. Joe was born in upstate New York, near a small town east of Buffalo on the Erie Canal.

As a young teenager, he left home. The thought of being a lifelong a canal worker was not something he wanted. He did not want to spend his life looking at the back end of a donkey. He didn't care if that donkey was doing an important and useful job pulling a barge along the canal. Joe Eggers had more in him than herding a boat pulling animal from dawn to dusk for the next thirty or forty years. No way! It was the big city for him.

Buffalo was at the center of things in those days. It was a big, cosmopolitan place, at least compared to the village he had come from. Ships came in off Lake Erie, hauling raw materials and other basic supplies. Manufacturing plants sprung up. People had to be housed, fed, clothed. The railroad had come to the area, drawn to the growing economy as bees to blossoms. Buffalo was an entrepot, a place where sailors, freighters, buyers, sellers, women of the night, builders, brokers, seamstresses, transporters, merchants, lawyers, and con men all did their business. The prospects were exciting! There were contacts to be made. Money was there for the earning, and there was a country to be built.

Joe chose to concentrate on the railroad. The high technology fascinated him. He knew he didn't have the education to design, engineer, or build even a simple machine. And the locomotives and rail cars were not simple. They had thousands of close fitting, moving parts. It didn't take long for him to see that even learning to maintain or operate one was beyond him.

His skills were in another arena. He was able to work with people. He could talk to them, relate to them, read their interests, desires, and intentions. It was like a bolt of lightning, realizing that he could read people. From there it was a short step to seeing that he could make money with those skills. Most of the time, he was able to persuade them to do what he wanted them to do. And quite often he was able to make them think that it was their idea, not his. He did well with this, getting people to do what he wanted them to do.

In Buffalo you could trip over all the shippers. People were looking to move any sort of goods and materials imaginable. Wheat, ore, furniture, livestock, people, mail, iron and steel. You name it, some one wanted to buy or sell it. And then they needed it delivered somewhere.

Joe Eggers developed a knack for negotiating rates and shipping contracts. He would work with any and all shippers, but his specialty became railroad freight. He was able to get his customers a good package, timely delivery at a good price. It didn't take long for the railroads to notice. Every railway company wanted the talented young men out there working for them. They wanted to maximize their efficiency and revenues rather than have talented competitors.

Joe found himself with a job offer from the trust that owned the biggest railroad in the region. The railway company needed able men, and he filled the bill. How far from watching an ass's ass pulling a barge! Soon he came to see Buffalo as a medium place, almost a backwater. He set his sights on New York City.

Before long, he was there. He loved the City. It was the business capital of the country and it was in the running to knock London off as the business capital of the world. He got himself a job working for one of the most powerful men in the most powerful city. His boss was Edward Henry Harriman, financier and businessman extraordinaire.

Like Joe, E.H. Harriman's background wasn't a rich one by any means. He was a minister's son. Even as a boy, E.H.

was not interested in the cloth. At about age fourteen, he got an uncle's help. Together they wangled the young man a position on Wall Street. His start was not as a mover and shaker. Nor was he a well connected blueblood. Young Edward started at the bottom of the pile. His first job on the Street was office boy for a stock broker. This office boy was smart, energetic, and determined. He did well. Within a few years he had built contacts and scraped up enough money to buy his own seat on the New York Stock Exchange.

From that seat, he started out financing business deals of all kinds for most any business. It didn't take long before he too got interested in railroads. In the 1880's and 1890's railroads were the cutting edge. They were the disruptive technology, the companies which opened vast new areas of commerce and social change. Steam railroads had a similar effect for (and on) the late nineteenth century that dot coms did for the late twentieth.

Not unlike in the late twentieth century, there were just too many companies trying to use the new technology. Too many railroads. A certain need for track and hauling was evident. But there were more railway companies than the economy could support. Many of them sprung up overnight. Quite a few of those were shoddily built and weakly financed. The industry was ripe for consolidation.

Harriman became a consolidator. He was to play a key role in reducing overhead and gaining efficiency. His first exposure to the iron rooster was working on a small upstate New York line. His father in law had part ownership and the company needed attention. With that entrée, E.H. stepped in and learned the ropes. He streamlined the financing, cut costs, increased revenues, eliminated competition. Before long the line was showing profits.

He had cut his teeth, and found a niche. Harriman started looking for other lines in need of attention. He took control of and turned around a number of ailing railroad lines. At first his specialty was in the financial and cash flow end of things. Before long he picked up operations and management skills. Not least among his early trophies was the Illinois Central, a line which serviced the all important Chicago hub and surrounding markets.

In the early 1890s Harriman stepped onto the national stage. He got involved in the Union Pacific Railroad. This proud old road was built in the 1860s from Sacramento to Utah, over the Sierra Nevada. In 1869 the UP met the Central Pacific in Utah. The Central Pacific was built west from Omaha as the UP worked east. Both were encouraged and partly funded by the federal government, starting during the Civil War. The idea was to tie the nation together and settle the west before the Confederacy could. In any case, by the late 1860s, the nation was joined coast to coast by rail. Travelers could experience speeds up to thirty or forty miles per hour! A person could go from New York City to San Francisco in about a week!

But thirty years later, in the 90's, the UP was in sad shape. Track needed replacing. Its locomotives and cars were old and wearing out. Worse, the line was hemorrhaging money. It had to be reorganized. The company was in such straits that Morgan, Gould, and other robber barons turned up their noses. Conventional thinking had it that the Union Pacific was too far gone to be salvaged.

Harriman thought differently. He arranged financing and jumped deeply into operations. Before long, in Union Pacific country, the trains were running on time and the line was actually making money. In fact, it was on the way to becoming the proverbial eight hundred pound gorilla in the room. Soon it would be taking over other lines.

By the early 1900s Harriman controlled more miles of track than anyone else. Anyone. Even the Czar of All the Russias with his colossal Trans Siberian Railway took second place to E.H.Harriman.

Harriman did not get where he was by being soft, nice, or even particularly honest. He considered all as fair in the railroad wars. His deal with Senator Clark for access to Los Angeles through Salt Lake was typical. He knew that Moffat might or might not push a road through the Rockies all the way to Salt Lake City. Even if he did, he would still need access to the west coast.

But Harriman controlled the Union Pacific. And he wanted to control access to the Pacific coast. So he made sure he tied up Clark's San Pedro Los Angeles and Salt Lake Road. Whether or not Moffat made it to Salt Lake, Harriman figured, he was little threat to the UP. At most Moffat's road would be a feeder line, a local railroad. And if he could delay or stop Moffat before he ever got to Salt Lake, so much the better.

So even though he knew Clark and Moffat had a handshake deal, he secretly offered a better deal to Clark. Clark was not a particularly scrupulous man himself. He took Harriman's deal despite his gentlemen's agreement with Moffat. This encounter, this transaction, was business as usual for Harriman and the UP. He didn't even give this deal a second thought.

Joe Eggers would come to know such tactics and ruses. After coming to the City from Buffalo, Joe learned at the feet of the master. He was drawn to the underside of railroad business dealings. He became the guy who E.H. Harriman relied on work the competition. Joe knew how to slow, stop, or at least cause problems for the other lines. Sixty or seventy years later, Joe Eggers would have been able to step right in and run Dick Nixon's "Dirty Tricks" campaign. And he wouldn't have let his people get caught inside the Watergate Apartments. He was good at what he did.

Right now, in 1903, Joe was in Colorado. He was in Colorado because of David Moffat and his road. To be precise, he was sent to Colorado because of David Moffat. Harriman sent him west to make trouble. He was to make as much trouble as possible for Mr. Moffat and his road.

Joe was a long way from New York City and the industrial northeast. Out west was a different world, new and interesting. It was not nearly as primitive as he had first feared it would be. There were brick buildings, schools, churches, and stores. He saw no stockades to protect from stampeding buffaloes or Indians on the warpath. No gunfights in the streets.

As part of the job, and out of curiosity, he intended to learn as much about the local scene as he could. He kind of liked what he was seeing. It was fresh and new, with lots of opportunities. Seemed like some of the mistakes made back east could be avoided out here.

He mused on his own future. He was here to do Harriman's bidding to confound the Denver Northwestern and Pacific people. Fair enough. There were plenty of ways to cause slowdowns, problems, barriers. Now, if he could also make some money slide into his own pocket, all the better...

Of a sudden it occurred to him that he had something unique he could use to build and improve his life. He had current knowledge of Mr. Harriman and the Union Pacific

Railroad. Very few people knew his boss's likes and dislikes, his personal strengths and weaknesses, the way Joe did. Not to mention, he had unparalleled insights and personal knowledge of the Union Pacific and its operations. Joe figured if he could use those to his benefit, why not? After all, he had exclusive and valuable knowledge. There was no reason not to make himself some money and establish himself in the Rockies, was there? A man had to look after himself, did he not?

Joe pushed back from the breakfast table. Not a bad meal, even if he was a long way from the City, out in the west. Being a New Yorker, he had the prejudice, or sure knowledge, that civilization stopped a little ways west of the Hudson River. When planning his trip he thought he was going to the ends of the earth. He figured he would be giving up the advantages of early twentieth century civilization.

Not so. The two people who met him on arrival were surprisingly educated and civilized. Dale Smertz actually had some railroad experience. And Ella, the one named woman. She was well read and strong. She had traveled, he could tell by her occasional remark. Her vocabulary was not that of an uneducated country girl. Yet she wore drab, often men's clothing. While she had a rough side to her, she was definitely a woman. They had joined him for breakfast.

He looked at the two sitting across the table. They didn't know it yet, but they would be working under his guidance. They would be the primary operatives for any ruses or stratagems New York would direct against the Denver Northwestern. Joe generally didn't get his hands dirty if he could avoid it. It was time to go to work. So he started at the beginning.

"Now tell me again about this rockslide in a tunnel along the front grade of Moffat's road."

He made himself comfortable, settling in for a morning's conversation.

Back on Eldorado Mountain, Mik was on his way up to that tunnel worksite. The supply wagon took the same route up the hill as he had walked down yesterday. The driver was friendly enough. He didn't seem to know much about the railroad. Nonetheless, he rambled amiably about things he did know.

"I just got hired. Mr. Pruden interviewed me because I will haul from his ranch. But I actually work for the Good Construction Company. That is whose camp we are going to. They have the contract to build this part of the line. My job is to take care of the teams and make these deliveries up to the construction camp every few days."

He stopped talking. They approached an obstacle and he needed to focus. His attention was entirely on steering the team around an empty wagon stopped and askew on the road. Somehow the driver had lost control coming down the hill.

The barrier safely negotiated, he continued. "I hear the railroad is hiring. They don't need more drivers or laborers. People like me are a nickel a dozen. What they do need is surveyors, carpenters and such skilled jobs. Mechanics and craftsmen are what they seek, not warm bodies." He smiled kind of shyly, and changed the subject.

"This is a great thing for Colorado, this new railroad. The whole of north western Colorado will soon be open for development. Ranches, towns, logging...And it will be good for this area, right around Eldorado Springs. It will be opened up so people can come up for the day if they want to. There is a hotel to be built up above town, did you hear?" Mik was half listening, instead he was thinking of Sula, and where he was, and what year it was, and what he should do.

The driver didn't even notice his rider wasn't responding. He was happy to have company and was still talking.

"Say, did you read what President Roosevelt said? He is proposing we make parks, national parks, of scenic areas around the country. They will be closed to logging, mining, and development. They will be owned by the people and open to all. And the rest of the forests will belong to the government, called national forests. Big steps, but they make sense. I like most of the ideas the old Rough Rider comes up with!"

The amiably talking driver saw a baseball sized rock tumble down the side of the road. That brought him back to the Front Range of the Rocky Mountains. He tore himself away from thoughts of Yosemite Valley Park and Teddy Roosevelt.

"Seeing that rock reminds me. I guess there was a rock-slide on the grade yesterday. At first they thought it got a man but I guess not. Have you heard anything about that?"

Mik just shrugged and gave the unvarnished truth. "Yeah, I heard that too. I really don't know what happened or anything." He thought, *God knows what happened to Michael Mast.*

Past the portal they went, but only Mik knew it. Portal. What a word, a doorway to go from here to there in the universe, and no one but he knew it. He was half tempted to just jump off the wagon and step back through it. Wouldn't that give the poor driver something to tell his grandkids! Maybe he should. He could go back to Sula, and the world he knew. The world of the internet and airplanes and cellphones.

But what if he jumped off and tried to step through, and it wasn't there? What if he was trapped in 1903? Besides, this was too good an adventure. He was one, probably the only one in history, to have such a window on a strange new world. He couldn't let this chance pass. He would come back to the portal and he would return to Sula and his life in another then. But not today, not yet.

On up the road the bumping wagon went. The driver had lapsed into silence. Soon they heard work being done. Voices shouting instructions, horses neighing, mules braying, men pounding and sawing. They came around a curve and there was the site. Mik was half envious of those who stayed up here all the time. But he was also more than half glad he had a room, a bed and full sit down meals in a proper house.

The site consisted of tents, some rough looking sheds, and several makeshift corrals. All the buildings and pens looked like they were thrown together in an afternoon. The site crawled with men coming and going. Supply wagons like theirs were coming up from Pruden's. There was also wagon traffic coming up from the south, along the newly cut railroad grade. Those wagons hauled timbers and other heavy materials. Such supplies had been brought to the railhead by steam and iron. Mik supposed the rails would soon be extended up to this camp.

Mik's driver slowed his team, then stopped.

"I have to take this shipment of meat and dairy to the cook tent, down the line a ways. I expect you want to hop off here. Good talking with you. See you around."

"Thanks, for the ride and dropping me off here. See you."

As Mik climbed down, he saw his friend Cam. The big guy was usually the one giving orders and having people wait, sometimes in line, to talk to him. Not today. This morning, Cam looked for all the world like he was standing at attention. He could have been in the service, standing in front of a senior officer getting orders for an operation or raid. But there was no officer, no saluting. There was, however, a distinguished looking man wearing a business suit. The man was talking to Cam, not dressing him down or giving commands, but talking. Another man, also in business dress, watched.

Now is not the time to try to get Cam's attention, thought Mik. He watched as the two well dressed men unrolled a sheaf of papers which looked like plans or blueprints.

Mik was unable to contain his curiosity. Even though he knew it was not appropriate, he tried to look inconspicuous as he edged close to the trio. The man who had been talking looked sharply at him, clearly not expecting or appreciating the interruption. He asked pointedly, "Yes, can I help you?"

Cam spoke up.

"Mr. Moffat, this is Myron Mast. The man who we feared was lost in the rockslide. He is working for a few days as my assistant until he gets his feet back under him. Mast, this is Mr. Moffat."

Looking at the other man, he continued, "This is Mr. Sumner, the Chief Engineer of the railroad."

Moffat relaxed and his expression softened.

"Mast, we are glad you are still with us." He looked Mik over, not rudely but sympathetically, as if checking to see he was uninjured. He thought for a quick moment.

"I understand you have good field experience. Join us for a moment. You should be in on this with Cam." With that, he looked at Sumner. "I'm done, Horace. Go ahead."

Sumner cleared his throat.

"Thank you, David. To recap and summarize, and I probably don't need to say this, but I will. We need to keep the basics in mind. We will be driving rail along the grade we are standing on. We are standing here, south and west of Eldorado Springs."

He pointed at the map. Then he swept his hand up and to the left. "Our goal is to keep this grade at two percent which will initially put us high above South Boulder Creek's mouth. Keeping that same gradient will take us to the level of the creek some nine or ten miles west. From there we will run along the creek to the continental divide." He jabbed a finger towards the top of the map.

Moffat made a wry face and said, "And that is when the fun starts."

Cam smiled and Mik followed his lead. Sumner did not see the humor and didn't crack even a little smile. "Keeping that grade and the hitting the creek where we intend is well and good. Things ought to ease up a bit for us there, at least for a ways. This stretch we're on now will require us to drive a dozen or more tunnels." He looked up at Cam, over to Mik.

"We cannot let that become a problem. We can't be having a rockslide on every tunnel. If we suffer that, well, it will put us way behind schedule. After all there will be many more holes to bore before we get to the level of the creek." He glanced at Moffat then looked Cam firmly in the eye.

"Mr. Braun. I want you to send crews to drill and sample the rock cliffs at every proposed tunnel. If you already have done so for some, all the better. Use what resources you need. I need a report on the geological stability of each site. I do not expect stability or geological problems but must know for certain."

Sumner made sure his wishes were clear. "Any questions, or any problems I should know about?"

Cam nodded no. "I will get on it right away, Mr. Sumner."

Sumner nodded in turn. "Good. As always, call or wire if you need anything." He and Moffat marched off down the grade towards waiting wagon. It would take them to the rail head from where they would take a train back to Denver.

Cam blew out a big breath. He relaxed his stance and looked at Mik.

"Man, it is a good thing I have you as a new assistant. This is an unexpected addition to my workload." He thought for a moment.

"I didn't want to tell them, but we are nearly done with the job. It turns out we already have geological reports on all but a handful of the tunnel sites. So at least we don't have to send teams all over the countryside. Mik, it is your job now. You work on gathering up the reports and information from the site office. I say office, you do realize it is a tent, right?"

He started to turn away but had a thought. He turned back and spoke.

"If someone gives you trouble or stalls you, use my name. Don't bring the actual reports out here in the open. Just assemble them one to a folder. I will get crews going to the few remaining sites. Come see me when you are done."

With that Mik moved on to start the job. Cam turned on to other tasks. He noticed a worker who was waiting to talk to him, and faced him. Just then he also saw a man he needed to see, and talk to privately. Cam called to him. "Steu, I need to see you in my office. I'll be done here in just a shake."

Cam didn't have an office either. He had a corner of a small tent set up next to the big wall tent that was the main office. Mr. Sumner used this big wall tent for his office when on site. It had a telephone, which was an unusual innovation for a construction project. Of course it allowed instant contact with the Denver office and other sites along the road. This company was ahead of its time.

Steuben Wentz came in to Cam's space as requested. He was a big man, not young, not old. From his appearance, his age could be anywhere between twenty five and forty. His title was Company Inspector. He was a Deputy Sheriff. His real job was company dick, the bull. Steu was the enforcer, the patrolman, the guy who kept peace in camp at night and after payday. His job also was to keep track of everyone on the site, those who belonged and those who did not. Not surprisingly for a construction camp, he occasionally was forced to crack a few heads. Every now and then, he had to have a private session with a troublemaker. Said troublemaker was later reported to have "fallen down and gotten bruised and scraped while returning to his tent." This didn't happen a lot. The "private sessions" came down just often enough to keep people in line. By design, of course.

Another part of Steu's job, which was understood by all but discussed by none, was company spy. He was paid to know what was going on. The Company Inspector was expected to know the gamblers and drinkers. He was aware of the unfortunate few who had marital problems. He saw through the goldbricks, ignored the whiners and watched the troublemakers. The man had a database in his head. Each man on the crew was known, strengths and weaknesses, as were regular delivery drivers. He also knew and watched when an outsider came on or around the site.

Steu was that rare Coloradan, a native. The Gregory Gulch diggings on Clear Creek, later known as Idaho Springs, were just being discovered in 1859. The same year, his parents fled Bavaria for a new life in America. The Pikes Peak Gold

Rush was at its height when they landed in New York City. The two stout Germans had several children already. Even so, they ignored opportunities in the east. They wanted to go west. They did so and ended up in the fledgling city of Denver. It treated them well. There were jobs for all willing to work. Several years later young Steuben came along.

Steu's parents wanted him to go to school. He went. Being able to read, write, and do basic arithmetic was enough for him. He got the basics in the class room but excelled on the playground. Being a big boy for his age, he learned early how to get his way. In those days a thirteen or fourteen year old was almost a man. Around that age he fell in with a gang. Steuben Wentz seemed to be on the way to a life, probably a short one, of street punkery and minor crime.

It wasn't long before he was caught in the act, a burglary. This was before the days of worrying about self esteem, of social services and juvenile court. Police on the street had wide latitude in dealing with their citizens. The cop who caught him gave him a choice—go behind bars or turn informant. Wentz avoided jail. He found he couldn't sell information to the cop, but there were many who would pay well for the right knowledge. Steu learned to work people. He built up a network of contacts and as a teenager did well working in back alleys and the underside of Denver.

The young man grew tired of that life, always looking over his shoulder. Plus it got complicated. It was just too much, having to carefully weigh every word, remembering who he had lied to about what. He knew if he kept at it things would not end well. He would end up in jail or stabbed in the gutter.

Fortunately for him, about that time, he met a woman who brought out the better in him. With her support he took a job with the railroad. Steu was not looking for a career working with his hands. He lacked the skills. For that matter he wasn't interested in being a mechanic, brakeman, or engineer. Instead he looked for ways to capitalize on his experience and contacts. He of course started as a laborer, moving ties and materials here and there.

Before long, he got promoted to being a yard bull, a company dick. These unglamorous names went to the man who kept the railyard in order. The company dick chased away hobos and made sure rail cars sitting in switch yards weren't broken into. Steu had a big advantage. He knew the tricks of the trade. He had worked both sides of the street, having spent years working with and against the cops. So he did well foiling loiterers, freeriders, and would be thieves.

His good work was rewarded. He was offered a position with the new railroad abuilding. Providing security for a construction camp on the new Denver Northwest and Pacific line would be a challenge. He felt qualified and was confident he could do the job well.

Steu didn't think of all this history as he walked up to the tent. He was on the job, thinking about a fight he had broken up the previous night. He made a note to check to see that the two guys were over whatever they fought about. And he was thinking about a couple of strangers who may have been lurking around camp. Pushing the tent flap back as he entered, he saw no one but Cam so spoke up.

"You wanted to see me, Braun?"

"Yes. Anything unusual going on I should know about?"

"Not really. Business as usual."

Cam nodded. "Good. Now, something new. You may have heard that Mast did survive somehow. I found him down the hill yesterday afternoon. He was dressed differently than I recall but my memory for that kind of thing is poor. Anyway, he was kind of wandering and didn't know how he got there. He seemed dazed and doesn't remember the rockslide at all."

A worker stuck his head in. "A load of shoring timber is coming in. Put it next to the shed up the hill? The big shed, next to the tunnel mouth?"

Cam nodded. "Yeah, that is where you ought to put it." The man left.

The foreman continued his news of Myron Mast.

"It is almost as if he isn't the same person. He looks much the same but just acts a little different than he used to. His choice of words is a little different. Nothing I can point to, but he is just a little different. I suppose the hard knocks had an effect. Anyway, I'm keeping him out of the line for now."

Another man stuck his head in, but clearly didn't want to talk to either the foreman or the company dick, at least not at the same time. He pulled his head back as if stung by a bee.

Cam smiled thinly at the man's reaction and went on, "He'll act as my assistant for a while. At least until I'm sure that his head has cleared. I want you to keep an eye on him too, if you would. He should be alright and act safely, but you never know...And if you have tasks for him let's us talk. Maybe he can help you too."

Steu nodded. "I heard many rumors, both that Mast was lost and that he somehow came through. Last I heard, he was coming up from Pruden's with a supply wagon this morning. I am glad to see he is with us." He thought for a moment.

"Right now, I have nothing for him to do. I may think of some suitable job but none are at hand. Of course I'll keep an eye on him for anything unsafe or unusual."

He cleared his throat, ready to bring up a delicate subject.

"About the slide. The dynamite inventory is at the correct level. I don't think the hole was overloaded for the blast. So that part has been accounted for. Assuming we have had correct figures all along, which I think we have had. Maybe we need to go back and be sure?"

He paused, another delicate subject on his mind.

"Oh, and something else. There were two strangers seen lurking around camp. Not just one man. It was, they were, a man and a woman, we think. He was slender with kind of intense, bright eyes. His companion looked like a woman in men's clothes. Or I guess it could have been a chubby man with long hair. No one got close enough to be sure about that. They were spotted but it was not close up, not a great distance but not close enough to speak with."

The cop got a frustrated look on his face.

"No one talked to them or saw them face to face. If they went near the tunnel they did it unseen. I doubt they did but I guess you never know for sure. In any case, I'll talk to Mast to get his memories and impressions. Maybe he saw or better yet talked to them."

Summing up, Steu looked Cam straight on. "I have to say, from what have been able to learn, that slide looks like an accident, pure and simple. Nothing intentional."

Cam nodded.

"Mr. Sumner will be reviewing the geology of the area to double check safety and stability. I too think that slide was no more than an unfortunate mishap. It will cost us a few days' time is all, thank God no injuries or worse. Even so, keep a sharp eye out."

He picked up a list of some sort, ready to tackle the day. Cam looked at Steu, smiling to soften the implied insult. "I don't want to tell you how to do your job, Steu. You know better than I what to look for, unusual incidents, intruder, and so on...Just keep me informed."

Steu nodded.

Cam continued. "Now we are making progress on the road, laying track, every day making feet in the tunnels, and so on. It is good visible progress. We are gaining ground on the timetables and deadlines for construction of the road. We are doing well and this may well attract troublemakers of one sort or another. If not them, hangers on and reporters will likely start to show up. If any newsmen or reporters do come around, have them sent to me. I don't want any of the men making comments or offering opinions. That goes for after hours too. Make sure the men don't talk. Of course you know what to do with the others."

Steu nodded again, eyes hard and a trace of a smile on his face.

Back in Boulder, three people were talking. One had asked, "Now tell me again about this rockslide in a tunnel along the front grade of Moffat's road."

Each knew that he or she had been sent out from the east to keep an eye on and slow the progress of the new railroad. The thing was, they didn't all know what the others were up to. Joe Eggers reported to senior management. Dale Smertz and Ella worked at a significantly lower level. So the three were fencing a little, fishing for what the others knew. Dale and Ella had more or less leveled with each other and considered themselves a team. But Joe was not part of that picture. He was not in the same loop they were in and so all three were asking themselves "who knows what here, and why?"

They were talking about recent occurrences and mishaps.

At this point Joe wanted to know more about the tunnel four rockslide.

He was direct. "You say you didn't cause the mishap. Do you know what did? Or who did? Is there someone out there causing problems?"

Ella glanced at Dale before speaking. No harm in telling the truth here, they had nothing to hide at this point.

"We were in the area, looking over the layout of the camp and tunnel. That is all we were doing, looking, trying to learn the layout. And watching to see how the animals were treated. Poor animals on many construction sites are cruelly whipped and starved. It is a shame and something should be done about it."

She realized she was heading into the weeds, so got back to his question. "We did absolutely nothing to cause a rockslide."

That said, she found herself veering from fact to wishful thinking. "The rocks along the front range there are rotten. That is all you need to know. Any geologist can tell you that, and that tunnels won't last. The mighty David Moffat will find it difficult or impossible to build a grade through that area. Even if he does find a way it will cost him money and lives."

She paused, and came back to the question. "We did nothing but look, from afar. I don't think we were even seen by anyone when we were up there."

Dale eyed Joe. "Like Ella said, probably bad rock and poor engineering work are behind the rockslide. Now, you ask, is someone causing problems? I don't know. Why do you ask? Do you think someone may be making trouble for the Denver Northwestern & Pacific?"

VI

Dale was trying to figure Joe's angle. What was this guy up to? Everybody knew the Moffat road would be good for Denver and Colorado, and eastern Utah. And everyone also knew that if the road was successful it would cut into the business and profits of the Union Pacific Line. Ella and Dale both wondered, what did Mr. Josephus Eggers care? Why was he even out here? Who did he work for, if anyone?

For his part, Dale knew why he cared about the progress of the Denver Northwestern and Pacific Railway. It was the enemy. He worked for a man who worked for a man who was an assistant officer who helped run security for the Union Pacific. Dale didn't know the name of his boss's boss but he did know that the man was pretty high up. Could be, he was high enough up that he maybe worked for someone in New York. Maybe that man even knew Mr. Harriman. It didn't really matter.

The fact was, Dale had a job to do. He had been sent out here to find out what the Denver Northwestern people were up to. Once he knew about that he was to gum things up and make life difficult for them. He was supposed to stir things up generally, try to encourage unions and workers' rights, question the need for another railroad, and so on.

And he was to cause problems for the railway itself. Not just any railway. His target for that was the Denver Northwestern and Pacific Railway, the new line abuilding across Colorado. His boss had not come out and told him that, of course.

He said, "Go out there and look after the interests of Mr. Harriman and the Union Pacific Railroad. You have a virtually unlimited expense account. Ella will be going with you. You can put her to work too. She has a knack for finding and building worker discontent. She has a heart for animals, and can stir up indignation about work horse abuse."

With a wink but saying nothing, the boss then made gestures. The pantomime showed trouble being made. First he was handing out money. Then someone got smacked with a fist. Explosions or collisions, Dale wasn't sure just which, were next. Dale Smertz got the message. He was to do all he could to slow or stop the progress of Moffat's road, by any means at hand. He knew the Union Pacific would look after him as long as he didn't cross too far over legal lines. The UP had a lot of good lawyers. They knew sheriffs and mayors and governors and could pull strings if need be.

But still, here in Boulder Colorado, far from his boss, he wondered. He always liked to know the competition. Good to be aware of who else was out there. So, what was this Joe Eggers about? What was he doing? Who had hired him? Why was he out here? Did Ella know anything about it? Dale knew what he was supposed to do. He sure didn't want to get tripped up by some guy just in from the east. This Joe guy kind of seemed like some dandy maverick type asking questions and upsetting things. He decided he would have to look into Eggers' background.

Then he figured the best thing to do was to confront the man, get things out in the open for good or ill. Dale did this never dreaming that Eggers worked directly for Mr. E. H. Harriman. The out of towner sitting across from him reported directly to the top in New York. Unlike Ella and Dale, Joe did not work for a man several rungs down in the pecking order. But Dale did not know that and wasn't about to learn it. Joe very much liked to work in the background. He really enjoyed creating problems in a way that no one could tell who caused them.

Dale cleared his throat, ready to throw down the gauntlet. He used his professional engineering voice, confident and steady.

"This road they are trying to build is technically a difficult job. Moffat is driving a railroad through the rock ribs of the front range, above rivers, and over the mountains. I am here to observe and report for the Union Pacific Rail Road."

He paused, reading whatever reaction Joe gave him, none, then continued.

"What is your interest? Who are you associated with? Frankly, I wonder why we should share the information we have gathered. Perhaps you can persuade us."

Joe was a little surprised by this direct challenge. He considered his answer and decided the way to handle this was to go soft. Let Smertz think he had the upper hand. Eggers knew the man that Dale's boss answered to. He was aware of company politics. Circles within circles and all that. There were some in New York who wanted him to work at cross purposes to Dale and Ella. Joe wasn't prepared to do that at least not yet. And he didn't want to make waves. The last thing he wanted was have that man, the person Dale's boss worked for, find out that Joe was in the field. It made sense to let Dale think he was bigger than he in fact was.

For a moment Joe was wistful. He sure would like to work on railroading, laying track and managing freight flow. He kind of wished he didn't have to be maneuvering among employees of E.H Harriman's Union Pacific Railway. An idea occurred to him. There were ways to get out of this unending dance of coworkers and opponents. He'd have to give it more thought later…

Suddenly back in reality in Boulder, Colorado, he responded.

"My interest in all of this, sir, is similar to yours. The area I am looking at is the general progress of the road backed by David Moffat. Specifically I am to learn what I can about how he and his men overcome technical problems. Tunnels, bridges, rockslides and other hazards of building. And the sheer supply problems they face, in rough uninhabited country."

He intentionally fuzzed over who he worked for. "How to build a railroad across flat, even terrain is well understood. Extended construction through mountains is a lesser known discipline. Those who know it don't like to share it. Any information you can give or advice you can offer will be appreciated."

Ella and Dale exchanged glances. They thought they had Joe's number.

"Good to have you on board, Eggers. Or should I call you Joe?"

"Joe, please. Josephus is just the name that my mama saddled me with!"

"Joe it is. As we turn up facts, Joe, we will be in touch. We will likely work our way on west, looking at the projected route and the overall progress on the project."

Joe nodded and offered his hand in agreement. Dale stood and shook it, looking Joe in the eye. He and Ella left the hotel. As they got out the door, Ella chuckled. She offered her thoughts.

"That guy is a feather merchant. We can feed him a morsel from time to time, something we learn or make up about the railroad. He will be happy to take whatever we give him. That should keep him out of our way. I don't think he will make trouble for us."

Dale wanted to agree. But that was more out of hope than conviction.

"I'm not so sure he really is a light weight. Not sure who he is working for, himself or some other railroad. Or maybe he works for the UP—I've heard stories of field agents at cross purposes. No doubt he'll be happy to let us do the dirty work. We just need to be sure he doesn't try to take the credit."

He shrugged. "In any case we need to keep an eye on him, find out who he really works for. For all we know Moffat sent him out to watch us. If that's the case he may try to steer us away with false leads. We need to keep that in mind."

They were out on the boardwalk now, and they needed to decide on a course of action.

Ella went on a tangent. "Boy, these wooden boardwalks sure are an improvement over dirt paths in front of stores and along the streets. Much cleaner and less dusty."

Then she got to the heart of the matter. "True that, Dale, we need to keep watching this Joe guy. But more important, what I want to do is come up with action plans. Things we can do to further the goal, slow Moffat down and help the UP. But to do that well, we need to stay out of everyone's sight. That way we keep our freedom to move."

They were strolling down the way, for all appearances talking about the weather or crops. She was on a roll.

"I think causing rockslides or other accidents is too risky. Especially now. The workers will be watching the dynamite supplies and pay extra attention to the drilling. So will the bosses." She grimaced because she disliked even the idea of bosses, of people telling others what to do. That was momentary, and she continued.

"With their guard up, there is no way we can get in to the site much less near a tunnel face. We probably can't get close enough for anything like that. I don't see any way. No way to set an extra blast or cause a tent fire or animal stampede or anything like that now. And I can think of no way to cause mishaps from a distance. Can you?"

"No, I don't think so. But we can talk to workers. Catch them coming and going, away from the worksite. Stir them up against unsafe conditions. And we have money. We can buy ranchers along the way." He warmed up to this strategy. "We can buy the right of way from some of the hicks out there. Buy them right out from under the railroad." He grinned.

"And maybe there are other obstacles we can throw up. You know, file for rights to build a hotel or something smack where they want to go. We can do that and never get close to their precious construction camps. They won't even know it until it is too late!"

Ella had been thinking as he spoke. "And I like your idea to stir up trouble among the workers. Even if we didn't cause that slide we can use it. We can plant seeds of doubt about safety. And about how the railway doesn't care about its workers or their health and welfare."

This was one of her favorite topics and listening to her, you could tell. "The corporation cares for nothing but its profits, workers be damned. And maybe there are men who want to demand an eight hour day. They should! Maybe we can get a strike going! Anything that slows work is good for us. And we need to shine a light on the plight of those poor horses and other animals being put to work, abused and not fed."

Dale and Ella continued to brainstorm plans in Boulder. At about that time, above Eldorado Springs, Mik was starting to work. He'd heard Mr. Sumner and he had some ideas about how to go about the job. Cam had told him to go through tunnel construction and geological reports. The idea was to find one on each tunnel job which spoke to the geology and stability of the site. For most jobs there was one report but for some he had to compile two or more.

He was grateful for the assignment. Being out talking to people who thought he was Myron Mast was kind of nerve wracking. Better to be in an office reviewing reports and listening to people talk around him. That helped him learn what was going on day to day around the place. It also helped him to speak and act the way expected. He didn't want to come out with a phrase like "under the radar" or "google it." Plus reviewing reports on all the tunnels helped him to see the big picture. He needed to get background, in a hurry. Mik was starting to pick up what Myron Mast was expected to know.

For him, the big picture was slowly came into focus. The railroad project itself was fascinating. The Denver

Northwestern and Pacific Railway was a spectacular vision. Mr. Moffat was building a steam railroad, mainline gauge. No electric cars or small time narrow gauge spindling for him. He intended to construct and operate a road that the industries and businesses of the region could rely on and build around.

By now, 1903, there were already tracks in use at the originating end of the road. They started at Utah Junction, a small railyard. It was just outside of Denver, about three miles northeast of where Cherry Creek runs into the Platte River. From there the iron rails, set on a good stable consistent grade, ran northwest. At the base of the foothills, they gained vertical by making a huge "S." This was carved into the land and crossed Coal Creek just south of a high plain area called Rocky Flats. The tracks went no further for the time being. But they would be extended bit by bit, soon. At present the road grade was being built north from Coal Creek, climbing across the face of Eldorado Mountain. The two percent grade was maintained. To be consistent and usable, the road would have to go through tunnels. There would be about a dozen of them in this stretch.

The tunnels weren't being built one at a time. Almost all were under construction at once. There were crews working on both ends of each tunnel. Mik marveled at the calculations which allowed men to, first of all, be at the right altitude and place on the mountain. Then, they could hammer and blast big holes into the right place on both sides of a big rock rib. They invariably met up in the middle, usually not more than an inch or two off. And still all the tunnel jobs were at the right height to make the required two percent grade.

It was a job to be respected. Doubly so when he realized this was all done by boots on the ground eye surveys supported by pencil and paper calculations. No GPS, satellite images, or computer aided design here!

From the reports Mik saw that there was more going on than just work on the tunnels. Surveying and preliminary grading was being done on up the planned route. Even up along South Boulder Creek. Indeed, preparatory work was being done all the way up to the continental divide. The tunnels on Eldorado Mountain would be done in a month or two. Track would be laid and put to use along that stretch. By then the grade along South Boulder Creek would be almost ready for rail too. Before fall, before the snow flew, the train would likely be ready to run clear to the foot of the continental divide. Then work would start in earnest to conquer the crest of the Rockies.

He found reports on the geology and locations of the tunnels as Cam had told him to. Truth be told he took some time to read background on the entire road. Then he stacked up the reports Sumner had ordered, and made sure they'd stay by putting a paper weight on them. Then he went out to find Cam.

A big stump of a man stood outside the tent. Oh no! Another doppelganger! Mik's knees actually almost buckled from the unpleasant surprise. Another surprise experience he really did not want to have or acknowledge!

His thoughts whirled. *My God! It is that musclebound oaf Steven!* The image of Steven shooting at him and his friends on a snowy starlit night raged back at Mik. Steven was an accomplice of Ulora and Del back in Sula time. One time Steve had tried to pick a fight. No big deal, he and a friend had deflected that easily enough. But another time, later, he had shot at that friend. And later still, the big guy had fired a shot right at Mik. Not pleasant memories!

Mik tried not to stare. He was fidgeting and had to stop himself from grabbing a shovel and going after the big guy. The man approached.

Steu smiled. “Mast, I feared you were lost in the slide. Damned glad to see you weren’t. How are you feeling now?”

He paused. “You do remember me, don’t you? Steuben Wentz. I’m the company security man. We want to find out what happened. What do you remember about that day? Can you tell me anything about what happened?”

Mik didn’t know what to expect. Last thing he thought he’d get is questions, from a cordial and concerned coworker. He was truly surprised and involuntarily took a step back. This guy brought back horrible images and memories. He wasn’t sure what he should say, if he should even acknowledge the question. How did this guy know him, and why did he ask questions? Cam came out of his tent just then.

“Mik, you may remember Wentz. Steu Wentz. I think I mentioned him the other day.”

He glanced at Mik, who looked a bit paler than he had the day before.

Cam continued, “He is the inspector, the company bull. You know, the man responsible to keep us and the jobsite safe. A good man to know, and to have in your corner. He is looking into the rockslide you escaped. Anything you can tell him will help us all.”

Mik nodded, acknowledging Cam. He forced himself to look at Steu. He tried to see just a company dick doing his job, not a man who had tried to kill him and others. He almost stuttered.

“Well, to tell the truth, there isn’t a lot I can tell you. I really don’t remember much. Everything before seeing

Cam come riding down the road is, well, kind of blank." He frankly hoped Wentz would go away.

Steu gave him a sympathetic but penetrating look.

"Alright. If you remember anything about that day, anything at all, you know where to find me. Even the smallest detail might be the last piece of the puzzle. I spend a lot of time just walking around the jobsite and watching things. Finding me isn't hard, just ask around. Now, I'll let you go as I have business to do."

He turned away then hesitated. Turning back, he asked "Say, you haven't seen a slender man with bright, almost feverish eyes, have you? He may be in the company of a mannish woman. Or perhaps not a woman but a chunky man with George Armstrong Custer like hair but no goatee..."

Mik immediately thought of the pair he met after Cam left him. What were the names they used? Ella and Dale, right? Dale sure had intense eyes. And Ella answered to the description! But he still wasn't one hundred percent sure about Steu's loyalties. He looked so much like the Steven who had shot at him before...But Cam vouched for him. Should he tell about the encounter? The turmoil in Mik's mind caused a number of expressions to cross his face.

Wentz saw that something was going on. He was experienced at interrogation and reading people's eyes and facial movements. He prodded at Mik ever so subtly.

"These people were seen near our jobsite just before the slide. Anything you can tell me about them will help us keep you and others safe." He fixed Mik with an "I'm waiting" look. Cam nodded, watching Mik closely.

What the hell, Mik thought. *This is clearly different from Sula time. The people here look like those in Sula time, with different names. No reason they will have all the same traits and friendships here as there. Cam trusts him, I guess I had better trust him too.* He didn't dare look into the abyss of thinking how preposterous the whole experience was. He just edged along its side. He sorted out what he knew about the couple and what he should tell Steu and Cam about them.

Mik kind of gulped. He knew he was somehow crossing a line, involving himself more and more in this strange new present. He hoped he wouldn't regret it.

"Now that you mention it, Steu, yes. I may have seen them yesterday after I came to. You know, when Cam came down the trail and told me who I was and what had happened. It was after he left and I had just started down towards Prudens' and Eldorado Springs." Mik was looking into the distance, concentrating on the memory and what he saw.

He looked Steu in the eye.

"Up the trail came a pair. Your description of them pretty well fits what I saw of them. Slender man, bright eyes, seemed pretty smart when he talked. Said he was some kind of an engineer, I think. With him was a woman dressed in a man's clothing. Like you said, from a distance, she could have been a chubby, curvy, short version of George Armstrong Custer."

He paused, remembering how outlandish the woman looked.

"Of course she had no beard but her hair was long like Custer or many women. There was no doubt about her being a she when she opened her mouth. She had a woman's voice and mannerisms."

He paused. Steu waited a moment, then asked, "What else?"

Mik thought, then continued. "They seemed to know that there had been a rockslide. And they knew something about the project. Looking back now it is odd that they knew anything. Rumors fly and all, but they seemed to know more than they said. For that matter, they seemed to know something about me. She mentioned my name and said she'd heard that I was lost, killed in the slide. Brain fog surrounded me still and I don't remember much other than that."

"Ah," said Steu. "That is helpful. Can you describe them or their clothing better? Where did they go?"

"She was wearing mans trousers and a work shirt. Suspenders. The clothes hung loosely on her, not form fitting or snug. I don't recall what he wore. Her hair is blondish. She seemed agitated. Like she was ready to pick a fight about "working conditions." Mentioned something about unsafe conditions on the job here. Also said something about animals. Strangest combination of attitudes."

Mik smiled, remembering that even then her rant had taken him aback. "Then they headed up the road towards the site. I started down so don't know what happened next."

Steu looked at Cam. "I'll ask around in town. I have a friend in the Sheriff's office who may know something as well. This pair probably went through Eldo or Boulder recently. A couple dressed like that will probably be remembered. That should make running them down easy enough."

With that the security man strode off to find and saddle his horse. His destinations, Eldorado Springs then Boulder. Cam watched as he faded down the hill. He turned to Mik and praised Steu.

"He's a good man, knows his business. He'll find out what there is to know about those two. Now, do you have a summary of the reports you can give me? I mean tell me, not read."

Suddenly Mik found himself, almost, back in Sula time. He was ready to sum up a case to a friendly jury. It was momentarily so real that he had to stop from clearing his throat and glancing at the judge for a nodded permission to proceed.

Proceed he did, but not with trying to impress and convince a jury.

"There are no faults or intrusions of soft rock in any of the tunnels. The geology is solid." He looked at Cam to see if he had a question. He went on.

"Tunnels one two and three are done. They are shored, stable, and safe, and in use. Track has actually been laid. Supply trains run as far forward as just past the uphill end of three. Four is recently holed through and the damage from the rockslide repaired. Shoring is in progress. It will be done and in use soon."

Cam nodded. None of this was news but it was good to step back and look at the big scene.

The recap continued. "Tunnels five through twelve are in process. Five is about twenty feet from holing through. The others are anything from the same to about a hundred feet to go."

Mik was gaining confidence in his grasp of the subject. He felt he was on a roll.

"At present rates, all the tunnels will be done, shored, safe and ready for track in about three weeks. The road grade between the tunnels is roughed out all the way out to South Boulder Creek."

Here, Mik deliberately did not say "down to South Boulder Creek," but "out to." The grade stayed with its two percent climb along the side of the mountain. The road didn't descend to the creek, rather the creek took its normal course down the canyon. At some point the two converged. The grade then ran at its two percent, parallel with the creek bed.

"The further tracks are actually laid the faster work can go. Having the road to bring up supplies and material will step up the pace of progress quite a bit."

Cam again nodded. He knew the status of each job well. He knew how far from holing through each tunnel was, down to the inch. And he knew how much faster the work went forward with supplies coming by rail not horse and wagon. He should know this, it was his job, his responsibility. The air he breathed and dreams he had were imbued with the road, its progress and problems. He loved it.

Hearing this concise and accurate rundown from Mik, working only from the reports, was good. That meant Mr. Sumner and others would draw the same conclusions too. "That was a good summary, Mik. Put the report on my desk."

He looked appraisingly at his friend. After a moment he decided the man was recovering and was emotionally and physically strong enough to do some independent work.

"Tomorrow, Mik, I want you to go up the grade. Walk it. No, on second thought, take a company horse and ride it. You'll need to switch, that is leave the horse and walk above or below tunnel work then pick up another horse on the other side. By riding, you'll make better time than if you walk. On horse you are still close to the job and will see everything that needs seeing."

Mik nodded, trying to look like he got it. Really, he was wondering what he would be looking for and at.

Cam continued.

"From here go as far up as you can get by noon. Turn back right after lunch. You can go to the cook tent in the morning. Get something to take for lunch, bread, cheese, and an apple or whatever you can get out of him. When you come back, give me an update tomorrow afternoon. It is very important that I have your report tomorrow."

Deciding to be blunt, Mik asked his questions.

"So what specifically do you want me to see? What am I looking for? Will I need a notebook or sketchpad, or just a good memory?"

Cam was glad to give details. Better to do that than assume, and have to send someone else out later.

"I will need several things. First, your views on ways to improve and speed along the grading. Not the rough work. The Irish and Swedes have that down well. I'm particularly interested in the actual smoothing and leveling of the ground. Taking it down to smooth enough to play tenpins on. If it is flat enough for that, its flat enough to spread and tamp ballast. Then we can lay rail! We need to work faster getting the surface suitable for that. It has been a bottleneck for us and we need new ideas. Plus general progress, any spots needing lots of fill, unusual hazards, and so on."

He paused and gave his friend a searching look. Had he made his wishes clear?

"Any questions on that? No? Good. If any questions or anything comes up, ask me today. I'd rather answer questions now than have you do a half baked job tomorrow..."

"Sure, Cam, I think I understand, but if not I'll ask."

"Alright. Now, for the rest of today, keep an eye on the work in the tunnel. Since we're holed through there should be no blasting. At this stage mostly it should be cleanup, shoring, and leveling for the grade. Matter of fact, I want no blasting on tunnel four. Talk to me if you think there is need for it. Do not drop in, tamp, or fuse any dynamite before you ask me."

Cam went back to his tent and Mik headed towards the hole in the mountain, tunnel four.

VII

STEU PONDERED WHAT HE KNEW ABOUT MYRON MAST AS HE rode down the hill towards Eldorado Springs. He thought, *The man looked almost frightened when he first saw me. I wonder what caused that? We've known each other for a while and had no problems. Maybe it is the slide...*

He pulled his thoughts away from the man who he believed had escaped a rock slide. Time to find out what he could about that pair who had been lurking. He wondered what the man and woman were about. Were they money lenders? Troublemakers? Maybe they were relatives of a worker? No, they would have come forth if so. Was he a pimp and she a woman of the night, trying to disguise herself? Then why the man's getup? Maybe they were just curious bystanders, wanting to see the project...

The two were shadowy and hard to figure out. They were reported to be hanging somewhere around or near the camp and tents, but no one could say when or exactly where. And no one saw them come or go. And not a soul had actually seen them in the camp or even near the tunnel works. But from what Mik said, they were darn well informed for unknown people. Mik had said they knew who he was and what had happened to him. That meant they were very observant or had an informant. Or both, he worried.

And then there was the woman's talk with Mik about workers and work conditions. Steu turned the problem over and over in his head. The more he did, the more he wondered if he had some socialist troublemakers on his hands. Damn dreamers with their "eight hour workday" nonsense. He made a mental note to keep an eye on several of the crew who he knew to be malcontents. If anyone was susceptible to labor agitation, they would be.

As he neared Eldorado Springs, he turned to the next part of the problem. Who, he wondered, in the town might know of the couple's comings and goings? He decided to start not with the town marshal. He usually had his hands full. The one to talk to was the postmaster. He saw and talked to almost everyone in town every day. If there was information floating around, he would know it.

The postmaster was a useful guy for a security agent to know. He was also owner of the boarding house, Charlie Pruden.

Steu entered the post office. A woman was talking with the postmaster so he waited, looking at the Army recruiting posters. The Army was always looking for men, needing more bodies. Occupation duty on Caribbean islands and in Latin America called for many soldiers. Not to mention an active, hot, ugly war in the Philippines. Plus, these were all regions with tropical diseases and harsh climate. The Army had lots casualties, not just from bullets but also from mosquito bites and jungle rot.

He also looked at the "Most Wanted" posters on the wall. The security agent was glad that he didn't recognize any of the characters pictured or described. That was no joke. Laborers drifting through the area looking for work sometimes had a bigger reputation and record than Steu wanted to deal with.

The woman finished her business and left. Steu stepped up to the counter.

"Mr. Pruden, you look well. How is the postal business doing today?"

"Busy as usual, Mr. Wentz. You caught me practically going out the door. I am headed to Denver on some business. What can I do for you? I understand the railroad work is going pretty well. I hear it is progressing more or less to schedule. How are things up your jobsite?"

Proprieties aside, Steu lapsed to more familiar terms. "We actually are progressing pretty well, Charlie. At this rate trains will be running on our section well before snow flies." He fidgeted and shrugged.

"As you may know we had a delay with a rockslide. I'm still looking into the why and how of that, which is why I need to talk with you."

Pruden nodded, waiting for Steu to open up.

"I am looking for two people. A pair was seen in the area beforehand. I do not know who or where they are. For that matter, I'm not even sure if they came down here. Seems likely, but you never know. It is two people, a pair like I said. I did not see them but they have been described to me. The man is slender, with prominent, bright eyes. And the other is, by all accounts, a woman dressed in men's clothing. I'm told she has longish blond hair. Or maybe shorter hair, but blond. Reports vary. They may or may not be involved, I don't know. But I sure would like to talk to them. Have you seen them, or heard anything about these people?"

Charlie nodded again.

"Matter of fact, Steu, yes, I think I did see them. Yesterday afternoon. The woman came into the Post Office and waited in line. She showed no sense of urgency or of having a problem. She asked if anyone was going to Boulder. A lot of folks do that so I didn't think much of it. But like you said, she was dressed like a man. She talked and walked like a woman, if you know what I mean. That is, she didn't seem to want to pass herself off as a man. It is just that she wasn't wearing what you expect a woman to wear."

"Do you remember what time she came in, Charlie?"

"What I do remember is she made some comment about the stables across the way, about how they were cruel to their horses. Not sure where she got that idea…" Pruden thought, looking at the wanted posters without seeing. "Seems like it was about two o'clock or so. I remember now putting the day's outgoing mail in the wagon not long after she left. Come to think about it, she said something about a meeting." He paused.

"Yes, she said she needed to meet someone at the James Hotel. I sent her over to the stables as I knew they had a wagon going into town which would go right by the James. Not the regular mail shipment wagon, but something sooner and usually faster. I saw her and a tall man get on the wagon and ride away. I guess she got over her feelings of the horses being mistreated."

"Thanks, Charlie! I myself am going next to Boulder. Can I do anything for you while I'm there?"

"Not today thanks, Steu. If you need anything from Denver, I'm headed that way. Good luck!"

Steu formulated a plan of what to do. First, get to Boulder. Then ask around, learn what he could about the pair.

Find them. Then talk with them, hopefully find out what they were up to. Or at least take their measure.

He picked up his horse at the stables and started down the road. The horse pretty well knew the way so he didn't need to guide her. The cop could concentrate. He parsed what Pruden said about a meeting. What could that be about? He continued to push and shove at different ideas about the blond and her slender partner. Who did he know at the James Hotel? Were the two staying there or somewhere else? Where in Boulder might they be? Well, he'd do his best to find out.

The hypnotic gait and the comforting rhythm of the horse's motion soon made his mind wander. His thoughts turned to how long his trip would take. *I sure hope we get a train to Eldorado Springs. It would be very nice to get to Boulder in under an hour, or Denver in under two hours. I wonder when that will happen. Maybe someone will put one of those new electric trains. I hear those are fast, quiet, and economical. And no cinders to burn holes in your clothes or singe your hair.*

First stop in Boulder was the city jail. Steu talked with a friend there he knew from the Sheriff's office. Unfortunately the man gave him nothing new. But he did know people in town. He gave Steu the name of the James Hotel's manager. The man owed Steu's friend a favor. His friend said to be sure to use his name. So now Steu owed his friend a favor. *Oh well, that is alright*, he thought as he headed to the hotel. *Go along to get along and all. That is really how it works. He'll call my favor in some time, and using it will help to get a bad guy off the streets.* Soon he was at the James.

The manager was correct and stiffly courteous before Steu mentioned his friend. On hearing the name, the man turned positively helpful. In fact, his memory suddenly improved quite a bit. Steu wasn't surprised, he had seen this type of behavior before. He often experienced such a change of attitude when he dropped a name.

The first time it happened to him it was a surprise. Going from being a cop, the enemy, to being a cop who knew someone, a potential friend, was always a welcome change. By now it was old hat. Even so, he always tried to smile and build on the positive aspects of it. It was sometimes hard not to be cynical about it.

Today, the manager was making a clean sweep, telling all he knew about the people in question.

"Yes, two people looking like that were here. They met with one of our guests this morning. Or I should say the three of them ate breakfast together. As far as I know the man they met is still registered with us." He looked at a man entering the lobby and his eyes lit up. "Ah, in fact, he is still around. There he is."

Joe Eggers was walking through the lobby. He heard his name and looked around to find who was talking. It was someone behind the desk. "Mr. Eggers, there is someone here who needs to talk to you," said the manager.

Joe had been on his way out the door, going to Denver. He intended to call on First National Bank, David Moffat's financial and business base. He had perfected an act as a supposedly interested investor. Of course he hoped to learn more of the project. Now the hotel manager wanted him to talk to someone.

Joe approached the desk. He wondered who wanted to talk to him. His guard was always up. Particularly now, since no one was supposed to know he was here. Any questions asked would likely be hostile or interrogative. They would not be friendly or innocent, he was sure.

The man with the manager was big, with hard eyes. He had seen security people and cops his whole life. This guy was not another UP guy in the field. Definitely not a fellow traveler asking for directions. And he certainly was not a representative from the Chamber of Commerce. "Cop!" the guy's demeanor screamed.

Joe believed in meeting problems boldly. He found often they disappeared when he did so. Plus he loved having the upper hand in any encounter. So, up he strode, stuck out his hand, and introduced himself. "Hello, I'm Joe Eggers. And you are...?"

Steu was wrongfooted by this. Not having the initiative made him hesitate for just a moment. Then he regained his ease. He was usually the one asking the questions, but he could go with the flow for a moment or two.

"Steuben Wentz, agent for the Denver Northwestern and Pacific. Nice to meet you. Sir, we have had some incidents on the jobsite. I need to speak with you if have a moment."

Joe was about to brush him off. He needed to talk to a railroad dick like he needed a wart on his nose. Then it occurred to him that maybe he could play this guy. Mr. Steuben Wentz might be a source of information, knowingly or unknowingly. For that matter, he might even become a useful ally. And it wasn't smart to make an enemy of him now that they had met. The company bull was not a person you wanted against you in any case. He could make life miserable on and even off the railroad's property. So it was worth a few minute's conversation. Maybe it would pay off.

Joe smiled an insincere flip of the lips. "Certainly I have time. What do you need to speak to me about?"

Steu went through the description of the pair. He mentioned that they had been sighted around the worksite and the tunnel before the slide. "We would like to speak to these two. We are not accusing anyone or saying they had anything to do with the rockslide. It was most likely an accident. Still, we would like to get their side of the story."

"I can see why. A rockslide is a serious matter. Have you had many of them?"

Steu ignored the attempt at sidetracking him. He parried with his own questions.

"I understand that you met with them, the man and the woman. Do you know who they are? Where they are staying? Did they tell you of their plans? Do you know how I can reach them?"

Eggers thought fast. He wanted to build some credibility with this man. He could prove useful in many ways. It was also a chance to kill the proverbial two birds with one stone. If he played it right, he could build goodwill, learn something, and take Smertz down a notch or two. All that aside, he wanted to divert attention away from himself. He needed figure things out, try to see what was in all this for him. He made a show of concentrating, dredging his memory.

"Well, Mr. Wentz, I don't know. I am not quite sure about this odd pair. They told me they were agents of another railroad. In fact, if I remember right, he said they were, and I think I have it right, they were sent here to look after the interests of the Union Pacific."

He stopped, concentrating with a puzzled look on his face. "Whatever that may mean. I don't pretend to understand that. They then questioned me about conditions on your worksites. Why they thought I would know is beyond me. Actually, looking back, it seemed like they were looking for problems or loose ends they could tug at. They also asked about the rockslide you mentioned. Of course, I know nothing of that unfortunate accident either."

Joe thought he was doing well, so he added, "I just arrived last night. When you stopped me I was leaving. In fact this morning I am on my way to Denver. My intent was, is, to meet with people and do some research. I am looking into investing into this very road, your company."

He paused, trying to read Steu's eyes and expression. The man said nothing, waiting him out. Joe decided to lay out a clue or two for this man to follow. The sooner this guy left him alone, the better. Best way to do that was to sic him on this Smertz character and his dippy sidekick. Maybe this railroad dick would go chase them. That way all three of them would be out of the picture and he could act as he chose. And it couldn't happen too soon. He continued, spinning a tale.

"They did not tell me their specific plans or intentions. As I think back, I see that things they said and didn't say gave me some ideas. I got the impression they were going to follow the Denver & Northwestern road west, on over the mountains. They implied they were headed to western Colorado and maybe even into Utah. Why, I do not know, but I think it fair to say that is what they were going to do."

Joe did not feel bad for not telling Steu everything. After all, he knew their names and more about their plans and intentions than he let on. That was for him to know and use for his own ends. Let the company dick figure it out for himself.

Steu listened closely to all of this. A commentary ran in his mind as Joe talked. *Who is this guy? Why should I believe him? But what he says makes sense. Agents of the UP! He may know what he's talking about. Can't say I'm surprised—those two just don't add up somehow. They are trouble. The last thing we need out here is competitors trying to see what we are doing. Not to mention stirring things or throwing a wrench in the works.* A mental image of someone literally throwing a big monkey wrench into a gearbox fleeted across his mind.

But why, he wondered, *would they head west if there isn't any road being constructed yet? There's nothing going on out there but our guys buying rights of way. And surveying for the road... Of course! They want to head off construction entirely, or make it difficult! They may get out there and try to block our rights of way. Or they will go looking for people out there who don't want our railroad in their county.*

Joe watched as the wheels turned in Steu's head. He felt sure he had succeeded in throwing suspicion off of him, on to the man and woman.

Steu decided what to do. *I have to follow up on those two out there. Wait, did this guy say he was an investor? Maybe he can give me some idea of what is happening in Denver.*

"Thank you, Mr. Eggers. You have been most helpful. Let me give you my card. If you hear, see, or learn anything else please contact me. I am generally at the worksite and if you ask for me I can give you a tour. If you are looking to invest that may be of interest." He smiled at Joe.

"Or you can cable or visit the main office in Denver. They will call or cable me. Is there some way for me to contact you should the need arise?"

Joe had a selection of business cards. One showed him as affiliated with the Union Pacific Railroad's New York offices. One had just his name and a New York City address. He gave Steu one of the latter. "You can wire me there. For the next week or so I will be here at the James. If I'm not in leave word at the desk and I will get in touch."

The two shook hands and each went off on his way.

A whole afternoon of watching others work for several hours made Mik tired. He didn't know enough to pitch in. If someone looked like they were going to ask him to, he hid behind his "I'm still upset and foggy" façade. After it all, he was more tired than if he had actually doing something. It was late in the day when he returned to Pruden's. Tomorrow would be better, he was sure. The prospect of riding up the road grade, to go actually do something useful, was good. He was ready to stop being a fifth wheel even if he didn't yet know enough about railroads or being Myron Mast.

The next day, Mik got up a little early. He was awake anyway, may as well get up. After again avoiding bloodshed from the straight razor, he dressed and went downstairs. He needed to clear his head. On one hand, life with Sula in modern Denver. On the other hand, he somehow found himself in 1903 Eldorado Springs. Reconciling or even making sense of the two was not an easy task!

He also wanted to keep the players straight, that is remember who was who and what their story was. Not to mention keeping his own story straight and free of twenty first century phrases. He hoped he wouldn't say something too stupid or wildly out of context. The hope, the plan, was to find a little quiet time at the morning table. As he came in he saw Seth Pruden was already seated, eating breakfast.

Seth glanced up and smiled. "Good morning, Mik. How are you? Are you starting to regain your bearings? You looked pretty darn pale at dinner the other night. I have to say you do look like you feel better this morning."

He pushed a chair out with his foot. "Grab a cup of coffee and join me."

Mik stood, not taking the seat. "Yes, I do feel better. Still a little foggy about specific memories. Frankly I can't recall a lot about my past. This time of my life is kind of unsettling, even frightening sometimes. That said, overall I think I'm better." He walked over to the sideboard, took a cup of coffee, then returned and sat.

Seth seemed trustworthy. Mik opened up a bit, looking him in the eye.

"Today, I am going to ride out along the grade, be a set of eyes and ears for Cam and all. That trek will probably refresh my memory some. But enough about me. Tell me, Seth, how are you doing? Remind me, just what type of work are you doing?"

"My survey team is doing the final grade markings. We're working up past tunnel five or six. There is one team at each so I am not sure which segment I'll be assigned to today. The work is interesting but difficult. We've been placing final grade markers, the pins to mark the actual desired level of the road grade. It is exacting work in a grand location." He paused, looking satisfied with the description and the work. Then he switched subjects.

"One of the hard things about this job is the access. It is poor, and the further west, the worse it gets. I guess that is why we need a railroad, isn't it?! This whole the project sure is grand and exciting. When we get this road done it help the whole region." His thoughts wandered and conversation lagged for a moment. Both took swallows of coffee.

"Hey, Mik, look me up when you come by today. If you make it up to tunnel six. I'll show you the surveying equipment and ropes. That is, if you want to." He looked wan, and his smile was genuine but weak.

"Sure, Seth, I'll do that if I have time, not sure how pressed I'll be. You mentioned final grade markers. One of the items I'm supposed to keep in mind today is final grading methods. That is, ways to make the grade match your markers. If you have any thoughts on speeding and improving that work, let me know. I will appreciate it. Who knows, if it is a good idea you may come to the attention of Mr. Sumner or even Mr. Moffat!"

The two finished their meal in amiable silence and went their ways.

This morning Mik wanted to ride up to the site alone. It was all well and good to hitch a ride yesterday but he wanted to look and think today. As his horse ambled along, he reflected on the breakfast conversation. He felt a twinge of concern for Seth. The young man seemed listless and a little depressed. Overall he seemed less energetic than most nineteen year olds.

When he got to camp he hoped he could talk with Cam about it. But today Cam was not in a listening mood; rather he did the talking.

"I thought you might have started early. You had better get moving. Remember, I'm particularly interested in the progress of the grade."

Mik did a quick mental review of what he knew about railroad construction. The term "grade" is railroad speak for the wide, long, level bed the tracks and train run on. To make it, the ground is filled and leveled then a layer of gravel, called ballast, is put down. On top of that go the cross ties which hold the actual steel track. The grade should be well scraped, even, well drained, and smoothly filled in. It follows the surveyors' stakes and markers. If this work is done well, the train will run smoothly and efficiently. If not it will be an unpleasant, bumpy ride. Worse, washouts may occur after even a small storm. No railroad needs the danger, delay, and expense of having and repairing washouts. He summarized it all to himself by thinking that grade is like a building's foundation.

Cam continued, "Also, out towards the end of the line: Before we even get to final grade, we'll need to fill and stabilize some areas. This is even before we can scrape the pioneer grade. You know, we're crossing ravines, canyons and such. Over the big ones we'll have to build a trestle. But we can fill the many smaller ones. Give me your estimate of the amount of rock and dirt needed for each of those. Often we can use the rubble from the tunnel but may need more. In that case give me an idea of where we can get it from. And take note of any non company people you meet. There are a few ranchers in the area but you likely won't see anyone else."

As Cam talked they were making their way to the tunnel face, the actual rock wall being holed through. The crews were working to shore the tunnel up with timber frames set every six or so feet. Hammering, sawing, and general commotion hung over the site. Men were already busy. There was an undercurrent of exhilaration in the air and morale felt high. The craftsmen here knew they were working on a new, exciting and significant project. They were happy to be there.

They stopped and both got off their horses. "Mik, you go on about your business. The crews know you are coming and will help as needed. Good luck."

A hostler came and took the horse Mik had ridden. The man's job was to take care of all the horses at this site. There was someone at each site to do that. Mik was glad, that way he didn't have to tend to that detail.

Note book in hand, pencil, matches and knife in pocket, jacket over his shoulder, Mik felt ready to go. He set out. First obstacle was the rock rib tunnel four had penetrated. Since the rockmen had holed through he walked in and up to the face. He warned the rockmen he was coming, and with little effort he was able to scramble up the small cliff face and through to the other side. Out the other end was a mirror image of the busy work area at his back.

The grade to the next tunnel was already flat and fairly smooth. It was only a few hundred yards and there was no point in saddling up a horse for that distance. Here the grade was starting to shape up. The bed seemed solid and final fill was being put on and tamped. It wasn't level enough to roll a billiard ball down the center but it was getting there.

He went on like this. Through, over or around the tunnel sites and along the road. He started high above Rocky Flats with a view out over the plains. As he neared where the grade met the creek the view closed in. There he was at the bottom of a steep rocky canyon. But before that, as he moved along the grade, the views opened up and were incredible. Plains, mountains, cliffs, sky…

He found his mind wandering from grade requirements, fill, tunnels holing through, and so forth.

Instead, he remembered. He recalled enjoying these very views back in his other life time. How distant and strange that seemed to him today! He and Sula had once ridden the train, going from Denver to the mountain town of Glenwood Springs, near Aspen. They sat in a vista dome car, with seats under a big bubble of window, and three hundred sixty degree views. They had gone along this selfsame route, past this very spot, over a hundred years later. Later.

But wait, he was looking back, remembering. How could it be later? That thought started to spook him. Would he ever get back to see Sula? Or was he stuck in the early 1900s? He almost shuddered with the weirdness of it all. It was time to shut those swirling thoughts out, and concentrate on the here and now. Whenever and wherever that was!

As he made his way, he looked east over the great plains and north to Eldorado Canyon with its big cliffs. As the route swung west, he got an occasional glimpse of snow. The high peaks along the continental divide never melted off completely. That in itself would complicate things when the road was pushed into the high mountains. But those issues were for another day.

The tunnels along this section were the heart of the job. In this stretch of the road there were rock ribs every several hundred yards, and a tunnel was being put through each of them. Work was proceeding on each, from both ends. None were as far along as tunnel four. Some were holed through but most were not yet. The grade between tunnels got rougher and less finished the further he went. Looking at the sun, he realized it was almost noon. He decided to go to the next tunnel site, eat, and turn around. He had several pages of notes, observations, and ideas to report to Cam. The outline of the report was forming in his mind as he rode.

From down Boulder way, the cop was on the hunt. Steu Wentz had caught the scent of his prey and was on the move. The slender man and mannishly dressed woman were his quarry. Acting on a hunch and trusting Joe's information, Steu had decided to go west. He was confident he'd run them down somewhere up there.

Seth and Mik had talked early that morning over breakfast, the start of the day for them. It was early for them. By that hour, Steu had already been on the chase for almost a full day. He was hard at work, far from Eldorado Springs, Tunnel four, and the railroad. The previous afternoon he had taken the train from Boulder down to Denver. From there he took another ride on the rails, up to the mountain town of Dumont. Fortunately for him he found a room at a local hotel. By breakfast time, when Mik and Seth talked, he had already caught the first stagecoach out. It lurched and bumped up the Berthoud Pass wagon road, over the divide to Fraser and points west.

Before getting on, he had asked around at the stage stop. Yes, he was told, a tall slender man and an oddly dressed person, a "he-she," had come through the day before. The station agent had sold them tickets through to the settlement of Fraser. Steu was glad to confirm that he wasn't running down a blind alley. His quarry was ahead of him. How far he did not know, but he was sure he'd find out.

The stage ride over Berthoud Pass was bumpy, crowded, and tiring. *A railroad over to the Fraser valley will be so much easier. The sooner we get the Denver Northwestern and Pacific built, the better*, thought Wentz. This as they reached the top of the pass, and the driver stopped.

"Time to put on the brakes!" he said. With that he started to chain a log to the stage. He used two chains so the log would stay parallel to the back axle. It would drag behind the stage and slow their descent. At least that was the driver's earnest hope! This made Steu proud he worked for a railroad which would put an end to such makeshift attempts at safety. It also made him take a seat by the door so he could bail out if things started to go bad.

Ella and Dale had come to Fraser the day before. They spent the night in town. The inn was hardly luxurious. It was a roof over their head and the food was edible if not tasty. Discussing and deciding their next steps took up the evening. Dale knew would have to report something to his boss, and fairly soon too. He wanted to have some plans in mind. When he reported, it was important to sound like he had things under control.

"We need to stir up the workers." Ella was sure that was the way to slow work on the road down. She was always ready to play on people's fears, suspicions and jealousies.

"If we can get them to strike maybe we can string things out until winter. Construction season is short, especially the higher into the mountains they go. The harder the company presses the more the workers suffer. Or, I know! We can sneak into camp and turn the work animals loose. That will give them a rest and slow the work while the railroad men round them up."

Dale was skeptical.

"Second idea first. How can we sneak into camp undetected? And do you really think that will do any good? Come on, El, let's be serious." He paused, thinking about her first suggestion.

"Labor agitation is a possibility. But again, how do we go about that? You think they will just let us go on site? When we want to talk about safety or long hours? Do you really think they would allow a woman to roam around? With blasting, horses, and other work going on? And don't forget, there are just two of us, Ella. We need to find something else, some other way."

Ella scowled. Dale thought some more then continued.

"I say we work our way on down the valley. As we go, we try to find poor ranchers. We offer buy up a right of way here and there, cash money. If we are able to buy even just a few rights of way, job is done. The railroad will have trouble coming through. Cheap, easy, quick. Totally legal and above-board. I think that is a good strategy."

He grinned as he went on. "We have money but not a lot of people to attack the problem. And we don't have tons of time. And this way, we don't need to trespass. Not that I am afraid to do that, but why ask for trouble? Plus we won't have to worry about a company dick throwing us off the worksite. They always manage to give an elbow or a knee. At the least, you end up with scrapes and bruises when they do that. Sometimes worse, blood and broken bones. So, what do you think?"

Ella didn't care for that plan. It was too simple, too civil. She preferred to rile people up. She really liked to spew venom. Whether against Moffat and other rich men, companies, or managers, she didn't care. She just liked to talk trash. If she could make workers feel unhappy and down tools, so much the better. But she couldn't come up with reasons to do it differently. Dale was right this time. They didn't have the resources or time for her preferred tactics here and now.

"I guess you are right, Dale. I'd love to go to the tunnel site and talk to workers and help animals. But that isn't practical for now. I agree that the best thing the two of us can do is start talking to landowners."

Business done for the evening, the two got down to more personal and intimate enjoyment.

The next morning, they prepared to go talk with ranchers about money and rights of way. The pair walked out of the inn. Standing across the way by the stage depot was a big man. The stage had just arrived and it looked like he had come in on it. He looked at them with a glint in his eye. It could have been simple recognition, or the excitement and knowledge of a hunter eying nearby prey.

Ella was onto him immediately.

"Dale. Don't look, but that big guy across the road. He is a cop. Probably a company dick. He smells of the law." She continued to look at him, trying not to seem like she was.

"I'm almost sure I saw him roaming around the tunnel work site. Yeah, I saw him when we spied on it, that day the rockslide happened. He is a company dick for Moffat! I don't like the way he is looking at us."

Dale glanced across the street. "Yes, I agree, he is a cop. But we are doing nothing wrong. I don't know what he is doing here but we have nothing to hide. Let him talk to us if he wants."

Steu couldn't believe his luck. He had just climbed down from the stage, shaking dust and stretching aching muscles. He got his head cleared and looked across the street. There they were, the slender man and his woman friend! What was up with her and her baggy canvas overalls?

Wasting no time, he walked over to them. He wanted to stride quickly but slowed himself. No use in stampeding them, he figured. *Easy does it, don't come on too strong. Be nice...* His thoughts were curious and intent but not angry or hostile. *Keep an open mind, follow the evidence*, he reminded himself.

Ella watched with alarm as he approached. She reminded herself, she was just a traveler, had nothing to be ashamed of, no reason to be afraid. Still, she had an instinctive dislike for the law. She wanted to turn away, to snub this tall man coming their way. Dale watched impassively as the man came across the street towards them. He calmly weighed whether to be courteous, or to put his guard up and be antagonistic.

"Good afternoon. Or I should say, good morning!" Wentz stopped near enough to have a conversation but not aggressively close. He gave them space to retreat or leave.

"I am a railroad agent. Can I ask you a few questions?"

He proceeded as if they had no problem at all with that. He extended his hand and introduced himself, looking Dale in the eye and expecting a response.

"My name is Steuben Wentz."

A pause, no response. "And you are…?," he asked.

Dale didn't speak, he just stared back. Finally Ella jumped in.

"Why should we talk to a railroad dick? And who we are is not your business." Her eyes flared and she stepped forward pugnaciously.

"You say you're a railroad agent, well for which road? And just what kind of prying are you up to? What do you want to know?" Ella was working herself up, not a hard thing to accomplish.

Steu wasn't surprised. He had hoped the encounter would be civil but apparently this wasn't going to happen. He could use her anger to his advantage.

"Ma'am, I work for David Moffat, the Denver Northwestern and Pacific Railway. The railroad you soon will be able to ride here to Fraser, direct from Denver." He paused, proud and a little surprised that description had come from his mouth, unscripted and unplanned.

"As you may know, we are building west from Denver. There was a rockslide at one of our worksites. No one was hurt, fortunately."

He paused, hoping for some response, a nod, any acknowledgement at all. He got none.

"I have to tell you that two persons answering to your descriptions were seen near the site the day of the slide." Still no acknowledgment, nothing.

"In fact you—or they—were reported to be there at the site just before the slide occurred. Now, don't misunderstand. I am not accusing anyone. We need to talk. It is just that we want to know your whereabouts and actions that day. Perhaps you saw or noticed someone or something."

He may as well have flicked Ella with a riding crop. She didn't jump but she definitely reacted.

"Why, you have nerve. Have you nothing better to do than chase all over Colorado, accosting innocent travelers? You should be putting your business in order instead."

And they're off! thought Dale. *Here she goes again.*

Ella was off and running. She looked Steu in the eye, stepping up near to his face. "You need to be looking at your worker safety and not talking to people on the street! You have men being kept away from home for days at a time. You make then do hard manual labor and handle dynamite. Let them be trampled by underfed, ill treated horses. Its no wonder accidents happen. And now you try to shift blame for shoddy planning and work to someone you don't even know...."

Dale stepped in, trying to slow Ella. She was not exactly forgettable even if she didn't speak. He sure hoped her rant didn't make her, and him, even more memorable to this railroad dick. He wanted the two them to remain anonymous. Plus he wanted to put Steu on the defensive.

"Mr. ah, West is it?"

Steu's eyes had met Ella's, and they lingered there for a moment then he looked at Dale. "Wentz. Steuben Wentz."

Having taken control from Ella, Dale went on, wapid fire. Thirty years later he would have been mimicking Porky Pig. His sentences stuttered out too fast for Steu to respond.

"Why do you think we know anything about your rock-slide? What makes you think we had anything to do with it? Who told you we were around Eldorado Springs? We know nothing about your problems. We are just traveling through this fair state. We think you should leave us and go on about your business. Why don't you find someone else to harass?"

Steu listened, letting the protests go past like water down a rapids. His mind clamped onto Dale's reference to Eldorado Springs. He had purposefully not told them the location. They didn't need to know it. If they did, maybe they'd let it slip. Sure enough, the slender man with bright eyes blurted it out. Steu was sure now that he had the right people. He sharpened his eyes and voice, and took a small step towards the two. He didn't want to threaten them, but he did want to take the initiative back.

"I have reliable witnesses who saw you there. Why were you spying on our construction camp? Were you bothering our workers? You were trespassing. But you knew that, didn't you? Did you go near the tunnel?" He paused, easing up. Suddenly he was the good cop, the courteous guy just trying to help.

"I'm sorry, but I didn't get your names. We can clear this matter up easily if you will work with me."

Dale wasn't about to give out any names. He put his hand at Ella's elbow and was ready to walk her away. She, not surprisingly, had other ideas. Her voice was shrill and loud.

"You think you are so smart, mister company agent. Well, you aren't. We will fix your railroad project. We have friends in New York who have money to burn. We will stop your fancy Mr. Moffat's road. You just watch! And your animals and workers will help..."

By now Dale was not guiding her away with hand on elbow, he was literally propelling her.

Steu had enough to work with for now. He watched them go, knowing that he'd get nothing further today anyway. The cop stood and thoughtfully observed for a moment, then went into the hotel. He took a room. Taking a dollar bill out of his pocket, he slid it across the counter, keeping it barely visible under his hand. Then he asked the clerk the names of the two people who had just left. They had registered as Mr. and Mrs. Dale Smertz, he was told.

As soon as he got to his room pen and paper came out. Names, impressions of behavior, and quotes got written out. He wanted to get it down while his memory was fresh. The guy seemed a cool customer but the woman, well, the woman had a screw loose. She seemed to have only a ragged control of her mouth and her feelings. Looking out the window when he finished, he saw the pair get aboard the down valley stage. They seemed to be arguing.

Eighty or so miles east, Mik was on the northeast side of Eldorado Mountain. He figured the last site was near, probably just a few hundred yards away around a few curves. He was on horse for this stretch, a horse which knew the road and needed little handling. Mik was alternating his attention between his empty stomach and the condition of the grade. Then of a sudden he saw a man on foot, coming towards him.

Mik looked twice, then yet a third time at the person approaching. "Not again!" he said out loud. Another doppelganger! This guy looked a lot like his best friend Joe Abrams, back in Sula time. This screwy, bizarre routine was getting tiresome. It made him weary and edgy, and homesick. These strange encounters with people he knew but didn't know were really something.

Joe Abrams was a close friend. The guy was his hiking and climbing buddy. He was, at least back in Sula time, a retired ranger, a man with a sharp sense of humor. It ran through Mik's head that Joe was born in Egypt but had accumulated a wide and deep knowledge of the Rocky Mountains. *Now, what will be this guy's story?* Mik wondered incredulously, resigned to another dose of the bizarre. He just hoped the man was friendly.

Joe Eggers had no idea about Joe Abrams. Or Sula. Or Mik Mas. What he was doing was thinking about the big J himself, and railroads and making money in the new century. Deep in thought, he was walking the rough grade when in the distance saw a man ahorse. It kind of surprised him but he was too deep in thought to really consider that he'd need to be aware and talk to him.

After his talk with Steu at the James Hotel, Joe had made the trek to Moffat's lair Denver. There he had managed to pass himself off as a potential investor from the East. He had even been able to wangle an invitation to go look at the road. And he was allowed to go solo, no company chaperone. This was unusual for Moffat's shop. Joe mused that Mr. Harriman would never ever let an unknown man come in to the offices. Much less talk his way to an unaccompanied scouting trip of a company project. What a difference in the two!

Actually Joe found it refreshing that he was taken at his word. He liked being treated as an honorable man. He had been busy for most of the day after seeing Moffat's office. Time was taken up by making notes and running figures on paper and in his head. The more he saw of the Denver

Northwestern and Pacific project the more he liked it. He figured Mr.Harriman might be interested in investing. Maybe would be willing to put in a few million to make more millions. A few million was small potatoes for the likes of him.

Then the thought occurred to Joe that he could paint the picture so that Harriman would not be interested. And he realized that this could be his ticket to independence. If he could scrape up some money maybe he could become a part owner, a junior partner in the Denver Northwestern. If that worked out, the future was his. He was ruthless and coldly analytical enough to know he had valuable knowledge. After all, Joe knew that he had a lot of inside information on Harriman's methods. If he was careful, he could parlay that lore, his familiarity, into something of value to Mr. Moffat. Joe Eggers rationalized this betrayal of his employer. It didn't take long to convince himself that anyone would do the same. Most any successful businessmen would not hesitate to do such a thing if offered the chance. Or so he proclaimed to his conscience.

The next day Joe took the invitation to heart. He went out and walked part of the project. Truly, he didn't expect to see anyone on the grade other than an occasional labor crew.

This man on a horse coming up the way was nearing him. He clearly was not your typical railroad worker. Who was he, Joe wondered, and what could be learned by talking with him?

VIII

HIGH UP THE SIDE OF A COLORADO MOUNTAIN, SOMEWHERE west of Denver and Boulder, two men approached each other. They were on a rough railroad grade.

The men were still a ways apart, one coming on foot from the north and west, the other riding a horse from the south and east. Mik kept one eye on the man walking. He was not visibly armed and acted peaceably. The guy didn't act like he was a threat. Damn, but he looked like his friend Joe Abrams back in Sula time!

Mik's eye was still on the job despite the stranger who looked like an old friend but couldn't be counted such. The grade here was no better than pioneer, maybe less than that. The trace was maybe ten feet wide, rutted and rocky but without a lot of ups and downs. A lot of gravel and soil would be needed to fill and level this stretch. Mik scratched a note of its condition then put his notebook away. Now he was fully focused on the approaching stranger who was unknowingly familiar.

He was a representative of the Road, and felt he should take the initiative. Mik reined the horse to a stop.

"Hello. You look a long way from home! How can I help you?"

Joe had a decision to make. Should he act lost, or carry himself like he belonged? If he belonged, he was someone who was allowed here, or better yet, was invited to be here. He eyed Mik, judging his audience. The man on the horse was dressed better than a common laborer. The fact that he was riding, wasn't on foot, said something about his status. He was alone, so he wasn't too important—Important with a capital I. Still, he probably wasn't one to be buffaloed either. Eggers made his decision. He would act as if he had every right to be here, act as if he belonged. After all, he had an invitation to be here.

Joe smiled, strode up to Mik, and extended his hand. Mik was still on his horse, preferring to be sure the interloper wasn't trouble. He looked, then leaned down and took the hand.

"Joe Eggers. Nice to see someone out here at the point of the job. I was wondering if I would meet anyone. This road is crossing some tough country up here. But it looks like it will develop into a profitable venture."

He paused, trying to see how he was coming across to Mik.

"Ownership of this road would be a good purchase. I myself may even be interested in buying stock in it. Of course the best way to learn if an investment is a good one is to get up close to it. In this case, I wanted to get my feet on the ground."

He repeated himself, partly to keep the conversation going and partly because he really believed what he was saying. "This is a difficult stretch of mountain you have tackled."

He paused. "You are with Mr. Moffat, are you not?

His choice to act the insider was the right one. The chess game was on.

Mik, leery of a stranger digging for details, nodded. He ignored the last question.

"Yes, there is a lot of rock to be moved. We have no shortage of that! At least there is plenty of fill uphill of the working grade. It should be easy enough to bring it down as needed."

He looked Joe over and asked, "You say you like to look on the ground—from where have you walked?"

"I came in from where the grade meets the creek."

"Oh. Well, that is quite a walk. Have you found what you wanted to know?"

Joe nodded, relaxing a little bit. "I was in Boulder and Denver, talking with some of the officers of the line about this stretch. I wanted to see and walk it, but they were short-handed and couldn't accompany me. I didn't want to impose. I wasn't sure they would agree, but I volunteered to come up alone and they did. It would have been good if one of them had been able to walk the grade with me. But I understand, they need to tend to business. First things first and all."

Eggers was stretching the truth. He had been in Denver and had seen some officers. He had talked briefly with one. He managed to wheedle a terse description of this stretch of the line from that man. Before long, in his mind, he exaggerated the brief statement into an invitation to inspect it. In point of fact he did not have explicit permission to be up here. On the other hand, he hadn't been warned to stay away either.

It would be a while, maybe never, Joe figured, before anyone he might meet up here learned that. By that time, either he would be in the company's good graces or he would be long gone. Either way it didn't matter that technically he was trespassing today. At least he hoped so. He figured if he handled it right, there would be no trouble with this man. He continued.

"Progress on this part of the project seems satisfactory."

He decided to fish a little.

"As I understand it, the line will go from here up South Boulder Creek to the head of the valley. Once there, a tunnel is planned. It will be driven under the crest of the continental divide. That job has been decided on, hasn't it? How is that all progressing?"

This guy seemed to be in the know. But Mik wasn't convinced. He surely wasn't up on the side of the mountain for his health. So why was he? Either he was a spy for a competitor or he really was a potential investor. Mik decided to toss out a little greed filled fib as bait. If Eggers nibbled he likely had money to put in. If he ran at it but avoided it at the last minute, he was likely up to no good.

"Interesting you should bring that up, Mr. Eggers. I hear contracts are about to be let for the tunnel. If things hold true to form, it will be good for stockholders. When that news gets out, the road's stock will most likely soar. You are right, this company offers a good opportunity. I myself am considering arranging my affairs to invest some of my own money."

Mik had absolutely, positively no intention of somehow gathering money to invest. He tried, only partly successfully, to stifle a grin when he had a mental image of him handing over a visa card. As if Denver bankers would know what to do with a small piece of weird synthetic material! He knew perfectly well that as far as the tunnel, its exact location had not been decided. In fact everything about it was up in the air, so to speak. The altitude, diameter, length, direction, grade, and most everything else about it were still up for grabs. Absolutely no contracts to build it had been let or even seriously discussed.

Mik watched Joe closely, not wanting to stare but wanting to read his reaction. He didn't know it, but his smile was taken by Joe not as a sneer but as encouragement. For his part, Joe's mind was racing. He liked the quality of the construction he had seen so far. And he liked the route. The project here was far from the crowded, urbanized east coast. It would open up new country and had the potential to be quite profitable.

If what he was hearing was true, this was his chance. Joe Eggers made a commitment. He decided he would step out on his own. He would put money into the Denver Northwestern and Pacific Railway Company. It would surely grow. Making that decision was actually declaring his independence. He would leave Mr. Harriman and his life back east. It felt good to make the break, and he was happy about it.

Joe looked back at Mik with his own smile. "The tunnel started, already! In that case, I will contact my banker. By the way, I never did get your name, Mr...?"

Mik once again shook the hand Joe extended. "Mast. Myron Mast. Nice to meet you."

Mik was pretty sure this Joe was on the up and up. Nonetheless, he'd need to see what he could find out about him.

"Well, Mr. Eggers, I need to get back to work. Have to get back to tunnel four yet today. And you need to talk to your banker, so I'll let you go. Best of luck to you."

He turned his horse around and headed back down the line.

Joe watched him go, then turned around and started back the way he had come. He knew he had crossed his Rubicon.

His energy and loyalty would no longer go to E.H. Harriman and the Union Pacific system. From here on in he would be looking out for number one, old Joe the good Egg. He had lots to do. First, he would learn all he could about Moffat's line. And he would actually put some of his money into stock. He wanted to be able to identify himself as a stockholder in talks with Moffat and others. Most of his money would be invested elsewhere. The main thing was to buy some property along the route. The right building or plot of land would surely increase in value with the road's coming.

As Joe walked west, he was thinking hard. He realized that he couldn't make the change from E.H. Harriman's man to independent in one fell swoop. He would need to buy some time. Reports would need to be continued. It was essential that he keep some information going back to New York. He couldn't let them find out that he was even thinking of switching loyalties. If they found out he had in fact done so, no telling what might happen. It wouldn't be good in any case.

Plus he wanted to keep on the inside of the UP as long as he could. Information, current information, about the giant railroad was valuable. The more that he could bring with him over to Denver, the better. Joe also realized that he had to find that man Dale Smertz and the woman Ella, and divert their attention somehow. He didn't want them reporting back to New York on him. And he didn't want them to be making trouble for him and his new investment project.

As Mik rode off, he made a mental note to tell the company security agent about this encounter. Steu had specifically asked to know about any strangers he met around the jobsite. With that he banished thoughts of the stranger. As the horse swayed and gyrated under him, he organized his thoughts for the report he would write. The weather held and soon enough he was back at the tunnel four site. He saw Cam go into his tent and followed there.

The big man tended to some details and people asking him questions. He fixed Mik with a look and unleashed a stream of questions.

"And how is the road progressing up the line? How far did you get? Did you see anything unusual or needing attention? We're about done with tunnel four and will be moving the camp up the line. Did you see any good sites to relocate it to? What do you think?"

"Whoa, slow down. Your questions are coming like water from a fire hose."

Cam smirked. "That's a city phrase if I've ever heard one! We don't have fancy fire hoses out here, just buckets."

Mik shrugged and smiled. "Just an expression. Anyhow, progress looks pretty steady to me. Of course the grade gets worse—less finished—the further up you go. That's to be expected. I saw no insurmountable problems. Fill over and above the tunnel debris is generally available. Heck, just pull it down the hill, there is puh-lenty of it."

He had a sudden thought. "This just occurred to me. I may be all wet, not sure."

He smirked and said, "Maybe your firehose of questions splashed me."

Cam groaned.

Mik apologized, "Sorry, bad joke. But think about this: If there is a problem with rock, it may be, at least at first, rockfall down onto the track. The noise and motion of the train may dislodge rocks for a while. Until the slides and debris slopes get stabilized again."

"Good point. You may be right. We will likely need to send crews up to inspect and if need be dislodge loose rocks. That and maybe put up rock fence by the tracks in problem areas. The operations people will have to factor that in," Cam agreed.

Mik continued.

"Yeah, it may be something to consider. Anyway, my report will give specifics. Have to say, I was concentrating on the grade and fill, but wasn't really looking for good sites to move camp. Offhand, I'd say move it past tunnel five or maybe just past six. As I think of it, there are flats, more or less, and water is running in the small creek just past six."

He paused. "Oh, yeah. There was one unexpected thing. Just this side of tunnel eleven I came around a corner and got a surprise. There was a man coming towards me on foot. Kind of a dandy, not really dressed to be out walking a pioneer railroad grade. He introduced himself as..." here Mik consulted his notebook to remember— "as Josephus Eggers."

He shut the notebook and laid it down.

"Said he was a potential investor. At first I was skeptical, but he seemed to know some things about railroads and some details about this project. I didn't tell him anything new, just kind of confirmed things that are general knowledge. His eyes lit up with dollar signs after he brought up the big tunnel under the divide. I think he is for real, not a spy or troublemaker. Should I tell Steu about him or do you want to?"

Cam nodded thoughtfully. "Josephus Eggers, you say? I'll mention him to Mr. Sumner. You go ahead and tell Steu about it too. Firsthand impressions and all that. But you'll have to wait a day or two. He's off chasing that man and woman he asked about. He wasn't sure when he'd return."

"Alright, I'll do it. Your report will be ready tomorrow mid morning. I'll work on it tonight. At that, I think I'll ride down to Pruden's now." Mik stood, ready to leave.

Cam winced. "Oh. That reminds me. I forgot to tell you in the rush. Prudens. Bad news."

He paused and gulped.

"The young Seth Pruden was found this morning, sprawled along the trail. He apparently was walking up to camp. He was dead."

Cam shook his head as Mik slumped back to the chair.

"Damn shame. Nineteen years old...He could have followed his father's footsteps, taken over their ranch. Might have become a big part of the community. I haven't heard exactly what he died of, but apparently he wasn't injured, shot or stabbed. I am afraid you will find no happiness at the Pruden home tonight."

Shocking news. Mik sat silent. He and Seth had talked just this morning. The guy had looked a bit pale and sounded a little blue. But he seemed healthy enough, and acted strong enough to meet life on its terms.

"Those poor people. They don't need a boarder, a stranger not kin, coming around tonight. God, it has to be awful for them. I think maybe I should eat up here and find a spot to sleep in one of the workers' tents."

Cam disagreed.

"No, don't do that. I think Mrs. Pruden and Odessa, and Mr. Pruden, and Ted too, will welcome having some company. Tonight of all nights. It can be comforting for them to have a routine to keep busy with. I suggest you just go down like usual. That's what I intend to do when I'm done here. Of course we'll want to offer condolences and help where we can. But I think taking care of their boarders will give them something to do. They'll probably want to keep busy and take their mind off the loss. It has to be terrible to lose a child."

Mik thought a moment and saw the wisdom of it.

"Yeah, you are right. I should go. See you down there tonight." Weary, grim thoughts gripped him as he rode down the mountain. He was not looking forward to going into the house. Still, he had the easy end of the bargain compared to what the Prudens had to deal with.

Day's end approached across the mountains as well. Up in the town of Fraser, the day was about gone. It was too late for Steu to return to Denver. He was stranded for the night. The stage over Berthoud Pass was gone. It had departed several hours back. Options were limited. He was going to have to spend the night. Tomorrow, he could return to Eldorado Springs and the work camp. Before he left he decided he would talk with the local sheriff's office. Ask them to alert him if the two troublemakers came back through towards Denver or Boulder.

Or he could pursue them on down the valley tomorrow morning on the local stage. The thing was, he didn't know how far they were going. He surely didn't want to hop off at every stop to check it out. Decision: return to the worksite on Eldorado Mountain. He half expected the camp would be moved up the line before he got back. After all, tunnel four was holed through and the grade was looking good. The rails would be laid up to that spot pretty soon. He wanted to stop chasing suspected agitators across the country and get back to his work. It was his job to keep the site secure and safe. He could sure do that better by being there than running after yahoos who dressed funny.

Dale and Ella did in fact go down the valley. And they actually wanted and intended to get off at every stop. They didn't stay for long at any one place. While there, though, they talked to anyone they could find. From Fraser, through Hot Sulphur Springs, to Kremmling, following the Colorado River, they worked their way.

Ella in particular liked to talk with folks. She loved to fire people up. The woman had a knack. She could quickly judge what a person's hot button was.

"Did you hear that the railroad will be coming through the valley? They have people out buying up rights of way for the track. I heard that they are trying to beat down the price they pay to landowners. The road demands a long contract. They want to get the right of way but end up paying the owners next to nothing. Someone told me that here and there, ranchers have actually been kicked off their own homestead! Can you imagine?"

Of course this last was untrue but that didn't concern her. It spread doubt and fueled opposition to Moffat's road. That was good enough for her.

Another thing Ella liked to do was look after animals. Often, after haranguing a rancher about the evils of the railroad right of way, she would challenge them not to mistreat animals. She didn't understand or didn't care that this undid much of the good will she had just worked so hard to earn. She would jump right in.

"I see your horse has ribs showing. Why don't you feed him enough? And the poor animal is panting and thirsty. Animals have feelings just like people. You must see that your horses are treated kindly!"

Ranchers and townsfolk certainly had reason to remember Ella.

While Ella was on her rants, Dale hung back. He was thinking a little bigger. The question he tried to answer was straightforward. It was, simply, how can we block the railroad from this route? He wondered if they could lay their hands on the deed for a big ranch which sat across the whole valley. The valley floor lands were settled and pretty much spoken for. Hay meadows and good grazing land lay on both sides of the river. Those who owned that land would not easily give it up.

Wrestling with the problem, Dale stopped thinking like an agitator or troublemaker. He shifted his point of view, looking at the problem as a railroad locating engineer. Was there a place where the valley narrowed and the options for track location were few? That would be the place to try to get a right of way or a deed! He'd have to check on that.

The rest of the day was deemed productive by Ella and Dale. Between them, they spread half truths, some lies, bile and animal advice at each stage stop. This bizarre combination of subjects cut a wide swath up there in the mountains. It made them easy to remember, even to snigger at.

In a way Steu lost an opportunity when he didn't follow in their footsteps. It would have been easy to know where they had been, and to quickly neutralize the damage they were doing. At every stop he could have countered with the truth, telling of Moffat's honest dealings. And he could have made points on the animal welfare issue. All he had to do was say something about how a rancher knows how to treat his own animals and easterners should not stick their noses in. But Steu missed this chance when he chose instead to return to his job.

In just one day, the pair made it from Fraser all the way to Kremmling, stops included. They arrived late in the afternoon. Kremmling was, and to this day is, a ranching and logging burg on the Colorado River. The town was located about forty miles west of the divide, maybe fifty miles north of the Breckenridge gold diggings. It was not large. As they drew into town, Dale saw a sign, and it confirmed what he had guessed. The population was listed as two hundred eighty three souls, hardly more than a village.

Dale sat and studied the land. He looked with the eye of a locating engineer. The horses pulling the stage clopped into town and he had a chance to study the surrounding hills. Kremmling is in a nice broad valley, lots of meadow and grazing space. He saw that the river valley seemed to narrow dramatically just west of town. He asked a fellow passenger about it. He was a local man returning home.

"I see the river canyon narrows to the west. Does that stretch of canyon have a name?"

The man thought a moment, chewing on a cud of tobacco.

"Gore Canyon. It is wild, narrow, steep sided. Or so I understand—it is too wild for me, have never been there. But I'm told that it goes on like that for a long way, twenty or thirty miles."

He spat out the window, and wiped his chin with the back of his hand.

"Then the valley opens up again for quite a ways. That, I have seen. It is nice there. A few lucky settlers have some damn fine ranches down there. Took my wife to see them. We went around the canyon over the mountain. The other end of the Gore Canyon looks as narrow and steep and tough as this one."

Dale nodded encouragingly. "So there is no road through the canyon now?"

"Nah. Just the river, I think, with rocky rapids. From town, the stage road leaves the river. It goes north and west over mountains. It takes you to the settlement at Steamboat Springs."

His eyes lit up. “I guess they have a hot springs which sometimes hoots like a steamboat’s whistle. That would be something to hear!”

He paused, and became more matter of fact. “And, I hear tell there are coal fields out there. I guess, maybe thirty or thirty five miles past the hot springs. The new railroad will go past those mines on the way to Salt Lake City. Like I said, the wagon road from here wanders north then west. Following the river then cutting north would be shorter in miles. If the railroad goes through there it will be a much more efficient route. That is tough country for them.”

His eyes lit up again. “Come to think of it, the Gore Canyon can’t be much tougher than a lot of the country they will have come through just to get here!”

“Yes, tough country, I see. Thank you.”

Thank you indeed, thought Dale. This could be the chokepoint he had been seeking. It seemed even better than the best case he had hoped for.

The two of them got out of the stage. They walked aimlessly in small circles, trying to shake the cobwebs out of their heads and aches out of their bodies. Soon they felt better and went to find a room. After freshening up, it was time to find a place to eat. As they walked, Dale filled Ella in.

“Here is where we can stop Moffat. Stop him cold. All we need to do is somehow block access to the Gore Canyon west of town.”

“Hey, by the way, Ella.” Dale screwed up his courage. “El, you do good riling people up. Get them angry about the rich men stealing their property and all. But then you undo most of that good when you preach to them about their animals. Can’t that talk wait until another time?

Ella was uncharacteristically quiet for a moment. "I know I should back off on that, Dale. But I find myself jumping in before I can stop. I feel so bad for an animal that isn't being treated right. If I don't speak up for them, who will? It is hard, I know we have to work on the railroad, but it is hard to stand by and see a poor animal get misused. I'll try to soften it but I just can't promise."

She felt bad, knowing that she was hurting their efforts to hinder the railroad. It was time, she felt, to try to make amends, and to make Dale smile. Maybe if she made light of her misplaced preaching and activism...

With a smile in her voice and on her face, she kiddingly continued.

"About the railroad. You're right, what we need is to just block access. Blocking access across an entire valley should be easy. I'll just throw myself down kicking and screaming. That'll do the job!"

Dale had an image of her doing just that, throwing a tantrum, turning blue, refusing to move. That would certainly divert attention from him. But right now they didn't need any more attention than they already had. For all he knew, that railroad agent might be on the next stage. That big guy with his questions and unspoken accusations. The sheriff would no doubt be happy to help him run a few troublemakers out of town.

Then the image of Ella throwing herself down changed. For some reason he got a mental image of her as a giant not a regular sized person. And in that image, the giantess Ella was laying across the valley. Gesturing to all that she would let nothing, no one pass. She was so big that no stage coaches or horses could get by. In fact water started to back up as she lay in the river, forming a big lake.

"That's it! El, you're a genius! That's how we can stop the road!"

She looked at him wide eyed. She knew he was very smart. He wasn't shy about showing it. But what on earth was he talking about? She knew that she didn't have his book learning. But, come on, what could he be thinking?

"Ella, a dam. We build a dam. We need to form a company and file to build a dam in the canyon."

"We don't know the first thing about dams. Or companies. Or filing. How can we do that?"

"It doesn't matter. We can figure it out. If we file and gain the rights to the canyon a railroad can't be built there. That closes off easy access to the lower Colorado River valley. And to the coal fields past Steamboat Springs. And we don't even have to build the thing. We just need to get the rights to do it! That's it!"

She nodded doubtfully, not really seeing how it could work. If he talked more about it maybe something would start to make sense.

Dale was hopping from one foot to the other, so excited he couldn't be still.

"We have to get back to Denver. To heck with spreading rumors up here. Hell, most of the ranchers welcome a railroad. I didn't tell you, but one old coot threatened me when I criticized it. No more of that, no more skulking around Eldorado Springs trying to make trouble. All we have to do is cable New York and have them draw up the papers. We can probably get it done with a telegram or two."

He grinned and rubbed his stomach. "Let's go eat. We have work to do back in the hotel tonight."

IX

The Pruden ranch looked deserted and sad to Mik. The life was gone out of it. There was none of the normal hustle of people coming and going. The ranch house was silent, perhaps grieving the loss of a young man it had watched and sheltered for years. Mik felt at a loss, a little unnerved. He chided himself for it. He hadn't unexpectedly lost a son and brother, just an acquaintance. And a recent one at that, although no one but he knew that. His sadness and loss were nothing compared to that of the community or especially the family. He squared his shoulders and went in.

Charlie and Jennie Pruden were sitting, huddled, in the living room. Ted and Odessa sat with them as did several of the long time boarders. Mik approached the shocked and gaunt pair.

"Cam told me about Seth. I am so sorry. What an awful, unexpected shock. My heart goes out to you."

He took Charlie's hand, then Jennie's, squeezing them. He did the same with Odessa and Ted. Mik didn't try to hug them. For one thing, he didn't feel comfortable trying to hug people he hadn't known for a long time. It was just as well. Only later did he remember that public hugging was not a custom in the early 1900's.

Jennie stirred. Her eyes were red from crying.

"Thank you, Mr. Mast. Your thoughts and concern are appreciated. I really don't know what to do or how I feel. My insides are numb."

She hesitated. "I am sorry that I cannot offer you a hot meal tonight. Our neighbor Mrs. Dunn helped us by bringing over a plate of cold cuts and cheese."

"Oh, Mrs. Pruden. Don't you worry about that. That is more than you should have to take on. If there is anything I can do please say so. I am at your service."

He glanced at Charlie as he said this, silently including him in the offer.

"Thank you, Mr. Mast. For this evening I believe Mrs. Pruden and I, with Odessa and Ted, will just sit together and try to come to grips."

With that somewhat awkward plea Mik left the room. He was depressed. He himself had taken a whole lot of knocks—falling down a rabbit hole into another world, being treated as someone who had somehow survived a rock slide, Seth dying suddenly...Of all things he had never expected, here he was in 1903, working on a railroad. Would he ever get back to Sula in the twenty first century?

He reflected on it all. It was weird beyond description to walk along the trace of a railroad that was about half done. It wasn't even built yet. As he walked, he couldn't help but be aware that he had ridden over it in a diesel electric train over a hundred years later. But as he walked, not only wasn't the road done, the diesel electric engine hadn't been invented! His mind sometimes felt like it was flying apart. There were just too many contradictory ideas and factoids floating around in it! He shook his head, trying to understand the inconsistencies. Mostly he had to get rid of the blues.

It was time to focus on the report he had to write. He grabbed some of the cold dinner. He scarfed it down and put the plate in the sink. Then he plodded up the stairs to his room. Or Mast's room, to be exact. He had nothing here but some clothes and a smart phone which was turned off and was of no use whatsoever anyway.

Whatever, he had to get to work. Thoughts of grade steepness and level and other items started to crowd out the blues. He was soon consumed with writing about road progress, tunnel holing, fill sources, and camp placement. For a while nothing else entered his consciousness.

Of a sudden, Seth's death rose out of the night. Mik wondered how many others had died or would die building this railroad. The cost of its progress in human lives was never discussed or studied. He shook that bleak thought off and went back to his report. Before long it was done and he turned in. Sleep came fairly soon and was not punctured with nightmares.

The next morning, in the village of Kremmling across the mountains, Ella and Dale rose early.

"I've been thinking, Dale, about your plan. It is a good approach, to try to block the road's right of way. We should pursue it. But let's not drop the other strategies." Ella looked at Dale, challenging him with a raised eyebrow.

He grinned. "Thanks. Yes, with a dam across the upper Gore Canyon we can stop Moffat in his tracks."

"Sure, if you get the telegrams off to New York. And if Moffat's men aren't somehow reading your telegrams. And if New York gets the corporation and permit filings done right and in time. And if Moffat doesn't already have rights to the Canyon. And if..."

"I see your point, El. Let's go whole hog to get this dam filing done for now. But yes, you are right, sugar. We should still talk to people. And try to purchase any other rights we can along the way. There have to be a few who will sell to us, cash on the barrelhead."

He stopped, trying to remember just how much cash he had left on him.

"And we—you, really, you're good at it—should still try to stir up labor trouble in the camps. And maybe that snoot Mr. Josephus, not Joe, not Joseph, not Joel, but Josephus, Eggers can help us somehow." He said this with a flourish of his hands as if he were parting the Red Sea or calling down a lightning bolt. Ella grinned and nodded.

Soon they got on the stagecoach headed back to Denver. It was the first of the day running out of Kremmling. The standard route was east along the banks of the Colorado River. It ran through Fraser where the driver stopped. Ella was disgusted by what she saw. There, by the stagestop stood the big railroad dick.

Steu was ready to go back. He had been ready to go back the day before, but couldn't. So first thing he bought a ticket in Fraser for the run back to Dumont. He really thought he was done with the odd couple. He expected that his encounter the day before with the man and woman was enough to run them off. Steu was surprised to see them when he climbed in the stagecoach as it readied to leave Fraser.

The cop's instincts that Steu had honed for several years were usually right. This time, his hunch was that the pair would be in Wyoming or Utah by now. Wrong. Dale and Ella were also unpleasantly surprised. They figured, hopefully, that they had seen the last of him. They had airily assumed that he would be in Denver. Or better yet, that he would be going the other way, fruitlessly chasing after them.

The two men eyed each other silently and warily. Ella glared. She was trying not to say anything, biting her tongue. She bit so hard that she actually tasted a little blood. Dale tried to take the edge off by talking a little. After all it would be a several hour ride over the pass to Dumont.

"We meet again. How was your evening in Fraser?"

Steu considered his response. As a youngster he had lived in the gangs and on the streets. He was not the imaginative type. But he did know how to get people to reveal themselves. Rather than answer Dale, he glanced at Ella. He nodded courteously. He decided to push and prod a little bit. Yesterday she had started to run off at the mouth. If he provoked her again maybe she would blurt out something of use to him.

Looking her in the eye, he talked blandly, as if chatting about the weather.

"Why are you so interested in our railroad? You're not just travelers passing through. I know that you and your man friend have been out trying to spread trouble. Talking to folks about rights of way down the valley. Spreading lies about how we treat ranchers. I ought to have you two arrested. Trespass and public nuisance."

Ella did not explode, didn't even nibble at the bait. She put on the sweet nothing act.

"Why, we are interested in the future of this region. The railroad, if successful, would be a benefit. When it is done we will be riding in comfort at high speeds, twenty five or more miles per hour. Not bouncing along like we are now, a stiff coach behind four horses."

"Yes indeed. And I would hate to see anyone try to stop the road from coming through. Why do you want to do that?"

"But why do you think that, Mr. Wentz? We are merely two citizens enjoying the scenery of Colorado."

The two sparred for another few minutes. Steu was getting nowhere and Ella was starting to enjoy frustrating him.

Dale might have left well enough alone, but didn't. He couldn't help but jump in.

"The thing is, chum, it is none of your business even if we don't like the railroad. The whole thing is an expensive, bad idea." He looked out the window at the mountains, in emphasis.

"The whole undertaking is backed by lightweight investors and run by amateur railroad men. There isn't enough business or settlement out here to justify the effort. Just look out the window! There are no cities, no factories, no mines. There's nothing but trees. Trees, rocks and mountains!"

Ella got her say in now, too. "And if the road does get through, the Union Pacific will cut rates to draw traffic. We will leave you high and dry. And broke."

This was the chink Steu was looking for. That guy in Boulder had told him they were with the UP. This confirmed it.

"We? We will leave you high and dry? So you are spies for the Harriman gang. Chinless wonders sent out from the east. Well, a fancy financier from the city doesn't know this country. He doesn't know how determined the people are out here. How we can grow into development and industry. The Union Pacific can't harm the Denver Northwestern Pacific."

Steu paused, feeling angry and contemptuous. He went on, half seriously, and was glad that he did.

"What are you going to do to stop us? Are you going to throw your body across the right of way, and throw a fit until we stop laying rail? Hold your breath until you turn blue? Call for daddy to come rescue you?"

Ella giggled and then laughed. Dale glared at her. He was angry at her for losing control, for talking and then laughing. And he was irritated that Steu had seen through them. His mouth ran away.

"You can make a joke about throwing our bodies across the valley. But we have something bigger and better to bar your precious right of way. You just wait and see." He knew he had said too much, but it was done. He ignored Steu the rest of the way.

The horses pulling the stage started out from Fraser at a trot. Soon the steepness of the road slowed them to a walk. Then a trudge. They climbed over Berthoud Pass towards Dumont. Just over the top, the driver stopped. He prepared to descend the south side of the pass. First he had to do the same thing Steu had witnessed the previous day. He stopped the coach and blocked the wheels. Then, asking the men inside for help, he chained the back to a big log. Dragging it behind, it acted as a crude but fairly effective brake.

Ella was aghast. "Those poor horses, having to drag a log besides pull the coach! That is asking too much of the dumb, overworked beasts!"

Dale said little. "Well, better that than have the whole rig run so fast the driver loses control. Then horses, driver, coach and we passengers would end up scrambled at the bottom of the mountain."

He had an "aha" moment, but wasn't sure if he should share it or not. He decided to wait, but the thought resounded in his head. *You know, if Moffat succeeds, the horses won't have to do this anymore. The train will do the heavy work. Much as I hate to say it, that ain't all bad.*

He pondered that as the coach bumped down the road.

Soon they neared the town of Dumont. There everyone could ride the train to points east. Or west, for that matter. One could go from the tiny mountain town to most anywhere. New York City, San Francisco, New Orleans, you name it. A train change here and there would be needed, but other than that it was clear going.

Dale wasn't thinking about miles of rail or convenient travel or about going anywhere. He was focused on his dam project. A firm plan of action is what he needed. He wanted to hit the ground running when he got to Denver. First Eggers needed to be found. He and El would likely need the elusive easterner's help.

It was very easy to say "just send a few telegrams." But to who? In what order? How to overcome the skepticism of people sitting in a skyscraper in Manhattan? Even with the UP's full backing, it wouldn't be easy. Better men than Dale had failed to get a reservoir company formed and obtain the rights to build a dam, even in easy country without opposition. Adding in Gore Canyon and the need for speed and secrecy...Maybe Eggers knew someone or had an in somewhere. Dale sure hoped so.

Joe wasn't in Denver, but in the spa town of Eldorado Springs. He wasn't thinking of ways to cause problems for the new railroad. Rather, ways to be productive and efficient took up his energy. The railroad of course dominated his thoughts. He was trying to look at the big picture, at least a bigger picture than Dale had. He was reviewing the previous day, trying to draw its lessons out.

Joe had been surprised to meet someone on the grade. He really expected to have the mountain to himself. Mr. Eggers prided himself on making the most of the hand he was dealt. Today was no different. He felt that the encounter on the grade had turned out pretty well. It looked dicey for a few moments. But it had turned out to be a civil and constructive conversation. It was odd how the guy had first reacted. The guy had looked at Joe like he was a ghost, or something.

That said, Joe wasn't sure about the man, what was his name, Mast? Joe wasn't positive that Mast had been telling the whole truth. He had heard rumors about the tunnel being underway but had heard the opposite as well. Enough stories on both sides that Joe couldn't really be sure. The day, and what Mast had told him, had kind of tilted the scale. It was clear that the road held promise.

After he met and talked with Mik, he turned back and went down to Eldorado Springs. It was late so he stopped for the night there at the Hotel Eldorado. Not a bad hotel for the west. He got into a conversation with the barman.

"This is a nice town. Spectacular cliffs, natural springs, roaring creek. Do you get many travelers?"

Joe may as well have flipped a switch. The barkeep smiled.

"We are getting more each year. And just wait until the railroad is done and the Crag Hotel is open. People will come by rail and spend time at the Crag. Some will come down to soak in the pool and eat in our restaurant! That railroad is the best thing to happen to Colorado since gold was discovered!"

"Oh, tell me about the Crag Hotel." Joe hadn't heard of this and it seemed to add to the promise of the road.

"It is a hotel being built high above Eldorado Springs. It will be located just below the railroad tracks. Have a fine view over the canyon and cliffs. People will be able to ride the train up from Denver, stop and get off. And a wagon road is being built to bring them down here. It will be a first class, fine establishment. It can't help but add to our business here in town as well!"

Joe finished his drink and went to his room. He was excited about the future prospects of the road and his part in it. Even more so to hear that development along the road was already being undertaken. There was a lot of money to be made, and he intended to get his share!

Deep sleep eluded him. Tons of information raced around his head. The bar keep's enthusiasm about the Crag Hotel and Eldorado Springs mixed with what the railroad man Mast had let slip about the road's progress. The news about the tunnel under the divide was so good it had to be true. Despite nagging doubts, the canny railroad man from the east convinced himself. If the tunnel was underway, the line would be making tons of money soon.

The next morning, Joe rose, breakfasted, and took a ride to Boulder. He had kept his room at the James and they expected his return. Most of the day there was spent at a desk. He wrote, rewrote, and discarded several reports to Mr. Harriman. It was a fine line he was walking. The report had to give good information. The trick was to give enough that Harriman was satisfied with the job he was doing.

On the other hand, he didn't want to paint too rosy a picture. No reason to give the New York boys any encouragement to come in and buy control. Or to send more people out to harm, literally derail, the project. Those were the last things he wanted. Here he was, about ready to jump ship. He definitely did not want to take that step and then end up finding that Harriman had bought control of the Denver Northwestern. That would be the absolute worst of all worlds.

Finally in the afternoon he gave up. It was time for him to go to Denver. He wanted to talk to someone, an officer or engineer. He felt the need to speak with someone, anyone, involved in the project. His mind was boiling with questions and ideas about the new road. With a shrug, he decided that he would write the report to Harriman later, tomorrow, the next day, sometime. That was the past. Now to go to Denver and greet the future! He gathered what he needed and started off.

A person sitting in the lobby would have seen a medium tall, expensively dressed businessman. He was deep in concentration and striding out of the building. But as he neared the door, the reception clerk called.

"Mr. Eggers. There is someone here to speak with you."

Joe saw a stocky, familiar looking man at the front desk, talking to the clerk. They both looked over at him. The clerk was relieved to have caught him for the other man. He was busy enough with all the guests and had other tasks and duties that needed done.

The big man standing in front of the desk looked appraisingly at Joe. Eggers smelled law. Oh yes, in fact he was the company dick he had sicced on Dale and Ella. Joe was clean but nonetheless he ran quickly through his recent acts and encounters. He was pretty sure there was nothing to be concerned about. Still, better to be sure. For all he knew this guy had a warrant or an accusation against him.

When he got back to town, Steu first had to catch up at work. He got himself up to date on the goings on at the camp while he had been up in Fraser. Among other things, Cam had told him about Mik's encounter along the grade.

Steu didn't really believe in coincidences. The guy wandering around out there on the grade had the same name as the man who had told him about the couple going west. The couple he had just chased to Fraser and back. Come to see him here at the James, he recognized that the two were in fact the same man. The security man wondered what this Eggers character was up to. He kept turning up at odd times in odd places. He would bear watching…

"Mr. Eggers, good to see you again. How are you?" Steu extended his hand.

"The information you gave me about the troublemakers was good. I tracked the man and woman down and found them in Fraser, over the mountain. Quite a trek, by train and stagecoach."

Joe nodded, unsure where this was heading. He took Steu's hand but said nothing.

Steu noticed the gesture, and noted that Joe had not volunteered anything. He went on.

"They were over there spreading trouble, a detective friend tells me. Trying to buy up rights of way, spreading lies about what the road will do, and so on. They are back over here somewhere now, I believe."

He probed to see what Joe knew but wasn't telling.

"I can't recall, did you give me their names?"

Joe decided, *in for a dime, in for a dollar.* He figured that he was going to leave Harriman and the Union Pacific. Since he was going to go to the other side and invest in the Denver Northwestern and Pacific, he should go all out. Or as far as he could—a good businessman never laid all his cards out at once. He decided he would tell Steu some of what he knew about Dale and Ella.

"I'm not sure about what trouble they may have intended to spread. Buying up rights of way, you say?" He wanted to separate himself from them, avoid any guilt by association.

"But I did learn names. He gave his name as Dale Smertz. He claims they are agents for the UP. He didn't say more, not sure if he is an engineering scout, or security, or what. Just "an agent." She goes by Ella. Her position is unclear and she said nothing to enlighten me. I'm not sure what she is doing. Maybe she's an agent, maybe just a hanger on, a biffy for her companion."

He smirked at this. He made up the term "biffy" but it fit.

"Or, given her garb and her attitude, could be she herself is a professional troublemaker. Someone like Mother Jones. Heck, maybe I'm all wrong and she is his wife. Anyway, that is the story on them."

By giving out this information, Joe earned a little trust and credibility from Steu. What Joe said tracked with what he knew. It matched with what Steu learned from talking to the couple. It also matched what he had gleaned from other sources. The railroad security man nodded. He decided to share a little of what he knew, tit for tat.

"I saw and talked a little with them up in Fraser. I stayed there but they got on the stage and headed west. They took the afternoon stage. The next day, yesterday, they were back. I think the likely place where they spent the night is Kremmling. Or I guess they could have paid some rancher for a room, but there are darn few ranches in that stretch."

Joe agreed.

"Probably they went to Kremmling and stayed in the hotel. I have trouble seeing them talking to a rancher nice about a room."

"Maybe so. Anyway, when they came back to Fraser we rode together over the mountain to Dumont and the train.

That was an experience! While bumping along the road, I prodded them a bit. At first they fenced, parrying and not answering. Then I got some off kilter answer."

Steu stopped, recalling the conversation.

"One thing he said, Mr. Eggers, puzzled me. Smertz said, and I'm not sure of the exact words but I got their intent."

He paused again to get it right.

"He said they would block the railroad right of way with something big. That's all he said, then clammed up. Do you have any idea what that could mean?"

He looked at Joe, raising an eyebrow, hoping for some help. He was talking about Dale and Ella and their plans. In the back of his mind he wondered just who and what Joe Eggers was. Would he shed any light on Dale's mysterious "something big"? And for that matter, what had happened when this guy met Mik up on the grade? He decided to change things up, be direct, and ask.

"Say, I understand you met one of our men up on the project yesterday. I'm told you were walking the grade east of tunnel eleven or so. Usually we send a company man out with guests. How did you get up there alone?" As he asked, his eyes narrowed. He didn't like strangers prowling around the job.

Joe had a stock answer for railroad security men. He just inserted the appropriate names and let it fly.

"I met with an engineer, an assistant to Mr. Sumner. Since he was busy he gave me directions and told me to go ahead."

Steu was skeptical, but accepted the answer for the moment. He would check it out later.

"Well, next time, you need to check in with the site boss before you go out wandering. You could have been injured, with blasting, filling, moving rock and so forth."

Joe nodded, glad that his answer had been accepted. And he tried to look appropriately chastened. Like the boy caught picking a tomato from a neighbor's vine.

Steu probed a bit. "What did you learn out there on the mountain?"

Joe smiled, knowing he had made it past the cop's initial skepticism.

"This is a momentous project, a huge complex job. I think it is being done well. The terrain is very difficult but the company seems to be getting the better of it. They are making good headway. I am impressed. In fact, I am considering making an investment in the Denver Northwestern and Pacific Railway."

Actually, he wasn't considering, he had already decided. The question now was how much and what he would sell to raise the money. But he wasn't ready to broadcast that, especially to a railroad cop.

"As to your question about Smertz and something big, that is a puzzle."

Eggers actually did have a fair idea, but kept it to himself.

"I do not know what he meant. If I see them again I will try to find out."

Not wanting to get a question about why he might see them again, he closed the conversation.

"My afternoon appointment is in Denver so I am afraid I must leave. Good day, Mr. Wentz."

Steu had hoped to learn the relationship, if any between Eggers and the couple. *Well,* he thought, *I need to look into Mr. Eggers. Who he is and why he is out here. And is he meeting with that couple? I wonder if he is an investor or a spy. Or maybe he is playing another game altogether. I'll give that job to someone, to find out.*

Earlier in the day, when the stage got to Dumont, Dale and Ella hurried off, not even looking at Steu. They bought tickets and boarded the train and went to Denver. They made sure not to sit in the same car as the railroad cop. They lost track of their tormentor at Union Station. Downtown Denver was busy.

Ella smirked, and jabbed.

"Usually it is me who says more than I want to. This time it was you, carrying on about blocking the road with something big. The only big thing is your mouth."

Dale couldn't disagree.

"Yes, I said too much. But that is one stupid cop. He is too dense to guess what I meant. Anyway, I didn't really to give anything away. He probably thought I was just blowing smoke."

He turned his attention to his big project. "We need to send a telegraph to New York about this. But first we need to find Eggers. He may know someone. I'll bet he will have helpful ideas. Where is he staying?"

Ella didn't want to involve Eggers. She didn't know who he was in it for. Instinct told her he worked for the UP, yes. But he just didn't ring true—something about him made her itchy. Over the years she had learned to pay heed to those feelings.

"The James Hotel in Boulder. At least that is where he was."

She frowned. "Let's not go to Boulder yet. I say we take a room here in Denver. The idea is fresh and we need to work on the project. We don't really need him to help us send a few telegrams, do we? Look, if we really need to, we can contact him later."

Dale thought a moment and nodded. "Alright. Let's go find a room."

X

The unlikely couple left the railroad station. They walked kind of aimlessly down Seventeenth Street looking for a decent place to stay. Ella didn't care where as long as it was reasonably clean. Dale wanted that and he wanted it to be close in.

"I don't want to walk for blocks and blocks, El. Let's find something nearby."

"That is alright with me. Just find something, please. I'm tired too. Last thing I want is to wander the town for hours looking for a room."

Even though they were apparently in agreement, their search wandered. They walked all over the station and business district.

Dale was already drafting telegrams in his head. He was captivated by the dam idea, utterly taken. So taken that he was having trouble focusing on the task of finding a hotel. His thoughts erupted out loud.

"I think we should go for the whole magilla. Tell them we want a dam, a reservoir, and a pipeline or power plant. And why we want to do this. May as well be specific. If we just tell them to file for ownership of land across the head of the canyon they'll wonder what we have been drinking."

He dodged a horse pulling a cart laden with dried cattle hides. The animal was skittish with all the noise and commotion of a downtown street. "What do you think about that, El?"

"I can't believe someone is using leather in this day and age! Those poor cattle," she wailed. The woman looked like she wanted to go scold the driver of the wagon. But she got her feelings under control, and redirected towards Dale's question.

"That sounds like a ..." Ella stopped mid sentence. Up the street, deep in thought, ambled Joe.

"Why hello, Mr. Eggers. We were just talking about you." She glanced at Dale who nodded imperceptibly. "Can we talk? You are clearly an experienced businessman. We need your advice and thoughts. It has to do with the railroad we discussed recently. The Denver Northwestern and Pacific. Is that something you can help us with?"

Joe was taken aback at seeing the two troublemakers. He had hoped they were long gone. If not long gone at least going. They were the last people he wanted to meet and talk with but he couldn't see a way to dodge them now.

He had been busy congratulating himself, savoring his new life. His thoughts: *I am good and I am lucky. Great to have both. I'm good because I talked with people in the know. I met them when I hung around Moffat's bank on Sixteenth Street. So now I know even more about the road and how I can make money off of it. But lucky too, heck yes. Meeting that man Mast up on the grade was a real fortunate thing. What he told me helps me even more. With what Wentz told me today...If this keeps up I will be a rich man soon. And an independent one!*

Joe had in fact been busy, and they actually were productive efforts. He had made contacts and learned much about the project. His luck held, and he was once again at the right place at the right time. He actually met and was able to talk briefly with Horace Sumner, chief engineer of the project. The man's comments and insights had bolstered Joe's decision to invest.

The potential for growth was exciting. The Colorado gold fields would yield freight. Also there for the picking were other low hanging fruit. Freight and passenger traffic would come from northwestern Colorado ranching, logging, coal and tourism. Not to mention the potential of eastern Utah. And the line would get its share of through traffic to and from the Pacific coast. Many shippers would be happy to give business to a competitor of the Union Pacific.

Joe intended to leverage his acquaintance with Sumner. He would do it by dropping tidbits of his knowledge of Harriman's Union Pacific operation. But, first things first. He had to secure a place at the table. He needed to become a stockholder or a prominent community investor. After he did that he would have more credibility. And timing was one of the most important things in life—good effort badly timed was almost as bad as no effort. Sometimes good effort exerted at the wrong time just made matters worse.

He had a volume of lore, gossip, history, and personalities of Harriman's eastern railroads. He could and would use that knowledge of the Harriman network to help Moffat and Sumner. And, of course, himself. But not yet, not yet.

The would be investor and Moffat confidante was jolted back to reality by Ella's greeting. His self congratulatory wool gathering stopped. He suddenly had to deal with the here and now. Joe faced the nitty gritty of troublemakers who could make big problems for him if he didn't handle them right.

Steu's mention of Dale came to mind. The man boasted, blurted out, that he had "something big" to hurt the road.

Joe was concerned about that. What on earth could bar the road? He needed to get to the bottom of that. And here she was, and he was. *Careful now, light touch, don't scare them off...*, he thought.

He acted as if he didn't see or recognize her at first. It gave him a chance to gather his thoughts and decide on how to approach the question of "something big."

"Ah, pardon me. I wasn't paying..." He made as if to step aside for them.

"Oh! Ella! Dale! Hello! I was just thinking about you two. I was wondering where I could find you. We need to talk about the..." He looked around, making a show of it. He wanted them to think he really did not want anyone to overhear. "...the subject we discussed the other day. Can we go find a restaurant where we can sit? We need privacy and quiet."

Another chess match: Dale and Ella wanted Joe's knowledge and contacts. Yet they didn't want to tell him their idea about a dam. They wanted to be sure that they, not Joe, received credit for it back east. Yet they hoped for some advice on how to propose it. For his part, Joe wanted to find out just how they planned to bar the road. If possible he wanted to stop or divert them. Preferably without their knowing he did it. In fact best if they got the blame somehow.

So everyone pretended they were sitting down for a friendly conversation. Yet each side had their own agenda, their own motives and moves. And each wanted the other to think them loyal. For their own reasons, Joe, Ella and Dale, wanted to seem to be on the same team. Or at least they didn't want to give the other reason to think they were on opposing teams.

Joe opened with a hint of his knowledge of local operations.

"I had a chance to walk part of the road above Eldorado Springs. Tough country, not easy to get to. Even so, it looked to me like that stretch of road will be well built. Tunnels are in solid rock, and will also be well shored. The grade will be filled and tamped. Rock walls are being put in where needed, both to support the grade and to stop rockfall from above. The route is ingenious. If they are able to push through clear to the west the line ought to do well."

Enough positives for now, he decided. Time to fish a little.

"Of course all I have seen in just west of Denver. Once, or I should say if, they get over the divide, it may be entirely different. No doubt, that part of the route has its own problems. It will be easy going for them at first. They can coast down along the upper Colorado River to the town of Kremmling. Then the country is more difficult and the choices not so easy."

Dale and Ella exchanged looks which told Joe he was on to something. He pushed on.

"They may have to wind west and north up and over the Park Range and Rabbit Ears Mountains. Or maybe they will bypass those barriers by heading down the Colorado through the Gore Canyon. From its lower end they could lay track to the north. It would run on the west side of the Park and Rabbit Ears ranges."

Dale nodded as if in understanding. He almost said something but bit it back. Joe continued after a moment.

"The problem with that route is, the canyon is a steep and narrow area. It would be really tough to build in." He let those statements lay. From the body language of the two, Ella in particular, he thought he had pay dirt. Maybe the Gore

Canyon was the area they somehow planned to block. Made sense, geographically it was a funnel. Plug the funnel and everything backs up. You could block movement on the road.

Dale seemed to agree but really had little good to say about the road.

"On the east side of the mountains we've seen only a small part of the road, on Eldorado Mountain. After that, there is a whole state, range after range of mountain, with canyons, cliffs, and other obstacles to face. Ingenious is one way to describe this route and this road. I'd say it is born of desperation."

Ella couldn't restrain herself. "My god, the whole project is folly. It is dangerous. It is a wonder they haven't lost more men than they already have. And horses! Oh the suffering of the animals on this railroad, it is criminal. And I can't believe the job hasn't been delayed more by slides and cave ins and so forth. The snows this winter will kill them off, or darn near. They will have avalanches all winter. Those won't be easy to fend off, especially when they get higher. And why do they need a road anyway?"

She was on a toot. "The Union Pacific Railroad can serve Denver and the Colorado goldfields. There is no need for another railroad. Another road just means one more snout at the trough. They will all be fighting over freight and passengers and slashing rates and competing on service and no one will win."

She returned to her favorite subjects. "And the working men need better jobsite conditions. We need to agitate for a forty hour work week. I know that is radical and will meet with resistance. It just doesn't make sense. We need to do something to slow them down."

Dale had watched Joe's expression as Ella gave her spiel. He wasn't sure how to read it. He responded,

"Now Ella, we have a plan for slowing them down. You and I have discussed ways we can get that done."

Joe's ears perked up, almost visibly. This is what he had hoped to hear. Casually, he spoke.

"Oh, really. What do you have going? Anything I can help with?" he softly asked Dale, glancing at Ella.

"I have been in touch with New York," he easily fibbed. "They are concerned with the progress of the road. They asked me if we had ideas on slowing or stopping it. I for one am at a loss on this subject."

He stopped for effect, and smiled ruefully. "Didn't tell them that, though. The fact is, I hoped to meet with you two. Thought that maybe the three of us could come up with something."

Dale read that to mean that no one in New York had plans or even any ideas how to stop or slow Moffat. *Jackpot!* he thought. This was an opportunity to make a name for himself. He could really score some points. If no one had any ideas, he would look all the better for coming up with a workable, inexpensive, well thought out, viable plan. His plan. He forged ahead without looking at Ella.

"Matter of fact, Eggers, or Joe…I can call you Joe can't I?" He was gratified to get a nod.

"Matter of fact, Joe, we do have a plan. The key to it all, like you said, is Gore Canyon. Whoever holds that stretch dictates what happens. Ella and I think we somehow have to stop the road from going down the Gore Canyon." He glanced her way and was glad to see she smiled, happy she would get credit too.

"If we can do that, stop them in the Gore, it will gum things up for them. That would force them to go up and over the mountains not around them. It will make them spend time and money to build. And once built, it will be expensive to maintain. Plus, forcing them to do that will likely keep them a regional not a national road. It will cut off their access to the roads and markets lower on the Colorado River. If they stay regional like that, they will have no choice but to feed traffic to the UP. Two birds with one stone! New York ought to like that!"

Joe raised an eyebrow. "Indeed. Good idea, but getting it done may not be easy. After all, barring a canyon that is thirty miles long and a thousand feet deep is quite a job. How do you propose to do that?"

Dale was on a roll. He couldn't resist his moment in the sun. After all, he had a chance to point out how he had solved the problem. He, Dale Smertz, had recognized and solved the problem he was sent out to handle. And it was something that not even the muckety mucks in New York could come up with. He all but burst with pride and excitement as he said it.

"A dam. We file for the rights to build a dam in the canyon. At its upper end, by Kremmling if possible. The beauty of that is, we don't even need to build the thing. If we just own the rights we control the canyon. No one else can build or do anything in there if we get there first."

Joe didn't show it, but he was a little shaken. This was a very good idea. Why hadn't he thought of it? For that matter, why hadn't Moffat thought of it? A simple glance at the map showed that control of the canyon was control of western Colorado, at least as far as railroads. He wanted to keep the duo talking, so he grinned widely.

"Say! That is a good one! We stop their access to markets. We make them go up and over yet more mountain ranges. And we hold rights to a potential money maker—selling water and power—in the bargain! Mr. Harriman will like that!"

His eyes met Ella's, which beamed proudly.

"Have you filed the papers yet?"

"No, no filing yet. Truth be told, maybe I am a little premature on this. I really shouldn't have said anything. As of now it is just an idea, a preliminary idea. First we need to form or buy a company. And get New York to agree to it. And draw up the papers. Much needs to be done to make this go."

He looked hopefully across the table. "Do you have any ideas, Joe, about how to go about all of this?"

Joe did in fact know something about the process. But he wasn't about to help this along. Quite the opposite as long as he could do it stealthily. He seemed to offer aid but sidestepped the last question.

"Yes, you had better get after all of that. Can I do anything to help?"

Dale knit his brow like he was birthing a calf, not an idea.

"Or maybe we could use one of the companies that the UP already owns. That would save time. The people, the officers and staff are already in place to handle paperwork. Do you have any idea who we'd talk to about that?"

Dale was determined to be sure he, and maybe Ella, got all the credit. He half frowned and changed his tack.

"You know, actually, forget that question. You are busy with plenty to do. Last thing you need is another project to get involved with. You probably don't know anyone, and I think we can manage it. We can reach you at the James Hotel in Boulder, right, if we need to?"

Eggers nodded doubtfully. Actually he was glad not to be ensnarled in forming a company and filing for rights. He had other things to do. First, he had to look out for number one and then he had to look out for the Denver Northwestern Pacific Railway, his new golden goose. He spoke as if reluctant, but actually he was relieved.

"Well, if you think so, I'll stay away from it. Let me know how it is progressing. I'll be at the James for a week or so yet. Good luck!"

With that, he nodded, stood up and left the restaurant. He felt as if he had discovered much. Better yet, he figured he had left them thinking he was kind of a dunce who realized nothing. Joe was already thinking of ways to use what he had learned.

Ella watched him go, a frown deepening on her face.

"That was too easy. You shouldn't have told him so much. You had to be mister big shot, didn't you?"

Several other ideas came to her at once. "What if he takes credit for this back in New York? We don't know who he really is or who he works for. Maybe he works for Moffat or Rockefeller or someone else who isn't Harriman's friend. And, thanks a lot. You didn't tell him you got the idea from me! Mister Big Shot! Big mouth big shot!"

She glared at him. She held the look for a few seconds but to him it felt like several minutes. Then her look softened.

"We had better get busy and beat him to the punch. I don't really trust this Mr. Josephus Eggers."

"Don't worry, El. That guy is a lightweight. He hasn't done anything but look at a few miles of grade. That and he has tried to get ideas and information out of us. We're the ones doing the work, and we are also the ones doing the thinking."

He put his arm around his companion. The gesture raised the eyebrows of some of the other diners. It was unseemly to see a man affectionately hugging another man.

Dale continued, oblivious to the glances and suppressed sneers.

"Let's telegraph New York and be sure they know it is us, you and me, who came up with the plan. And we need to find a company, or have one formed. Need to get the construction and water rights filed for. I have authority to spend money. Let's go round up a good lawyer to help us find a company."

Joe was glad to be done with the pair. Walking to the station to catch the train for Boulder, he mused on what he had heard. He had to hand it to this Dale guy. A dam in Gore Canyon was a good idea. Simple, cheap, straightforward, and final. If they succeeded the list of complications and problems for the new road would be long. It would be expensive, take time, and cause other issues for the Denver, Northwestern and Pacific.

On the other hand, if Moffat's people knew of it they could spike it. He turned over in his mind how he could tell someone at the Denver Northwestern but keep his distance. He intended to invest in the road. That is, he intended to invest if he headed this problem off. But things were getting complicated.

What if things went Dale's way and the road got blocked? Then Joe would need deniability that he had leaked the dam secret to the Denver Northwestern. If the road did get blocked by the Gore Canyon dam, he would need to stay and keep working for Mr. Harriman.

He did not want anyone to know he was working both sides of the street. If that came out he would soon have no street at all. He had to be sure that absolutely no one ever found out that he had tried to torpedo the UP's attempt to dam up Mister Moffat's Road.

Then the ideal solution to his problems came to him. Myron Mast. If Joe told him, he would know what to do. He could get the word to the Denver Northwestern. By going through him, Joe would keep enough distance that he could plausibly deny it if things went off the track (so to speak!).

Yes, getting hold of Mast was the way to go. He was the one riding a horse out on the grade. He was responsible, high enough in the company to be out inspecting line alone. But probably he was not so high up it would be difficult to get to him. And if things blew up Joe could create enough smoke that any accusation made would be suspect. How to get in touch with him? He thought hard, *Didn't he head back down the line to his camp? Did he say to where? Was it tunnel four?*

That morning, Mik had his handwritten report on the grade ready. It included a layout of his observations, opinions, and measurements. He felt that all in all it gave a fair snapshot of the line as it was the day before. Of course that changed literally daily, but it was as up to date as he could make it.

He had a thought zap through his head. *Careful, Mik. Snapshots haven't been invented yet. This report doesn't give a snapshot, it presents a good picture. Remember that!*

The kitchen at the Pruden's was quiet and deserted. Some kind soul had put out bread, cheese, fruit and coffee. He grabbed a few bites, numbly remembering his recent conversation with Seth, sitting at the very same table. Then he got a horse—grateful for the hostler who had one saddled and ready to go—and headed up to the site at tunnel four.

Before he left he ran in and grabbed an apple. As he rode up, he ate and enjoyed it. Done with it, he tossed the core to the side of the road.

Not long after that he got to the worksite. As he arrived Cam was talking to two or three men at once. They discussed the upcoming move of the camp. His friend gave out instructions, rapid fire. The camp would be moved up the line past tunnel six. The rails would soon be laid up through four since the tunnel was through and the grade nearly finished. A railhead was no place for a camp and worksite building pioneer grade.

Mik caught Cam's eye and held up the report. Then he took it into Cam's office tent and set it on the crate which doubled for a desk. As he was leaving, Cam came in.

"I'll review your paper, Mik. Any questions I'll let you know. I may have you take it with some other documents down to Denver."

"Alright. I'll be around." Mik nodded and went on out. He meant to go to the cook tent and get some real breakfast. His trip was interrupted. Someone was calling out for him, almost yelling.

"Mast, I need to talk with you." He turned and saw Steu, the company cop. Mik's first reaction was, this is the big guy who evoked bad memories. But he had to admit that Steu, unlike the man he resembled, didn't seem violent or forever ready to put up his dukes. Mik shivered, remembering the cop's doppelganger in Sula time. Steven something. He was a thug. One of those guys who was always and forever looking for any excuse to smack someone.

"Mik, how are you? Do you have a minute?"

"Sure." Mik glanced wistfully towards the cooktent then

faced Steu.

"Hey, you mentioned meeting someone on up the grade the other day. I guess he called himself Joe Eggers. What can you tell me about the meeting, and him?"

"It surprised me to see someone on foot. He was not dressed for a day walking the grade. He was in a coat and tie, and dress shoes. Even so, he seemed like he was at home out in the woods. He seemed fit, wasn't breathing hard or red faced or anything."

"Who told him he could go out there unaccompanied, did he say?"

"No, I asked. He just said he had talked with someone on Sixteenth Street, didn't say who. He was vague about that. The guy was unarmed, alone, and dressed for tea not railroad work. He didn't seem to be a threat. If he was intent on no good he wouldn't have been alone. And he would have dressed rougher, and maybe been armed. He acted like he belonged. He didn't act guilty like he was trespassing or doing anything wrong. I didn't worry too much about it at that point."

"You say he indicated he might want to invest in the road?"

"Yes, after a while, that is what he said. The more we talked, the more apparent it became that he was fairly knowledgeable about railroads and road construction. Still, his getup made me wonder if he was leveling with me."

The cop nodded. "Interesting. I did a little checking up on him. That was my conclusion too. He's from the east. At least one person I know thinks he may have ties to Harriman and the UP. But he acts like a legitimate investor and businessman. I'm not sure what his game is."

Mik nodded in turn. "I was a little skeptical of his intent. He was very subtly fishing for information. He brought up the tunnel, the big one to be drilled under the divide. Since he was fishing I let him believe it was further along than it in fact is. When he heard that, he brightened. Come to think of it, that is when he came out with his intention to invest."

Steu paused, taking that statement in. He was kind of thinking out loud.

"If he isn't genuine I don't see the picture. See, he pointed out the man and woman to me. The ones I was looking for and chased over the mountain. Told me they said they were agents of the UP. Why would he do that if he was a UP man as well? Apparently he isn't with them. Or maybe he is and for some reason he wants us to know about them. Very strange. It is hard to say. My advice: if you see him again, handle him carefully. He may or may not be a friend."

"Thanks, Steu. I appreciate the heads up," said Mik. He turned to go to the cook tent and eat some more breakfast. But just then Cam came out of his tent. He was smiling.

"This report is concise and complete, Mik. Good work. I need you to take it down to Denver, to Mr. Sumner, along with some other papers. Here, they are all in this case. Get going as soon as you can. He telephoned to have it brought down and is waiting on it."

"Alright, I am on my way. Is there anything else to take, or anything I can bring back?"

"Not that I think of. Main thing is get the papers in that case to Mr. Sumner."

Mik grumbled inwardly, but took the case, got on a horse, and headed back down the hill. If things went well, he could be in Boulder by mid morning. That meant arriving in Denver by two or so. Modern trains and all were quick and convenient, he figured. He brought himself up short: *What am I doing, thinking that six hours from here to Denver is fast and easy? My God, I have driven that stretch in forty five minutes. Am I settling into this 1903 world?*

This made him think that he had better try to get back to Sula time pretty quick. He feared that if he didn't do so soon, he might never escape.

The trains ran on time. Denver arrival was scheduled at 1:57 and the engineer hit that on the nose. He got his papers delivered promptly. Finally able to slow down, he found a restaurant and hungrily ate his first decent meal in days. Being in town on business he was able to sign as an employee of the Denver & Northwestern. That was good since he had no cash, at least none that would be acceptable in 1903. Trying to spend a bill with a date past the year 2000 would likely net him a visit—and a stay—with the sheriff.

Shortly after "arriving," he had pocketed his phone—he didn't wear a watch any more—and kept it out of sight. He looked around and saw a street clock. There was one on almost every block. If he hurried he could make the next train back to Boulder. It would be close but he'd try. It wasn't the last run of the day so he didn't have to hustle too hard. There was another one thirty or forty minutes later. The bill was ready and he was about to sign for it. Just then, in to the restaurant walked a vaguely familiar person.

It was Joe Eggers.

"Mr. Mast, I hoped to see you in here. I called at the Denver Northwestern offices to locate you. They said you had just been in and were going to stop here for a meal."

Mik's antenna went up. The guy wanted to talk to him, and had tracked him down. They had met once, and talked for only a few minutes. Something was up. And how did he persuade the people in the office to reveal where he was? He must have some gift of gab. *Why did he go to the trouble to locate me?* he wondered. He didn't let the questions cross his face. Calmly, he responded,

"You just caught me. I want to try for the next train to Boulder."

Joe repeated himself. "I hoped to find you here. But if I didn't, I planned to do the same thing, to catch the late train. I'm staying at the James Hotel there in Boulder. Maybe we can talk on the ride up there."

Mik was wary. He nodded.

"I imagine we can do that."

They made the train and got seated. Unseen, Dale and Ella were already on the train, at the end of the car. After meeting with Eggers they decided to return to Boulder after all. They were still working on wording of their telegram to New York and wanted to go back to their base.

Both were concerned to see Joe talking with Mast, the guy who had escaped the rockslide. What was up with that? They tried to look like just any passenger, scrunching down in their seats at the far end of the car. One pretended to read a newspaper and the other relaxed and seemed to be dozing. They did not want to be seen.

Mik decided he wanted to set the tone, and so started the conversation.

"You wanted to talk, Mr. Eggers? First answer me a few questions. Why me? How did you know I worked for the Denver Northwestern? How did you find me in Denver? Who do you work for?"

Joe considered his response. The tone of the questions wasn't quite hostile, but certainly was not amiable.

"You are right to be a bit wary, Mr. Mast. We have only briefly met. We do not know each other or our backgrounds.

Let me start by a simple statement. Not everyone is a friend to Mr. Moffat and his road."

Mik harrumphed. Not one of his questions had been answered, or even acknowledged. He replied,

"Too true. And are you friend or foe, Eggers?"

"Fair question." Joe meandered some more, sidestepping the matter.

"First let me explain why I sought you out. We met on the grade the other day. You were knowledgeable about the road. As you were out alone, I judged that you have a responsible position in the company which owns the grade. Railroads don't send laborers out alone to judge the general progress of work. And Mr. Moffat's head clerk told me where to find you there at the restaurant."

He looked at Mik and judged that the answers were satisfactory. Or at least that Mik still had an open mind.

"That said, I have information which could be of use to the Denver Northwestern and Pacific. It is knowledge which may well prove to be very important. I seek you out as a friend, or at least a neutral. I want to pass the information. After I gave it some thought, you seem like a very qualified, knowledgeable, appropriate person. You are the one I want to tell about it."

Mik thought *We'll see if you are friend or not.* Aloud, he softened a bit.

"That seems a reasonable explanation. Just what is this information you speak of?"

A deep breath calmed Joe. He realized that by saying the words he was committed. Goodbye, Mr. Harriman. Hello, a new life in the West.

"You may have met a couple, a tall thin man with intense, intelligent eyes, and a woman? She often dresses as a man, not in skirts. That in itself isn't important, nor are their mannerisms or even if you have met them." He slowed, trying to judge if Mik knew or knew of the pair.

"They have been lurking around the jobsite on Eldorado Mountain, tunnel four where the rockslide was. The thing is, they are agents for the Union Pacific. Not just people keeping tabs on the competition, no harm in that and everyone does it. No, these two were sent out for the sole purpose of making trouble for the new railroad, the Denver Northwestern and Pacific. They tell me this themselves. With pride."

Mik almost scoffed. "And just why should they tell you this? So what if they did? This is a competitive, cold business world. Everyone tries to throw roadblocks in the way of their competitors."

"Because, Mr. Mast—may I call you Mik? Because, Mik, they are serious. They aren't about spreading rumors or harassing workers. Their intent, their goal, is nothing less than slowing or stopping the building of your railroad line. By any means at hand, fair or otherwise."

He paused, taking in Mik's response, which was noncommittal. He continued, fudging the truth more than a little.

"I represented myself to them as an independent businessman generally interested in the progress of the line. Possibly an investor in it. For some reason they took me into their confidence. The two have concocted a plan to stop the line in western Colorado. Or at least to seriously disrupt it."

"Oh? How?" Mik figured this guy could well be playing games. Even so, it couldn't hurt to hear him out. It would be an hour before the train got to Boulder in any case. May as well listen and learn what he could. At worst it would be a dismal and ridiculous tale, at best he might find out something important.

"They are focused on the right of way, the legal right to scrape a grade and lay track. They are eying the right of way going through the Gore Canyon just west of the town of Kremmling. I am told that they are, or will shortly form a company. Or take over a company, depending on the easiest way to go. Not important. The thing is, the company they come up with will file for rights to build a dam in Gore Canyon. Let me repeat that—a dam in Gore Canyon. Their intent is to block access once and for all."

Joe thought again that this was actually a pretty good plan, and wished he had come up with it. He could have shopped it to the highest bidder. But now, he was committed, and had to tell all about it.

"If they succeed, it will force the Denver Northwestern to alter plans. Or maybe even stop altogether. At best, it will have to change its route. It will have to run its rails north up and over the Park Range and the Rabbit Ears Mountains rather than west around them. Mr. Moffat is already faced with one stretch of high mountains. Another would be an expensive, time consuming barrier. Perhaps an insurmountable one."

"And again, Mr. Eggers, and I don't want to put too fine a point on this question. But I will. Why should anyone believe you?"

"I tell you because you clearly have experience and judgment. And we met in neutral ground on the grade. And I intend to invest in the road. And if I am going to invest I will do what I can to protect it. Of course I want my investment and the company to succeed. If I have information germane to the success of the road, of course I want the right people to know."

"Why not take it to Mr. Moffat or Mr. Sumner direct?"

"Because I want this threat to be taken seriously. I recognize that I am an unknown, a potential investor just met. Again, you are right to be skeptical. It will mean more, be more credible, if word of this comes from someone in the organization."

Mik's body language and attitude remained defensive. His disbelief was evident.

"But don't just take me at face value. Look at new companies being established. Check into at new filings for water rights. Ask if any utility or dam companies are newly on the scene. Especially in and near Kremmling Colorado. You will see."

That made some sense. Mik was doubtful. Still, it wouldn't hurt to check it out.

"Alright, Mr. Eggers. I will pass the word. You say you are staying at the James. Can you be reached there? Someone else may want to talk with you."

The two men were concentrating on the other's talk and body language. So intent was the talk that they were oblivious to people around them. Dale and Ella still sat at the far end of the car. Ella couldn't contain herself. She put on her floppy man's hat. Using her best male stride, she walked by them. She was able to overhear railroad talk. And the word "dam" floated out as well.

She had two urges, both of which she resisted. First she wanted to yell at Eggers. She wanted to get in his face and ask him what he was doing talking to someone about their dam. Second, she wanted to turn right around and run back to Dale to tell him. But she calmly went to the far end of the car, turned around, and walked back, just a fellow stretching his legs. She took care not to look at either Mik or Joe.

"That snake is telling our plan!," she hissed at Dale. "He is spilling it to Myron Mast of the railroad. I heard someone say the word "dam." We'll need to watch them both. And we need to get our papers filed tomorrow!"

The train pulled into Boulder. Mik found a ride towards Eldorado Springs, intending to get off at Pruden's. Eggers left and walked towards the James Hotel. Dale and Ella watched. For a while they stayed huddled at the station. The discussion between them was, whether to split up and follow each, or go to their base and get a good night's sleep.

They decided to sleep and then pick up the trail in the morning.

XI

Long was the night. It was late before Mik arrived at Prudens and quietly climbed the stairs. The clock was already past midnight, almost an hour into the next day.

For a moment he hesitated. Then he roused Cam. The story as Eggers had given it to him came out quickly and clearly. The whole thing was important enough to risk the foreman's ire, which was short lived in any case. Mik longed to hit the rack but knew when he did he would have trouble falling asleep.

"So, actually, like Eggers said, it actually is a pretty good plan for what they want to accomplish," Mik finished up.

"A dam, huh? I find it hard to believe they can get even a filing done in a few days. Still, we can't take the chance..."

Cam, like Mik, was not entirely trusting of Eggers' motivations and loyalties. Whatever the reasons the man had for telling them, they couldn't sit on it. The information and how they got it needed to be sent on up the line. He figured he would go to camp early and telephone it in. The idea of calling brought home to him that he worked for a progressive company. Mr. Sumner made sure they had the latest communication and other technical devices. It was fun to be part of the cutting edge! With that thought, Cam dismissed Mik, rolled over and easily went back to sleep.

The next morning he went to work and did just that. Seldom did he have reason to use the phone, so it was kind of an adventure. He went into Sumner's office tent. There it was, on a crate, a box with wires sprouting from it. Cam hadn't telephoned so much that he was blasé. Still, he did know how to use it. He was pretty sure he did, anyway. He walked over and picked up the ear piece from a bracket on the phone. It was attached by a wire running to the box. Holding it to his ear, he cranked a handle on the side of the phone. In a few moments someone spoke and he heard the tinny sounding, disembodied person. This was a phone line direct to the Denver office. "Mr. Sumner's Office," said the voice.

He leaned in so his mouth was just by the horn, the microphone. Reminding himself to speak slowly and clearly, he started. "Cam Braun here. I have a confidential and urgent matter to report. I need to speak to Mr. Sumner."

It turned out that Mr. Sumner was away from the office. After a moment's pause, Cam started talking. He gave a concise rundown of the Gore Canyon dam plan and its source to one of Sumner's secretaries. Cam knew the man. Sumner put great faith in his people. Talking to this secretary was as good as talking to the boss himself. As he talked, Cam kept in mind that it was smart to stay on his good side. The secretary could make life miserable for anyone he wanted to.

The secretary acknowledged. "Alright, thank you, Braun. This is good to know. If you hear any more on the subject call me. I will get this information to Mr. Sumner. He will have an accurate account as soon as he returns."

Cam rang off and gave it no more thought. The main task of the day was preparing to move the camp. That and he needed to coordinate with the track layers. They were laying iron at the rate of hundreds of feet per day. Before long they would be at tunnel four. He needed to have his camp moved before they got there.

No one up on the hill gave more thought to Eggers' story of a dam. But the main office staff in Denver certainly did. The response from headquarters was quick and unexpected. Within an hour Cam was called away from organizing the move. He was called to the main office tent to take a phone call.

Cam never got phone calls. He wondered who was calling, and why. *It must be something important. Maybe another rock slide, or a derailment. Something where they need more bodies, where they need me to go help out. Or maybe Teddy Roosevelt has gotten the country into another war,* he thought.

Cam walked into the tent and picked up the phone.

"Braun here. Yes, Mr. Sumner, yes I did..."

He listened, fingers drumming on a desk.

"We are not sure of that. We do know something about the people who are supposed to be involved. They are not locals nor known characters. They seem to be hangers on of some kind. Yes, they well could be agents of the UP or another competitor. We are not sure of that. Steu Wentz has been out trying to meet them. I know that he had the chance to talk to them."

This went on for several minutes. Mostly he listened, some he talked. His fingers stopped drumming and picked up a pencil, scrawling some notes.

"Yes sir, the instructions are clear. We are to catch the mid day work train at the railhead and come to Denver. It will hold until we get there."

Cam scrawled a note summoning Mik and held it out to a clerk. The man read the note and left in a hurry to deliver it.

Cam continued, "It will have clearance for a quick run. Catching the mid day in good time should not be a problem. We can pick it up less than two miles from here, at the end of the rails. I am to call or wire if there is a problem with our getting to Denver. Yes. We will see you this afternoon."

Cam waited for Mik. Meanwhile he gathered a briefcase and a sidearm, finishing up as Mik entered.

"You wanted to see me, Cam?"

"Myron Mast. It is good that you woke me last night, Mik. I informed the office this morning. They said, and I agree, good work on running down that report on the dam."

Mik nodded and smiled. "I wasn't sure but decided to wake you. So they were happy to hear of it?"

"Not happy, not by any means. But it was something they definitely needed to know. Denver is up in arms about the whole thing. On top of our, or I should say, my, report this morning, it turns out that someone else is in on it."

He held Mik's eyes.

"It seems a filing has just been made to build a reservoir in Gore Canyon. The papers name the builder. The filing was made on behalf of an outfit called The New Century Power and Light Company. They are chartered out east, New Jersey or somewhere. Folks in Denver are trying to find out ownership details as we speak."

Cam shrugged. "Anyway, you and I need to go to Denver. Mr. Sumner and Mr. Moffat have a job for us."

"What kind of job?"

"They will give us the details when we get there. We may be gone for several days."

"I don't have any spare clothes up here. Should I stop at Pruden's and get some?"

"No. We will have to buy overnight supplies and a change of clothes when we get to Denver. This is a high priority. We won't be going by Pruden's. They are making space for us on the mid day work train. They are adding a car for us to ride in, so this issue is really important to someone up the line. The train will wait for us if need be, it is that important."

He took one last look in the briefcase and closed it. Then he smiled in anticipation.

"Usually we work on just a small stretch of the road. That is all we get to see. But today, we will get to ride over the entire length of our railroad. I wanted to take a look at the newest section anyway. And this is a rare opportunity to see and check out the rest of the line down to Denver. We have no responsibility on the train but to get to Denver. We can relax a bit, see and look at things we otherwise would have missed. For me this will be almost an afternoon's leisure outing!"

Mik was nonplussed. An extra car? For him and Cam? He was about to ask more questions but thought better of it.

Cam sensed his curiosity. "They will tell us more when we get down there and sit face to face. Now, you go and have two of the best horses saddled for us."

The big man turned away as Mik left. He turned to his clerk again.

"Call the main foremen and crew chiefs. They are to meet me here in twenty minutes. We need to assign out the work that needs done the next three or four days. I will be out for a while so you and they will have to step in. You are in charge; I will tell everyone so at the meeting. Something has come up and I need to go to Denver to get it taken care of."

Mik headed to the stables. He did not see two people lurking in trees at the edge of camp. They were watching the goings-on and taking notes. One was a tall man, the other was shorter and was almost plump, not bony and angular.

Ella and Dale had come up to camp before dawn. They wanted to get set so they could watch the camp's activity. Particularly they wanted to see and follow the comings and goings, if any, of Myron Mast. The way he and Eggers had been talking on the train really concerned, even worried them. It looked like the two were trading secrets and discussing important matters. Ella especially was suspicious. Mast might be in on their secret. If it came clear he was, they agreed that he needed to be delayed or diverted somehow. Maybe even stopped. The two stood in the trees and took turns watching the camp through binoculars.

"He is going into the foreman's tent." Ella watched. "Seems kind of in a hurry. Like he was called in or something. Or maybe he has something to tell."

Dale sniffed. "It is hard to say why he's in a hurry. You are guessing, El. Maybe he just wants a cup of coffee from the pot they keep on a stove in there. We need to be sure what is happening before we act."

Soon the man they were following came out in just as much a hurry as when went in. He made a beeline for the corral. There he talked and gestured earnestly to a hostler. They picked out two horses. The hostler called the blacksmith from his forge and the two of them saddled up the steeds. Their quarry—Mik, although they didn't know that was his nickname—went back in the foreman's tent. Two men came out, Mik and a tall burly freeman.

Both had seen him around but neither knew for sure that he was the job foreman. They noted that he and everyone around him acted like he was the one in charge. He was carrying a briefcase and had on a gunbelt with a big old Colt revolver.

Ella kept up a commentary on what was happening.

"They are going to ride out somewhere. And it looks like they are in a hurry. Mast doesn't look upset, rather he is almost smiling. Kind of like he is off on a fun outing or adventure." She put the binoculars down.

"I don't like it. I hope they don't ride those horses too hard."

Dale half listened, and thought out loud. "Why the foreman, or at least the guy who acts like the foreman? Did Mast tell him too? Why horses? They seem to be going somewhere in a hurry. The only place they would go in a hurry is Denver. Unless there is a problem up the line. But if there is, more men than two would be going up there. Plus, they are riding down the line not up. It must be Denver." He looked again at the camp.

"Look at that wire strung up from tree to tree to the main tent. I'll bet they have a phone line! I wonder if they called Denver about us and our plan. Do you think the higher-ups want to talk to them?"

They looked at each other. Dale was starting to get agitated, fidgeting and scowling. He was sure he was on the money. Ella put the brakes on.

"Like you said, Dale, we need to know for sure before we act. We can't even be certain that Mast knows our plan. For all we know they are headed off to help with a derailment or something."

"I guess you are right, El. Maybe Eggers was feeding him a line last night. Probably this coming and going this morning has nothing to do with those two talking last night on the train."

Ella became more confident and assertive of her opinions.

"They are fixing to move camp from the looks of things

there. People are packing up tents and so forth. Let's not jump to conclusions."

She dropped the binoculars and glanced at her partner.

"Let those two ride off to wherever they are going. I think we should stay around here. We know everything revolves around the construction of the grade and laying rail. People running off to meetings or something aren't important. This is the place to be. Not off on a chase to who knows where."

She looked her partner in the eye. "It is too easy to get lost or lose a person if we start moving. Better to sit here."

Dale wasn't so sure. "You may be right. I don't know, maybe we need to hedge our bets." He took the binoculars and scanned the camp yet again. He had an idea.

"How about this, El? You stay here and keep an eye on the camp. I'll go to Boulder and try to find Eggers. We really need to know what they were talking about last night. Then let's meet back in town this evening." He set the binoculars down and did not look at her. Of a sudden, he took off walking fast down the mountain. Ella was concentrating on the camp and by the time his idea got through to her, she had no time to object. She was not sorry to see him go anyway. Him and his dam, he couldn't focus on anything since he dreamed that up.

Mik and Cam rode away, heading down the grade. They caught the mid day work train easily. There was no need to hold it. The ride to Denver did turn out to be enjoyable. Cam studied the track and roadbed, lapping it up like a thirsty dog. Mik satisfied himself with watching the world go by. The mountains, high plains, and the outlying farms and then the city slid by. So much smaller than the Denver he knew! The train arrived at Union Station in the early afternoon. They went straight to Mr. Sumner's office in the Majestic Building on Sixteenth Street.

The two were immediately shown in to the engineer's office. Mik was surprised to see that Mr. Moffat was there as well. Hands were shaken all around. Moffat opened the conversation.

"Braun, Mast, glad you were able to get here promptly." He offered no small talk about the line, the weather, or anything else. "Tell me again about these two people and their plan."

Cam looked at Mik. Mik nodded, taking his cue to tell the tale. It took a while to tell it all. He started with his encounter with Eggers on the tracks and took it to his waking Cam the previous night.

He ended with, "I am told these two are agents of the Union Pacific. When I first met them they seemed almost out of place. They acted a little furtive, and were nosy, and bragging about his training, and so on. Their story didn't really make sense, it didn't come together. But that was just after the rockslide and I was having trouble fitting the pieces together anyway. Looking back now, I think they were up to no good. They were, I believe, not coming around to do anything positive."

Moffat and Sumner exchanged glances. Sumner took the floor.

"Thank you, Mr. Mast. That is good background information for us. Your story answers several questions. Good to hear it straight from the horse's mouth, so to speak." He paused, a thin smile on his face, awaiting Mik's nod of acknowledgment.

"Now, here is some background you two need to know. So listen carefully. We knew that an outfit called

Hydroelectric Power Company planned some kind of a pipeline in the Kremmling area. It posed problems but none we couldn't work around."

His expression gradually hardened, looking pained and worried.

"As we found out today, that has changed. Hydroelectric Power was just bought by another company. This new player is called the New Century Power and Light Company. They are based in New Jersey. This combination brings us troubles."

He paused, ordering his thoughts. "That outfit—New Century—has filed to build a reservoir at the head of Gore Canyon, just west of Kremmling. If successful that dam and reservoir would be a real problem for us, blocking our intended route. Also, but not so much of a problem, there have been mining claims filed on and within our rights of way."

Moffat interjected, "They appear to be nuisance filings, intended to slow or divert us."

Sumner continued, "Yes, we have clear prior rights to deny those claims. But these claims and filings are part of a bigger picture. This all tracks (no pun intended, gentlemen!) with your report and information from your sources." With that, the chief engineer sat down, his sudden relaxation looking as if delivering the news had exhausted him.

Moffat took over.

"Fortunately we have the whip hand, even over New Century Power and Light. We own senior, deeded right of way through the area. We have had it for over a year. The Denver Northwestern Pacific bought it from the Burlington Railroad. That is, we bought the rights they originally filed for."

Mik wanted to ask what happened to the Burlington, but thought better of it. Moffat continued.

"The Burlington parcel of deeds and contracts we own includes rights to trackage and access at all points for road, sidings, and whatever we want to put within two hundred feet either side of the center line. Our rights run from where the Eagle River runs into the Colorado River, back upstream through the Gore Canyon, into Grand County."

He looked appraisingly at the two men just in from the construction camp, then at Sumner. "Horace, they are your men. You take it from here. Good luck, gentlemen." With that, he shook their hands, nodded, and left the office.

Sumner gestured to a briefcase on a desk. "This case contains the deed. The Burlington deed David mentioned. It was just delivered here from Chicago. We need it taken to Hot Sulphur Springs, the county seat which governs the Gore Canyon."

He looked at the two men, making sure his instructions were clear.

"This document needs to be recorded at the County Courthouse. We want it put in the public record, for all to see and acknowledge. It is imperative that this be done quickly and without fail."

Cam asked, "Should we have a copy to file instead of the original?"

"No, we want a clean and unchallengeable transaction. You must file with the original document. Get it recorded and stamped for future reference. It is, like I said, here in this case. We have kept a copy in our files here in Denver. Again, it is the original that the County Clerk needs to have to make a proper record. Using a copy could cloud ownership. The last thing we want is to give someone the opportunity to claim that."

Sumner waited and watched to be sure they understood.

"We need you two to get this done. You must get the deed up to Grand County and have the Clerk file it. Just how you accomplish the task is up to you. You can both go, together or separately. Or just one of you. The important thing is to get the deed recorded as soon as possible. The success of the road, of your future and mine, may well depend on this."

He handed the case to Cam.

"Here are the documents. There is also a letter for each of you. The letter is over my name and requires all help possible from any employee or contractor of the Company. Do not hesitate to call on any company man if you need anything. If anyone refuses or dawdles, report that person's name and position to my secretary."

He took a key out of his vest pocket and gave it to Cam. "Here, the key to the case. Go now. Come back as soon as possible, day after tomorrow or maybe the next, with a signed affidavit from the Grand County Clerk. Like I said, all the resources of the road are available to you. Just show the letter. Don't give it up, just present it. If you don't get full cooperation I will have that person's job."

Horace Sumner and David Moffat were the senior officers of the railway. They thought they were talking with one of their trusted foremen and his assistant. They did not know that this second man was in fact from another time. The two prominent businessmen would have been pleasantly surprised to know what he already did.

In fact, the railroad was successful in protecting and keeping open the Gore Canyon route. But that was clouded in the mists of the future. No one would learn how the present would work out for a few days yet. In fact, had Mik said something he would have gotten, at best, cold looks. Perhaps it would have earned him a dismissal and maybe even a sheriff's escort to the insane asylum.

He of course said nothing, gave no hint to anyone about it. Actually, Mik was already going over pros and cons of ways to handle the deed in the case. He wanted the safest and quickest route to Hot Sulphur Springs and the County Clerk. He and his foreman friend clearly had their work cut out for them.

Before Mik and Cam left, Sumner's secretary approached them. He held out some papers.

"Here are tickets for you. These are open, round trip tickets for the train to Dumont. Also the stagecoach to and from Hot Sulphur Springs. You can use them at any time." The man paused, searching for the right words. He looked Mik in the eye, and the same for Cam. "Mr. Sumner and Mr. Moffat want this taken care of. If I were you I would waste no time."

Both men knew this man technically was just an assistant. But he had the ear of and spoke for the owners. This was a man who knew exactly what was going on in the organization, who were the workers and who the slackers, who had secrets and how they were trying to use those secrets. In a phrase, he knew where the bodies were buried.

The man's advice should be listened to and acted upon. Mik was momentarily reminded of one particular First Sergeant. He had gotten a similar warning from a grizzled vet he had known in the Army, way back in Sula time, way forward from Moffat time. He shook the thought off and came back to the task at hand.

Cam nodded. "You can be sure we will handle this quickly and discreetly."

"Good. Cable or call me if there are problems or you need me to smooth the way for you."

The pair left the Majestic Building. Cam looked at the clock outside the bank's lobby. He shook his head, disgusted and resigned.

"It is too late to catch the Dumont train today. The last one is pulling out about now."

Mik agreed. "No sense in going back to Boulder or Eldorado Springs. We had better spend the night here in Denver. We can catch the first run out tomorrow."

Cam thought a moment. "There is a hotel near the train station. Let's go there. We can be near the station and make it easy to get going tomorrow morning."

While Cam and Mik rode in their private train car to Denver to meet with management, Ella stayed at the camp. Dale made his way to Boulder. He wasted no time going towards the James Hotel. He needed to find Eggers. Dale watched the entrance for a few minutes then went and found a spot outside a café across the street. He parked himself and watched comings and goings from the hotel.

Dale felt sure, at least he hoped, that Joe was in town. The man had come back to Boulder last night. Dale saw him get off the train. He had to talk to Eggers to find out what Mast knew. What had they talked so earnestly and intently about? Time was crawling. He had been sitting across the street for over an hour and it was after noon already. Dale was impatient to find and talk to Joe. On one hand he was glad he had he hurried down from where he left Ella. On the other, time was running along and nothing seemed to be happening. *What the heck, the James has a dining room. I'll go in there. I'm hungry, will have something to eat. Maybe I'll see him*, he decided.

In fact, Joe was in there. He too was hungry and was having a bite. Lunch at the James was really pretty good. *This might be a good place to live for a while after I invest in the*

Denver Northwestern, thought Joe. He finished up leisurely. The would-be entrepreneur stood, stretched, and decided to take a walk with an eye to checking out houses he might buy.

He was heading out the door to do that. In strode Dale. "Well hello, Smertz," said Joe mildly. "What brings you storming in?"

Dale was surprised but regained his composure. He decided to be assertive and forthright.

His tone was accusing. "I saw you talking to Mast last night. El and I watched you two talking like old friends." He paused a moment, then charged on.

"What did you tell him? Why are you talking to railroad people? You didn't tell him anything about my, er, our plan did you?"

The direct, frank questions caught Joe off guard. Then things clicked.

"My *job* is to talk to railroad people. What of it?" He looked Dale in the eye, and took a step towards him.

"And who appointed you to spy on me? If you saw me, you must have been on the train. Why didn't you come say hello? Did you not want to be seen? Have you something to hide? Are you ashamed of something? What is it, Dale?"

He was on a roll now, he had the initiative. Joe did not want to tell this man what he had been up to, not even a little bit.

"What are you keeping hidden away, Smertz? Who are you to check up on me? I didn't see you on the train, or that buffoon who won't wear proper womens' clothes." From Dale's wince, Joe saw he had found a weak spot, and jabbed at it. "What does it call itself, Evelyn or something?"

Dale's face reddened at the reference to Ella. He had feelings for her even if she had quirks. He knew he was close to losing his temper.

"You leave El out of this!" He said it louder than intended, and passersby glanced his way. He realized it and lowered his volume.

"Stop trying to change the subject. What did you tell Mast? Did you talk about the dam? You two were acting pretty friendly there..."

"I'll not answer to a common employee. Who I talk to and why is none of your concern." He made to step around his confronter.

Dale almost snapped. He stepped in closer, putting his face inches from Joe's. He raised his voice again.

"Damn it, tell me! We are on the verge of blocking Moffat and his road! New York will reward us handsomely if we do that! If you told him anything about the dam it will ruin a stroke of genius, my stroke of genius! And it will cause you, me, and many others real problems. I need to know. Tell me what you told Mast!"

Eggers wasn't about to admit what he had revealed. It was no one's business anyway. If it came out that he had leaked Dale's plan, it would ruin his standing with Harriman. In fact, Mr. Harriman took employee disloyalty very badly. He would probably go out of his way to ruin Joe if he found out. And it would make Smertz and Ella redouble their efforts to stymie the project. He had to distract this increasingly angry and desperate man.

"Mast and I are not friends. If you must know, I was soft soaping him to find out plans for the mountain crest. The continental divide." He put out some disinformation, that is, he lied.

"Their long term plan is to run up and over the mountain. Any thought of a tunnel has been put aside. It would be too time consuming. And expensive—they can't recoup the investment. As you can see, he thinks I am a fine fellow. I have let him think I am a potential investor. That is how I have gotten him to open up. Now you too have a secret, my secret. See that you keep it!"

This seemed too glib, too easy, to Dale. Something told him this was just a story to shut him up and make him go away. What Joe was saying didn't make sense. It did not add up. Everything he had learned about the Denver & Northwestern's plans included a tunnel. Everything—he had heard repeatedly from several sources that a tunnel was in the plans. There was even at least one solid rumor that a location had actually been chosen, and work started.

Dale realized the situation was getting complicated. His job was to keep track of and make trouble for the Denver Northwestern Pacific. But now it seemed this Eggers guy was playing games. It was almost like he was working both ends somehow. Whatever he was doing, it was making things hard for him and Ella. He needed to figure out what game Joe was playing. He realized that the thing for now was to back off a little. He and El would follow Eggers or Mast, probably both. That was the sure way to see what they were really up to.

So Dale backpedaled. "Oh." He paused as if rethinking things. "I see. That's good information, good to know. Sounds like you have things in hand." He grinned kind of shyly, and stepped back out of Eggers' face.

"Sorry, old man, I got excited there. I shouldn't have accused you of spilling the secret." He stuck out his hand. "My apologies, Joe. No hard feelings? Let's shake and go about our business."

Joe wasn't sure that Dale had bought the story. Even so, he was glad to be rid of the gangly, pesky man.

"Accepted." He pasted on a smile and shook Dale's hand.

Making a show of looking at the time, he muttered an excuse. "I have a meeting to prepare for. Good day."

Dale figured he—and Ella if she came off the mountain—would make a show of checking on Mast. Maybe that would flush out Eggers and he could find out what the man was really up to.

"Good to talk with you. I have to go check on some things myself. Good day to you, too." He turned and left the lobby.

Joe watched him leave the hotel and cross the street. Then the tall man paused and walked towards the yard of the stage line to Eldorado Springs. Joe was torn. Should he warn Mast that Dale might be on to him?

Joe turned the encounter over and over, trying to read what Dale was up to. The guy seemed quite worked up there for a minute. But was he really worked up? He calmed down suspiciously easily. The thought occurred that maybe Dale was unbalanced. No telling, he might try to harm someone. He was very protective of his dam idea and he might do anything to protect it, keep it secret.

After all that, it was really about number one. Joe decided he needed to look after his own life and prospects. He wouldn't worry about Dale and his shenanigans. Let him do what he would. The important thing for Joe was, he had to protect his future. That meant safeguarding the target of his investment to be. He had to protect the Denver Northwestern and Pacific. It was time to act.

From his room, Joe grabbed his traveling coat and hat, and took the train for Denver. The plan was to try to find Mast. If he couldn't easily do that, he would go to the offices of the railroad. If need be, he would try to see Mr. Sumner. Someone needed to be warned about Dale and his plan.

Across the street, Dale hadn't gone far. He stopped where he was not obviously watching. He wanted to see what Eggers was up to. From his spot he could see the hotel entrance. Just as he feared and suspected, Eggers came out and briskly walked away. He seemed to be headed for the train station.

Dale wanted to bring Ella in. But he didn't think there was time. They would have to meet up somehow and compare notes later. The gangly man kept his intense eyes on Eggers and followed. He was ready to duck into a store or turn and look into a store window should his quarry look his way.

Joe went to the station and bought a ticket. Dale watched, then approached the ticket agent.

"Can you help me? My friend was supposed to meet me but I seem to have missed him. Perhaps he is already on the train. Well dressed man, supposed to go to Denver…"

The ticket agent gave him a stare. "I don't keep track of your social calendar."

Dale didn't wilt under the stare, just looked levelly back, not hostile, not servile.

The agent relented a bit. "But I will tell you I have sold no tickets to Jamestown or anywhere but Denver in the past hour. If your "friend" has come through here, he bought a ticket for Denver."

Dale smiled, he hoped pleasantly, and shoved money across the counter.

"Thank you. I need one too." He walked out to the waiting train and got in the first car, hoping Eggers wasn't in it. The more he thought about it, the more certain he was that the story Eggers told about no tunnel was horse manure. And so was the bit about his softsoaping Mast. They were up to something.

Dale was sure, felt it in his bones, that somehow, for some reason Mast was onto Gore Canyon dam plan. He was determined to see where his man was going and who he would talk to. He brooded as the train pulled out, gaining speed.

XII

THE TRAIN RIDE TO DENVER WOULD BE RELAXING, OR AT LEAST Joe hoped so. Usually he was soothed by the rocking rhythm of the train. The gentle swaying and the clickety clack usually acted as a lullaby for him. Not today. Today his thoughts were in turmoil. Ideas got torn apart, pieces of them rearranged like fitting a jigsaw puzzle together. Answers he was trying to come up with remained elusive.

He wanted to find Mik, wanted to talk to him. In fact he realized he had to find Mik. Joe had to know what Mik was doing with the information on Dale's dam project. If and how that information got out could ruin his plan to get aboard the Denver Northwestern and Pacific. It could also ruin his standing with Mr. Harriman. Not good, that.

And he wanted to warn Mik about Dale. The man had come across as batty, maybe unstable and dangerous. Keeping an eye on him was essential. As he relaxed a little, enjoying the rock and roll of the car, Joe was sure that his man was in Denver. He decided the place to start was the Majestic Building. Someone at the road's headquarters was bound to know where Mik was. He could act as Mik's new friend as well as the inside investor. Somehow he would finagle the information.

It was late afternoon by the time the train pulled in. Joe realized he would be spending the night. He needed to get a room. Fortunately there was a hotel just across the street. The Station Hotel had a good reputation, clean and upright. It would do. As a matter of habit, Joe was alert and tried to be aware of who was around him. He in fact did look around as he left the station. His mind was still jumbled with images and thoughts of railroads, tunnels, dams as well as Dale yelling in his face. He was preoccupied and just not as thorough as usual. He did not see the gangly man with bright eyes lurking back by the tracks. As Eggers crossed the street to the hotel Dale hurried forward, keeping him in sight.

Intense eyes watched Joe as he mounted the steps and went into the hotel. *Bingo!* thought Dale. *Now I know where Eggers will spend the night. I can scout around town a bit. I can either take a room there myself after he has settled in or find one nearby.* He thought he might wander down Sixteenth Street. He might find Mast or see someone else worth following, although who that would be he had no idea. Then he decided not to take a room at all. He thought, *Better yet, I'll stay here. People have to go through here. Tonight I'll sleep on a bench at the station. Keep track of comings and goings. Whether he leaves with someone or alone, that way no one can sneak by me.*

Joe Eggers took a room. Or actually, rooms. He signed for the Presidential Suite. No reason. Well, really, he had good reason. He was still on Harriman's dime. He probably wouldn't have that privilege for much longer. May as well enjoy it now, he figured. The suite was on the top floor with windows overlooking the station. Joe stood, curtains parted slightly, enjoying the dynamic urban view.

Across the way he saw Dale Smertz! How did he get

here? Joe couldn't believe it. The crazy tall man was down there, standing in the doorway of the station. And he was looking at this hotel. He was staring as if he expected the hotel building to get up and walk away or something. Or maybe he was just deep in thought. Either way, Joe was glad to have seen him. An unsettling question came to Joe—Does that guy have a gun on him?

Damn! Joe thought. *I looked and didn't see anyone following me in Boulder or on the train. Or when I got off and went through the station. When did he get here? He must have been on the train and I missed him.*

He watched as Dale took a last look across the street. His body language said he had made a decision. Then he didn't come out on the street. He disappeared back into the station. Joe did not want to be followed by anyone, Dale least of all. He was upset and was determined to give this guy the shake. Who did he think he was, anyway? Joe realized he had to become invisible. He needed to get out of the hotel unobserved. There had to be a side exit or a rear door or something he could use.

He went down to the lobby and approached the front desk. The clerk looked up.

"May I help you?"

"Yes, I will be meeting some friends here, but they don't know it. I want to surprise them after they get here. Is there a rear exit I can use to come and go so they don't see me? An exit not visible from the station?"

Like many hotel clerks, this one had heard an amazing variety of excuses and stories. He thought, *Surprise some friends, yeah right. I'll bet the guy is afraid of meeting a jealous husband or his own wife. He wants to know where the escape route is.* He kept a straight face. He nodded towards a corridor and answered, “Yes sir, down that hall and the exit is last door on the left. It will bring you out in back and you can’t see the station from there.”

Joe went off that direction to be sure he knew the route. As he started down the hall he thought he heard his name. Maybe he was hearing things, but to be sure he paused and looked around. It was someone trying to talk to him.

“Eggers!”

It was Myron Mast. Joe remembered he went by Mik as well as Myron. Next to him stood a big dark complected man. He was carrying a briefcase, holding it like it held the crown jewels. They each also carried what looked like a sack from a clothing store.

Mik asked tersely, “Eggers. Why are you here?”

Joe approached them. Mik glanced at his companion and said to him, “This is Josephus Eggers. He is the potential investor I met up on the grade. He is also the man who told me about the dam.”

Joe was surprised at the bald statement about the dam. Wasn’t that a secret?

Mik looked at Joe and nodded at his partner. He said “This is my friend.” He did not make an introduction. The man was not friendly, but not hostile either. He looked at Joe curiously with a hint of antagonism or maybe it was skepticism.

Joe decided to make quick work of it. “Mik, I am glad we happened to meet. I came to Denver in hopes of just that. I have a caution for you. It is very important for your railroad. Can you and I talk?” He pointedly looked at Cam.

“He is my friend and coworker. He knows what I know, and whatever you have to tell me he needs to hear too.”

Joe decided he was in all the way. He had no choice. He had to trust these two.

"Alright. Can we go somewhere private? We need to talk."

Cam and Mik traded glances. The unspoken but clear message was to be careful and watch each other's back.

Mik nodded. "Alright, where do you have in mind?"

"In fact I have taken the Presidential Suite here in the hotel. It has a sitting area room and three separate bedrooms. Perhaps we can go there? At least so I can tell you what I know, with no listening ears. I am in need of a meal. Maybe we can eat later, but let's get business done first."

Across the way, Dale was sprawled on a bench. He was trying with no success to get comfortable on a slab of oak eighteen by sixty inches. Since he was over seventy five inches in height, he couldn't even stretch out. He was not watching the hotel entrance. For that matter, he wouldn't be paying it much attention until morning. Most trains had come and gone for the day. At least the local and regional ones. For now he was sacking out, or at least trying to get rested. He figured if his quarry was up to something, whatever happened would go through or occur at the station. And he intended to be there to see, follow, and act.

Dale had gone to Boulder, found Joe, and followed him to Denver. Ella didn't know that, she just knew that he had left her on the mountainside. He had run off, saying something about going to town. She stayed up watching the camp above Eldorado Springs. And she was getting tired of watching routine, mindless activity. Nothing of note seemed to be happening. All Ella had seen was men working. They were moving tents, harnessing horses, and so on. She did not recognize any of them and no one did anything the least bit interesting.

Time for me to head for town too, she thought. As she started out, she wondered if Dale had had any success with finding Joe, and where he was now. She figured if her man friend wasn't at the hotel when she got back he would have left a note or word at the desk. No doubt he would show up sometime soon. At least that was her hope. Ella was walking down the hill but soon got a ride on a wagon. She looked forward to a bath and a hot meal. And she wanted to compare notes on the day with Dale. Soon enough she was in Boulder.

As Ella arrived she couldn't find Dale. She decided to rest up and maybe he would show. As she rested and got cleaned up, she didn't know Dale was in Denver. He himself was not cleaned up, but was trying to rest on a hard bench in Union Station. Of course she had no idea that the men he watched were across the street in a hotel.

Mik, Cam and Joe entered Joe's Suite and stood around uneasily. Joe noticed the big man held onto that case he had like it held the Holy Grail. He wondered. *Curious. I wonder why the death grip. What does he have in there? It must be real valuable.*

"Have a seat, gentlemen. We need to discuss the Denver Northwestern and Pacific. I am, or will be shortly, an investor. You two work for the Road. At least you do, Mik, and your trusted friend may too. In any case, we have interests in common even though we have just recently met."

Mik and Joe sat in the two easy chairs in the sitting room. Joe continued,

"I need to tell you what happened today. I was accosted by Dale Smertz, at my hotel in Boulder. It seems he saw you"—he looked at Mik—"Mik, and me on the train last night, talking. I didn't see him or his companion but he certainly saw us. He all but accused me of telling you about their plan for a dam."

Joe paused. "He became loud and almost violent. Of course I did not want to admit to anything of the sort. My word, he could have been armed. Anyway, I kept talking and got him slowed down. I passed our conversation off as my pumping you for information on the road, nothing more. I think he calmed down. He acted like I cooled his suspicions. But you need to know he is aware of you."

Mik exclaimed, "I didn't see him last night. Do you know, was he with that woman?"

"Apparently. Like I said, I didn't see either of them. Anyway, the more I thought about the scene he made this morning, the more upset it made me. I think the man is unbalanced, dangerous. I decided I had better warn you."

The two men sitting in front of him exchanged glances. Some message passed between them but Joe couldn't decipher what it was.

Joe wasn't done. "And, to make matters worse, that man Dale followed me down here. After I checked in I was looking out the window." He nodded towards them. "He was standing in the doors of the station, looking over at this hotel. Again, I did not see him on the train today. But he must have been on somewhere."

Mik again, "Is he alone?"

"Not sure. I saw only him. He is good at skulking! After I checked in here I took a moment to scan the view." Joe was becoming upset, and started repeating himself. "I was looking out that window," he gestured. "And then I saw him standing in the doorway of the station. He looked around then went back inside. He was purposeful in doing that, as if he intended to stay a while. Far as I know he is still in there. I have not seen the woman today."

There was silence.

The other man spoke up. "This changes things, Mik. If he is on your tail, we may need to make another plan."

Mik nodded. "Yes. Maybe we should split up."

The other man—Joe still didn't know who he was—thought for a moment.

"He doesn't know me. I'll go look in the station. See if he is there."

"No, if he doesn't know you, let's keep it that way. He may have seen you at the jobsite. Let's be sure he doesn't even know you are around. We want to keep every advantage we have. Better that you stay out of sight. How about I go. I'll be careful. I imagine I can get out of the hotel by a side or back door. Same for the station, I'll use a side entrance and avoid the front door he's probably watching. Plus, I'll stay behind the crowd. Plenty of people over there to blend in with." Mik made as if to stand up but didn't, waiting for Cam's agreement.

Cam pondered for a moment and nodded reluctantly. "Alright. Be careful."

Mik got up and started for the door then stopped. Looking at Joe, he decided to clear the air. He gave some background, enough hopefully to stop more questions. He still didn't trust Joe completely.

"The information you have on a dam near Kremmling has been corroborated separately."

Nodding towards Cam, he continued. "This man and I have the job of delivering information which will defeat that plan. Enough said: You don't need to know more. If you don't know who he is or what he is doing, you can't let it out inadvertently. If this Dale character is in fact unbalanced or violent, he might try to scare or beat it out of you. But, again, what you don't know you can't tell."

Quickly Mik went down to the lobby. Wanting to avoid the front door, he asked about the hotel's rear exit door. He asked the same clerk as Joe had. The clerk was amused and showed it. *I wonder just what kind of "meeting" those men are having*, he wondered, with a smirk. *They sure are concerned with how to sneak in and out of here.*

Mik ignored the man's sneer. He went down the hall and out the side door. Then to be safe he went long way around block. The crowds thickened and grew as he approached a side door of Union Station.

There was a party of five entering by the same door. It was a family with young children. They had bags galore, at least two for each person. He stood behind their chaotic little party and scanned the big central room. Far across the way, in a corner, he saw Dale. The man was thrashing around under a coat. It looked like he had a wildcat under there, holding it down while it was trying to get out. Mik smiled. He knew that Dale wasn't fighting anything, he was just trying to make himself comfortable lying back on the hard bench. He was intent on that and did not notice the comings and goings across the hall. And he was alone, no companion in sight anywhere in the hall.

Mik was free to watch undetected. He moved along behind the gaggle of travelers, struggling with their horde of suitcases and wandering children. After he watched a while, he was certain Dale was settling down. And was alone. He sure looked as if he were going nowhere. Mik backed out the door quickly. He was just an anonymous pedestrian as he returned to the hotel by the same route. No one was following him. Especially not a woman dressed as a man. He wanted to be sure of that.

The clerk almost laughed when he saw Mik return through the side door, looking upset and tense. *I wonder if he saw the husband, or the wife, or his wife*, the clerk thought. He was constantly amazed at what people would do. He would give his own wife a good laugh with the story of this guy.

Mik wasn't sure what he expected to find when he returned. He had been intent on seeking out Dale and checking if Ella was around. It had for the moment slipped his mind that Cam and Joe didn't know each other. He hoped neither had stormed out, or started an argument. He figured that the best he could hope for was quiet. He really expected to find Cam and Joe, sitting and stonily ignoring each other. Not so. They had found common ground. The two were talking technicalities of roadbed construction.

"I don't understand why so many roads put ballast two feet on either side of the track. What a waste!"

"You know, you are right. If you cut it back to ten or twelve inches on each side, you could save construction and maintenance time. Not to mention a fortune in costs!"

Mik stood at the door, bemused by the sudden camaraderie. He cleared his throat.

"I hate to break up this trade talk, gentlemen. Back to the matter of our pursuer. Here is my report. Dale Smertz is, or was as of two or three minutes ago, over there in Union Station." He pointed, half dramatically, to lighten the room.

"He seems to be alone. I did not see Ella at all. He is not

actively watching the door or the ramp. It looks like he is prepared to camp out, sleep on a bench. I expect he'll not get much rest on a hard oak bench with the noise. Not our problem. His spot is right by the ramp out to the tracks. It is well chosen. Anyone boarding the train has to go by him."

Joe asked, "Are you sure he was alone? Did you see the woman?"

"Yes, and no I did not. The usual crowd made it hard to see each person. If she is around they have separated and are acting like they don't know each other. If she is there and if she saw me, she definitely didn't follow me back here."

Cam calmly spoke.

"I've been thinking on this. Here's the plan for tomorrow morning. Mik, you and Joe here need to go back to Boulder. You need to get a briefcase and guard it like it holds the Queen's jewels. Don't be too obvious but be visible enough to entice him to follow you. Do what you have to do to get him out of the station. Somehow you need to get him to track after you to Boulder. That is the main thing."

Mik started to protest, and Cam held up a hand to silence it.

"With two of you, you can lose him out there somewhere. Or confront him. Only if you have to or it is to your advantage, but you can acknowledge and talk to him, challenge him, whatever. Just do it well away from Union Station, preferably in Boulder. It doesn't matter how you get him away from here. The thing is, you need to clear the way so I can go do what I need to do. Even if she is over there, she doesn't know me. You get Dale out of there and she won't matter. I will be free to do what I need to do. You know what that means, Mik."

He paused. "Does this make sense?"

Mik glanced at Joe. Joe wasn't sure about this "what I need to do" stuff the big guy kept saying. He knew he didn't dare press and ask questions. He could pump Mik later. He nodded but said nothing.

Mik slightly nodded himself, reluctantly.

"Yes, it makes sense. The two of us can go in early, just after sunup to catch the first train to Boulder. That gives you the rest of the day. Agreed?" Cam nodded, and Joe again wondered just what Cam would be doing.

The three sat back, relaxed with having a workable plan in place. Attention turned to other matters.

Stomachs were rumbling, enough to be heard. Mik was ravenous.

"How about some dinner? I know the back way out, we can come and go. Even if Dale is watching, he won't see us. Plus maybe I can buy a briefcase while we're out. The hotel clerk made odd faces when I used the rear door. I guess he isn't used to his guests being mysterious. Or that is his private entry, I don't know. As the saying goes, it takes all kinds."

He started towards the door but halted.

"By the way, Joe. You say you have three bedrooms in this Suite? Why don't the two of us stay here tonight. We can each have a room. That way we are near the station tomorrow morning, and C..." He almost said Cam's name but stopped himself with a guttural "k" sound, turning it into a cough. He quickly salvaged the mistake.

"That way you and I are close by, and can get going early. The earlier we roust Dale after his poor night's rest, the better for us. And he," nodding at Cam, "can watch. He can maybe see if Ella is lurking around, and if we are successful in getting Dale to follow us out of town."

The three had a dinner on Joe's expense account. The conversation was relaxed. They enjoyed an evening of nice, neutral train talk. It was over and they were back in the room early. By ten o'clock no one was awake in the Suite.

The clerk in the lobby amused himself by trying to figure out what was happening. First they left then came back, by the rear exit both times. The guy who earlier had looked tense was calm. Leaving, one of the men had a case which he clung to like it was life itself. Coming back, two of them toted carefully guarded cases. What was that about? And, who was with whom? Or were they just three businessmen? And if there were women involved, where were they?

Little did he know, there actually was one woman involved. But she wouldn't be coming through any of the hotel's doors, be it front, rear, or side.

Ella was in Boulder. And Ella was starting to worry. *Where is Dale? I hope he is alright. Or maybe*, she wondered suspiciously, *maybe he isn't chasing Eggers at all. Maybe he is with a woman in a saloon.* She banished these thoughts. *No, he is probably watching and waiting for Eggers to do something stupid. He'll come back to me as soon as he can.*

She went to bed, but didn't sleep well. Her dreams were not pleasant. They weren't terrible, sit up gasping nightmares but they were not sweet and restful. She was running down a track being chased by Eggers and another man on a hand cart. It was sort of like the kind of handcart moved by pumping a lever up and down. The men were laughing maniacally at her and at the handcart. How she knew that she wasn't sure, but they thought the cart was hilarious. As for El, she would get ahead of them and slow down. Then either a partly completed tunnel would loom up, scary and dark, or she would find herself among a herd of angry, mistreated horses. Then she was running again, being chased. It was not a restful night.

Morning. Dale didn't have a restful night either. His mouth was awful. It tasted like every train that had come to the station had detoured through his mouth, leaving cinders and grit. He blearily sat up, his back aching from the hard flat surface. He scanned the roomful of early morning travelers but saw no one of interest. Still, he forced himself to sit up and pay attention. He slowly gathered his coat and belongings, ready to move.

In the hotel across the way, Mik and Joe left the room. The clerk was about to go off shift but was glad to see them. He was bemused that they went out the front door this time. The two just sauntered out like they were simple businessmen with nothing to hide. It was almost like they wanted to be seen. He couldn't wait to tell his wife about this!

Cam stood at the windows of the Presidential Suite and watched as they crossed the road and entered the front doors of Union Station.

XIII

Before the two men left the lobby, Mik decided to clear the air. He stuck his hand out to Eggers.

"Since we are working together for now, let's get comfortable. As you seem to know, I go by Mik. How should I call you?"

Eggers was relieved he had been accepted, that they were pulling together. He was on the same side now. "Joe. Call me Joe." He smiled and reached to take the hand.

"And I know you can't say much. But I am curious about your friend. It looks like you have known each other for quite a while. He seems like a solid, dependable man."

Mik smiled and said, "We have worked together one way or another for years."

This was so in more ways than Joe could possibly know. Actually, that simple statement painted a picture that was outlandish and bizarre. So much so that neither Joe nor anyone else would even be able to even wrap their head around it. Mik fought off a sudden wave of feeling lost, alone and never able to get home. Memories of Sula and their life came in a torrent. They were followed by images of his friend Kwame, a double for Cam if ever there was one. And Joe Abrams, a double for Eggers. Yet other images of his previous life threatened to flood in as well.

He continued. "In fact, sometimes it seems like several lifetimes."

Mik then wrenched his thoughts back to the present. At least to the present present…he had to concentrate on Union Station, Dale Smertz, and the situation they faced.

The men ended the handshake, both glad to be in an amiable working relationship. They walked out of the lobby and paused at the street. Mik had given their actions some thought, in fact had not slept very well for dreaming of the morning's challenges. He had a plan.

"Joe, we need to act like we are deep in discussion. That way we can walk right by him and don't have to notice him. We want him to think we don't see him, that he has tricked us. But I want to know where he is. And I want to be sure he sees us."

"What do we do if he doesn't see us, or if he is gone?"

Mik glanced both ways and stepped out to cross the street. "I guess we'll have to make a ruckus or something. We can start a spirited discussion or argument or something. We'll figure that out as we go. Hopefully he is awake and on the lookout."

As usual the station was noisy and crowded. Passengers were sitting, standing, talking, waiting for loved ones to arrive or for their train to load and depart. Some poor souls were stretched out on the floor pretending that they were resting. Uniformed trainmen came through pulling carts loaded with baggage, barking to make way. Bells rang and the station master periodically bellowed announcements. Clerks chalked, erased, and rechalked arrival and departure times. It looked chaotic. Actually it was well organized and things ran predictably and smoothly. It was an example of American organizational and industrial might.

The two men paused briefly at the door. They were looking for Dale but trying not to be obvious about it. Mik saw him fumbling around, gathering his stuff, in the same spot as the previous evening. He said as much to Joe as they waded the crowds and joined the ticket line. A railroad ticket line in 1903 was a "lowest common denominator" experience. One met and saw all types of people while waiting to buy a ticket to ride the iron rooster. Mik was reminded of the DMV office a century later, waiting in line to renew your driver's license.

Joe offered to buy. "I am on an expense account, Mik. There is no reason for you to shell out."

"No. If you buy it looks like I am your stooge. Or worse, that you are buying me off. We should try to make him to think we are peers or equals. Or better yet, competing business associates. That will make him wonder which of us he should follow." Mik grinned. "Besides, I have an expense allowance too."

That half boastful admission surprised Joe a little. Maybe this Myron Mast was more than just a mid level field hand. If he had expenses covered he was upper level. Apparently he was a judgment level manager of some sort. Joe speculated around that for a moment. Then the cynical investor to be part of his brain spoke up. It wondered if perhaps this guy had connections. If so, he should be wooed a little. Joe pushed that back. He had things to do this morning besides schmooze with railroad people. Anyway, he saw the logic of separate tickets. Stepping up to the counter, he told the clerk loudly, "I need a one way to Boulder. Next train out."

Mik was next, and bought a round trip. He figured if Dale was watching it would further complicate his plans. Plus, he wouldn't mind a return trip to Denver for its own sake. He was finding that he liked to ride the train. The experience in and of itself was enjoyable. Much more relaxing than jockeying a car through traffic at high speeds.

Dale Smertz had indeed seen them. He was watching intently but intermittently. It was difficult to keep track without staring. It didn't help that his night on the bench was not the most restful. It was good to finally spot them. He had been awake and on the lookout for at least an hour and was ready for some action. Actually he was beginning to wonder if he had somehow missed them or something.

Dale was ready for just about anything so long as he could get moving. He wanted to think of something besides his aches and pangs. Plus he knew Ella was worried about him and he was concerned for her. That weighed on his mind too. It didn't help that his eyes felt like someone had poured sand in them, and his mouth still tasted bad.

The man he was on the lookout for, Joe Eggers, finally came in with a companion. Dale realized it wasn't really "finally" because it was early in the day. Just that he was ready to move. The two, Eggers and friend, paused for a heartbeat at the door, probably taking in the din and crowded hall. Dale was almost positive that the other man was that Mast guy, the one who somehow escaped the rockslide a few days back. The one Joe was talking to on the train! He was carrying a brief case, holding on tight. Dale wondered what was in it that caused such a death grip.

The two were talking intently. It seemed to be a conversation between equals. It was not an argument but it wasn't a friendly, laughing and smiling talk either. They were obviously discussing something important. Was it him, and Ella, and the dam?

The two got in the ticket line, seeming to dicker on some matter of importance to them. Otherwise they were oblivious to everything. It was hard for him not to gawk. He stopped himself, looking away. To keep busy and blend in, he fiddled and gathered his things. He wanted to look just like one of many. It wasn't too hard to blend in with the hordes waiting to ride the train.

The pair got to the head of the line. Joe bought a ticket then the other did too. Dale couldn't tell where or if they bought a one way or round trip.

They continued to talk. In fact they talked so much they walked right by him on the way out to the tracks. He overheard one of them, not sure which one. "That should bolster the stock price..."

Now, what did that mean, Dale wondered. Maybe Joe had been straight. Maybe he really didn't sell out him and Ella and their dam. It was possible that Eggers really was just trying to wheedle information about the project. The guy was on the up and up after all. But if that was the case, why were they together now? Why had they met in Denver not Boulder? What had they talked about? Dale knew he needed to find out if he could.

He noticed that Eggers carried nothing, no case or bag. He was empty handed. Mast, on the other hand, had a brief case. It had a lock securely keeping it shut. He held it close, and constantly looked at. Dale briefly wondered if the guy expected it might try to run away. That case must hold something important, maybe valuable. Had Eggers given or sold him something? It didn't look heavy. It must be papers or something light. His mind spun. Maybe that case held evidence of their filings for the dam! Or information on him and Ella!

Dale reflected back on his first meeting with Joe. The man was hard to read. Right now, Eggers acted like a man in charge. The way he walked, talked, and his body language all said "I am a man to be reckoned with." When he and El had first met him, he sent out mixed messages. At first he had talked like he was a boss, like he was used to being heard and heeded.

Then he had backed down, had started to act like an underling. He had almost knelt and pulled his forelock to Dale. At the time Dale had thought the man had suddenly figured out how important he and Ella were. It happened all of a sudden. Looking back, it almost seemed like Joe wanted to diminish his importance. Like he wanted to build up Dale and Ella's position, at least in their minds.

Joe had tried to act meek that day when they finished their meeting. But right now, this morning, the man sure acted different. Today he walked and acted like a person used to being listened to, to having and using authority. Maybe he had some hold over Mast. Or maybe he had just closed some deal and was strutting his stuff. Dale just couldn't puzzle it out. He needed to follow and find out more.

The previous night Dale had bought an open ticket, good for any train all day. He had to pay more than he liked, but wanted to be able to move quickly in the morning. Last thing he wanted to do was stand in line while the men he was watching disappeared onto a train or somewhere. No need to get in line this morning, and he was glad of it. He finished gathering his belongings. Not that he had a lot, really just a coat and hat. The two men had already walked past him as he stood.

As he stepped in behind his quarry, he made himself slow down. With a short night and the excitement of the chase, it was easy to let his imagination run away. What was happening might well have little or nothing to do with him, El, the dam, or anything.

Joe Eggers was probably just another hustler, one of hundreds in any city across the country. Dale could relate. Joe was likely looking to make money off the railroad, any railroad. One of those guys who used any influence or leverage he could to make money, get a commission or a job, or even a payoff. Dale told himself that whatever contents or papers or money that Mast had in that case, were meaningless. They likely had nothing to do with him and Ella or Eggers. Probably had nothing to do with their efforts to slow down the Moffat Road. Probably. But to be sure, he somehow needed to get a look at what was in there. He watched the two men walk the length of the train, still talking and ignoring the crowds.

Joe and Mik deliberately went to the front and got into the first car behind the engine. Once seated, they had a view of people coming on the platform to board the train. And it gave Dale several other cars to get into. They wanted to make it easy for him to follow.

"There he is, getting on two cars back. He must have already had a ticket, hasn't had time to stand in line." Joe looked at his watch. "Nine minutes until we pull out. Plenty of time. Shoot, I can even sit back and relax!"

"Too bad we can't let…my friend know Dale has taken the bait and is on the same train." Mik had an idea.

"Stay here Joe and keep my seat please. If he tries to leave the train do what you have to, we have to get him out of Denver." He stood up and grabbed the empty case he had been all but fondling for Dale's benefit. "I'll be right back." He walked up through the car towards the engine. A conductor looked sternly at him. "Sorry, sir, but you can't go any further."

Mik pulled out the letter from Sumner. As the conductor read it a look of surprise and curiosity chased across his face. Then it closed down with acceptance. He listened as Mik laid out what he wanted.

"I need you to send a quick telegram. Now, before the train leaves. Hold the departure if you must, but the message has to be sent. Memorize this; are you ready?"

The conductor, eyes widening, nodded.

"Yes, sir, I understand."

"The telegram goes to, are you ready? It goes to Cameron Braun, Presidential Suite, Station Hotel, Denver. Copy to Mr. Sumner at the Majestic Building. It should read, 'Tall man is with us stop Good luck at the waters stop Mik end.'" He had the conductor repeat it. He watched as the man got off the train, ran to the locomotive and had a word with the engineer. Then he hustled into the telegraph room.

Mik put in the reference to waters so Cam would know it was genuine, not a ruse. No one but he and Mr. Sumner knew Cam was headed to Hot Sulphur Springs.

The train lurched, ready to go, as Mik returned to his seat. The conductor ran from the telegraph office. He climbed on just as the cars started to move. Mik was satisfied that he had gotten word to Cam. All he and Eggers had to do now was keep Dale occupied for a while. Best case would be all day but the next two or three hours would suffice. Then he would be too far behind Cam to make any difference. The deal would be done.

Cam watched Mik and Joe enter the station, and a few people after them. Then he went down and ate breakfast. Afterwards, in the room, he sat back and relaxed, pondering the best way to go get the deed recorded. A knock on the door disturbed his reverie. He was startled enough that he actually jumped a little bit.

"Telegram for Mr. Braun."

He heard the announcement but was skeptical. The only telegrams he had ever received were news of momentous occasions. Births, deaths and so on. No one even knew he was here. Almost no one, he reminded himself. He cautiously cracked the door, opening it wide when he saw it was the hotel clerk. What was the telegram about? He hoped it was from Mr. Sumner, or more likely Mik, or even Eggers. No one else knew his whereabouts. And the whereabouts of the deed. At least he hoped no one else knew.

A hotel clerk's life is humdrum, with people coming and going but doing little of interest. There were exceptions, rare but they did occur. One exception was happening for the clerk at the Station Hotel. Cam, Mik and Joe's comings and goings were a memorable change in the man's daily grind. Most of the time people came and went, and the man couldn't remember them even minutes later. But these three...Said clerk never really did figure the situation out. For days afterward he wondered about it. Why were men coming and going from the back door? Why did one take a room for three? And then he and one of the others left early? Last of all, why did the man who was still there got a cryptic telegram?

Even though it could land him in hot water, he was nosy. The clerk made a practice of opening and reading incoming telegrams. He found it sometimes gave him leverage over guests and occasionally over his boss. He was careful about it; he knew he would have been fired and maybe run out of town had it become known.

In this case, the telegram made no sense. There was no advantage for him. He saw no way to collect an extra payment for his silence or anything else. But it sure gave him a good story to tell at the tavern after hours, and his wife when he went home.

The big man, Braun, took the envelope and opened it. He almost shut the door in the clerk's face but then didn't. Cam figured he might have to send a response somewhere. After he read the telegram a grin split his face. His whole demeanor changed, like an anvil had been taken off his shoulders.

"Thank you!"

He set down the briefcase he had held and dug in his pocket.

"Here, for your trouble."

The clerk was grateful for a big tip for just handing over a piece of paper. Two bits! A quarter wasn't bad for three or four minutes' work! And he didn't have to ask for it or threaten to tell someone about the contents of the telegram! This story got stranger and more interesting with every twist!

To be on the safe side, Cam closed the door and waited a while. He had some time, could catch the eight thirty train to Dumont. That was a good plan from the timing aspect. He wanted to be sure that Mik and Joe had cleared that Dale character out. Taking the 8:30 train would get him up to Grand County in good time. From Dumont he wanted to be sure to catch the mid day stage. That would give him ample time. He wouldn't have to worry during the entire ride over Berthoud Pass.

If everything ran on time, he would arrive in Hot Sulphur Springs by about four. Barring problems, there should be enough time to handle the filing yet today. He would go direct to the Courthouse and get the papers filed, recorded, whatever the term was, and done with. He made a mental note to wire ahead from Dumont to have someone waiting for him in Hot Sulphur. He needed to have a local man of good repute who knew the town ready take him direct to the courthouse.

Cam would be more than be glad to have the whole business over and finished.

Braun did himself proud that day. He couldn't imagine it, sitting in a hotel in Denver looking at a cryptic telegram. Much hung on how he did his job the next eight or ten hours. There were many results of his good work. First result was that the future of the Denver Northwestern and Pacific Railroad as a viable enterprise was assured. There were other benefits which flowed directly from his filing of a piece of paper.

The personal fortunes of many men would grow. Of course their families and heirs would benefit from having money and status. Those fortunes would in future be put to work for business and charitable use in Denver, Colorado, and the region. The most widespread result wasn't financial. It was the opening of western Colorado. Development and economic diversification came to the land. Thanks to the railroad many industries and activities became possible. Many of those were profitable, from ranching, coal mining, and (ironically) dam building, to year round resorts with many second homes. They opened up a host of recreational activities for many people—skiing, rafting, hiking, and mountain biking.

In fact, Cam made the trek over the mountain to Hot Sulphur Springs with no problems. The deed he carried so protectively was safely delivered. The papers owned by his employer were properly submitted, noted, and recorded in the public record.

The immediate effect was to reserve and hold open the route through the Gore Canyon. This allowed Moffat's company to bypass natural barriers. It let the rails take the path of least resistance, rather than go up and over the Park and Rabbit Ears mountains. This increased the viability and profitability of the road. Not to mention letting it stay alive and functioning.

Keeping this route open also allowed a later addition of perhaps twenty miles of track. Adding this relatively small amount of road yielded another host of economic and social benefits. The short cutoff at the west end of the Canyon joined the Rio Grande's route. This came from Pueblo, up the Arkansas River then across the divide and down the Grand River to Grand Junction. From there it was an easy run for traffic to and from central Utah and points beyond. Using this cutoff, people could come and go direct between Denver and Grand Junction. Ever more homes, resorts, ranches, mines, stores and mills became possible because the trains came through.

Because Mik and Joe kept Dale from interfering, Braun safely and easily got to Hot Sulphur Springs. Because of that, he delivered and caused to be filed to the public record one legal document. Because of that, the train came to western Colorado.

Cam would have snorted if someone told him all this. He would have disbelieved that he had an important albeit anonymous place in Colorado history. The man was just happy to have met Mr. Sumner's expectations, to have gotten the job done. Truth be told, he didn't like this business of riding on trains, carrying pieces of paper. He really disliked being an errand boy for the big shots. What he loved was building railroads, not using them. Even as he returned to Denver he looked forward to getting back to that.

But the story continues. While Cam was on the way west, the game was afoot on the train from Denver heading to Boulder.

Dale made sure he got onto the same train as Eggers, several cars back. The locomotive started to pull out of the station pretty much on time. Dale noticed a conductor run out of the telegraph office and climb on the train at the last minute. That sort of thing often happened and he didn't give it much thought. He idly wondered just how safe it was for a conductor to jump on to a moving train. For a moment his thoughts drifted to Ella and how outraged she would be at that practice. Good old El, always looking out for the little guy, and for animals...

He wrenched his mind back. Time to focus. He directed attention and energy towards the men two cars up the line, the one behind the engine. Having watched carefully he was sure they hadn't slipped off. It made sense to move one car closer to them. It would be easier there to keep track. He was punchy and chortled at the thought. *Keep track, on a train. Funny!* He moved up unobserved, he thought, by the two. Settling in, he watched, and eyes became heavy.

In Boulder Ella had slept later than usual. She woke alone, something she was not used to doing. It made her a little concerned, almost scared. Dale never spent the night away. He always came back to her. She hoped he was alright. At breakfast, she pushed her bacon and eggs around the plate. It felt like days since she had eaten a good meal. Her stomach told her she was hungry.

Her worries made her too preoccupied to eat. What to do? There were just a few options which made sense. After turning them over and tussling with each several times, she made a decision. Then the eggs, while grown cold, tasted good as she hurriedly snarfed them down. Ella was eager to go by the James Hotel this morning. That is where Eggers had been staying and maybe she could pick up his or Dale's trail there. She felt better for having a plan.

On the way up to Boulder the train sometimes got delayed. Today it was all running on schedule. Mik had expected things to take more time. He glanced at his watch and saw that today of all days everything had fallen in place for the railroad. No delays, no breakdowns, no traffic jams. The first runs of the day were sometimes like this.

They were approaching Marshall, the last big stop before Boulder. The town was almost as big as the home of the University a few miles north. This place disdained laboratories, poetry, reading and book learning. Marshall was a calloused hands, coal mining town. Its wealth was torn from inside the earth by strong, determined men who braved dark, wet and sickness to do their jobs.

It was early in the day. Miners going on shift were filing towards the mine entrances. Others came out, faces blackened by coal dust and sweat, their work done for a few hours. Mik watched, musing. Long and dangerous days they endured, toiling deep underground in damp, eternal night.

Something the woman Ella said the first day he was here came to his mind. She talked about trying to "organize" the workers. She didn't say it but he imagined he meant, not just railroad men but miners too. Saying they should work only forty hours a week. Mik knew a long bloody battle was coming over that issue. But he also knew that work schedule would be accepted, soon be taken as a right. He knew that Marshall and its coalfields would hear and feel its share of gunfire and strife. Fires would destroy much of the town before all was said and done.

But that was the future, known to him but unknowable to the Ellas of the world. The engineer slowed the train as he neared Marshall. The lurch brought Mik back to 1903. He was on the train to Boulder, with a man he hardly knew, trying to dupe another man into following him. It occurred to him that the best thing to do was split up, he and Joe. Dale could follow only of them and wondering about the man not followed would keep him occupied.

"Joe, we should split up."

Joe was relaxed, eyes half shut. He came awake and listened to Mik.

"His pal Ella will likely be waiting in Boulder. If one of us leaves the train now Smertz will have a decision to make. He'll have to either follow or wait and try to find and follow later. Either way he is occupied and" he paused, almost naming Cam, "… and my friend is clear to get his job done. What do you think?"

"Actually I was kind of thinking along the same lines. Yeah, it makes sense. Why don't you get off. Take the case and make a show of heading towards Eldorado Springs. I'll ride on into Boulder and take care of Ella, or both of them, there. I mean I'll do my best to occupy them, keep them guessing. No harm to anyone if it can be avoided any way. I'll delay as best I can."

Mik looked Joe Eggers in the eye and shook his hand. He stood and said good bye. It was so strange to look at the man.

In another life, in Sula time, he had looked at the same face. His friend Joe Abrams had sure looked him in the eye many times. They were adventuring and hiking partners. Mik had to turn his thoughts away. Thinking too much about such things got too convoluted and bizarre. And he wasn't afraid to admit that it was a little frightening.

"Okay. See you."

Joe wondered what "okay" meant. He had never heard that expression before. Whatever, Mik was leaving the train and Joe was on his own.

Briefcase firmly in hand, Mik stepped down off the train and walked over to waiting wagons. He ostentatiously asked around.

"I need a ride to the Springs. What'll it cost? What? Too much!"

And again, several times. Trying to cut a swath, he succeeded. If Dale asked anyone around the stop he would be sure to learn where Mik went. All the effort was for naught. Mik was not followed.

Dale had had a near sleepless night in the station. Not only was the bench hard and flat, but the place was noisy and lights were on all night. He was beat. The train wasn't even out of Denver before he was fighting to stay awake. The comfortable seat and the sweet sway of the cars running on smooth tracks worked their magic. He nodded off shortly and fell sound into rest. The man slept through every stop.

He was still out as they came down the hill to Marshall. As the train was ready to start up again, the conductor cried, "Next stop, Boulder." That word, Boulder, caused the tall gangly man to stir. He awoke gradually, then the lurch of the train brought him almost fully awake. He felt the engine labor as it started up the small hill leaving Marshall. It took a moment to realize where he was and what he was doing. Dale looked back at the stop and saw Mast there! The man got off early with his briefcase! Eggers wasn't on the platform, just Mast. Where was he? Was he lurking on the platform with Mast, or still on the train? What were these guys up to?

For a moment Dale thought of pulling the emergency stop cord. No, if he did that, everyone would stare at him. Last thing he wanted was a bunch of people looking at him and remembering him. He'd have to ride it out to Boulder. Better to find Ella there, run Eggers down, then go find Mast. As the train picked up speed, Dale watched Mik walk towards a wagon and talk to the driver. He receded into tininess as the train went around a curve and Marshall disappeared.

Joe, Dale, and the other passengers arrived in Boulder on time. Joe climbed down the metal stairs onto the platform. He glanced around as if not the least interested in anyone else, and strode off. Dale watched, unable to push his way to the door. Eggers was alone. His thoughts crowded frantically. *Where was he going? What had he told Mast? And what was in the briefcase Mast had so carefully held? Where could he find Ella?*

He could find Ella just where Joe was headed. The James Hotel.

XIV

Joe watched as Mik got off the train. He was making a point of finding a ride to Eldorado Springs while Joe watched. As the train pulled out he watched and didn't see Dale get off. So he decided to have a little fun when he got to Boulder. When the train arrived, he could go straight to his hotel. Or he could take a roundabout stroll through town. That way he could use up some time and see who followed him. Dale, Ella, both?

As he left the station Joe looked left then right, trying to decide where to go, then stepped left. He walked haphazardly, stopping to look up at the spectacular mountain scenery and into shop windows. Before long he saw Dale's reflection in a window. Dale was watching him from across and down the street. Joe decided to stroll to and through the campus of the University. It was up a hill about a mile south of downtown and the railroad station. So off he went.

There wasn't a lot to see. The school was not even thirty years old and the campus landscaping was not well established. There were some scraggly trees and a few greenish, uneven lawns. The Main classroom and administration building and a few other red stone structures stood out on the barren hill like Scottish castles. Over time, Joe mused, the trees would grow and the surroundings would blend in. Sometime down the road they would look as if they had always been there.

It took concentration to walk just slowly enough so that Dale kept him in sight. He went straight as much as he could, taking no sudden turns or evasions. In front of the main building, he stopped one professorly looking man and asked him several questions.

"Excuse me, sir, but is there a campus police force?"

"I believe we have one patrolman. Do you have a problem?"

"I'm not sure. A man is following me." Here, Joe glanced towards the corner of the courtyard where Dale was lurking. "At least I think he is. I came from downtown and so did he, staying the same distance back. I don't know who he is. Where might I find the patrolman?"

The conversation stretched out for five or six minutes. Joe had no intention of involving the campus cop, but wanted to buy time. Plus he wanted to make Dale wonder what was being said.

"Thank you, sir, you have been most helpful," Joe said. He was tiring of the game, and he had used up some time. He took one turn around the central quad, strolling like he hadn't a care in the world. Then he started the walk back towards downtown.

His hotel, the James, was on the main street. It enjoyed a good reputation and seldom had vacancies. Ella had been sitting in the lobby for a while. She tried to look purposeful and like she belonged. Nonetheless, she started to get looks from the lobby clerk who wondered just who or what she was waiting for.

"May I help you, ah, miss?" asked the bell captain. He hoped this person was a miss not a mister. "Are you waiting for someone?"

Ella got the hint. She got up and slowly walked to a restaurant across the street. There a newspaper caught her attention. She bought a copy. The headline screamed, "Roosevelt Asks Millions to Strengthen Navy." She ordered coffee and sipped on it while pretending to read. She would read a line or two at a time. She glanced up often to eye the people coming and going across the street.

The article in the newspaper was about an updated and modernized fleet. It was to be made up of new types of ships, cruisers and battleships. Odd, the new ships wouldn't be powered by coal or coal with sail supplement. The navy wanted them to be powered by something called fuel oil. She wondered idly what the advantages of the new fuel were. All the while she was watching the people around her. Almost everyone entering or leaving the hotel got her once over. She was kind of upset that there was not one familiar face among them.

Ella wondered how the sailors would like the new fuel. Would it make life easier or harder for them? How about coal miners and mining towns, idled because the Navy didn't want their coal? She went off on a tangent, thinking of miners thrown out of work and starving and animals used in the mines abandoned. The vivid images of suffering surrounded her and she felt her anger rising. She wanted to yell something out. But she realized of a sudden that she couldn't do anything about miners or the Navy not buying coal. What she could do is try to find her partner.

For lack of any better plan, she scanned the street again. It was with great relief that she saw Dale! He was coming up the sidewalk, not in a hurry or trying to get to the hotel. He was kind of stopping and starting, watching something on the other side. He was trailing someone. Ella looked the direction Dale seemed to be focused. There was Joe Eggers striding up the way, going into the hotel. She gestured and to her joy, got Dale's attention. He stopped looking at Joe and walked directly up to Ella in the restaurant.

"He kept you out all night! I was so worried about you. Are you alright? Where were you?" She stood and wanted to hug him. At the last minute she remembered she was dressed as a man and hadn't better get too close.

"What happened? Who were you with? Do you think he told anyone about us? Where were you?" She had a thousand questions.

"Mast. He met in Denver with that Myron Mast. They spent the night in a hotel. Don't know for sure what they talked about. Am I glad to see you!" He started to step close to hug her and had the same realization, two men did not hug. In public. In 1903. He stepped back a little.

"I followed them onto the train this morning. When they got on, Mast carried a case, a briefcase. He acted as if it were full of jewels. I mean, he wouldn't put it down or anything. He got off in Marshall, still carrying it."

They sat down and he ordered coffee for himself.

"I followed them onto the train. Promptly fell asleep. I didn't want to but you know how the motion and sound can do that. I slept on a bench in the station last night. Or I should say I kind of rested there, didn't sleep much. Anyway, I woke up just as the engineer started to pull out of Marshall. I couldn't get off then, we were moving too fast."

He paused. "I was worried about you too. Are you alright? Did you see or learn anything at the worksite yesterday? How did you get back?"

"There was nothing going on that that site. All I saw was a bunch of men moving stuff around and packing wagons. Just a bunch of workers preparing to move the camp. Tents coming down, wagons loaded then unloaded and reloaded, and so on. There was no indication of anyone doing anything out of the ordinary. I finally gave up and left. Started walking and was able to cadge a ride to Boulder with a hostler."

"Well, we have to find out what Eggers told Mast. And why they were on the train together after a night in Denver. I don't know where Mast stayed, but Eggers was in the Station Hotel across from Union Station. Like I said, Mast had a briefcase this morning which he cradled like it was the most valuable thing."

He swilled the rest of his coffee, grimacing as he felt a few grounds go down his throat.

"He wouldn't put that case down. Even though he had hold of it, he kept looking at it like it might run off or something. Strangest thing. Now, maybe he wasn't worried about it going away. Maybe he stood to gain something from what was inside. He took it with him when he left the train. Last I saw him there, in Marshall, he was talking to a wagoneer. Not sure where he was headed."

El was excited to hear about the night. "Just after I spotted you I saw Eggers go into the hotel. You're right, we have to find out what he knows. And who he told." She smiled. "I'm just glad to find you again, and that you are safe."

She allowed herself a vulnerable moment. "I was so worried, Dale. So worried."

Joe was tired from his walking tour. He was not yet completely comfortable with the altitude and the dry climate. And to be honest he seldom walked two or three miles at one time. It was good to be back at his base in the James. He knew that Dale had followed him all around. It was hard to miss the uniquely dressed Ella sitting across from the hotel. She stood out like a trumpet at a banjo fest. No doubt she saw him, at least he hoped so. The two of them were probably hovering somewhere around, trying to decide what to do next.

Sprawled on the bed, hands laced behind his head, he looked at the ceiling. He had to think the problem through. He didn't really care about Dale Smertz and Ella or what they did. There would always be agents for other railroads hanging around making trouble. Such people would always have some success. Mostly they spent a lot of time uselessly running around trying to sow discontent. Let them.

Joe was focused on Mik's friend, the one whose name he never learned. It seemed that he had a job to do. Somehow he would clear the road's way through western Colorado. At the same time he would stop the Union Pacific's effort to dam up the Gore Canyon. How, Joe wasn't sure. And it seemed he needed to go do it quickly.

Joe came to the same conclusion, that he and Mik had discussed. They had to buy time, just drag things out for as long as they could. Between them they needed to keep Ella and Dale occupied for only a day or two. And who knew where Mik was? What was he up to now? He couldn't do anything about that. It was up to him for now.

Joe was ready to move on. Literally, psychologically, socially, in all ways he was starting a new chapter in the story of Josephus Eggers. He had found a new city and a new life.

What he wanted, needed to do now was to wash his hands of Ella, Smertz, the Union Pacific, and all that. He wanted to be done with the entire situation.

For now his goal was to know and become known in Denver. He needed to hang around down at the Majestic Building, headquarters for the Denver Northwestern and Pacific Railway. He wanted to become trusted and respected. He wanted his participation to be welcomed when he actually put money into the Moffat road. The sooner he rid himself of working for Harriman and the UP and became his own man, the better. Joe couldn't just say good bye and expect to be left alone. Mr. Harriman wouldn't take his disloyalty lightly. Joe had to find a way to deflect that. Better yet, he had to find a way to put the blame elsewhere.

What he needed to do was tie up Ella and Dale for a day. Not literally, although that did cross his mind. And he also needed to find a way to exit from the UP in such a way that he wouldn't become a target for a Mr. Fixit security man like himself. Joe knew there were others like him in New York, just waiting for an opportunity to make a name for him or herself.

So, the deal was, he needed to find a way to make it look like the couple had made the mistake. Make it look like they were the ones who tipped the company's hand about the dam. And he had to make it look like he had tried to stop it. Why not make it look like Mik had outsmarted them and hoodwinked him? Make them focus on Mik, not him. Joe didn't know what Mik was up to and didn't care. He was just another pawn in the game.

Joe, and Dale and Ella, were all banging their heads against opposite sides of the same problem. They were close enough that if they listened, they might hear the thud of heads hitting against a knotty problem. Joe was in his room. Dale and Ella remained in the restaurant across the street, talking strategy and catching up.

Earlier, Mik had gone from wagon to wagon in Marshall, visibly haggling on a fare to Eldorado Springs. After three or four discussions, he agreed on a price and got on a wagon headed that direction.

Forty or so minutes later, the wagon approached the Pruden Ranch. He could see a group of people gathered in the small cemetery up the hill and west of the house. Seth Pruden was being buried. He would be forever nineteen years old. Poor Mr. and Mrs. Pruden, Ted and Odessa. How sad. As he watched, the people started to disperse.

The hostler dropped Mik off. He thought Mik was making a mistake. "Are you sure you want off here? Town is another mile or so, long walk…"

"Yes, I'm sure. Thanks. See you around."

He slowly walked up the lane to the house, carrying his briefcase still. He saw Steu Wentz among the mourners. Before he went into the house to again offer condolences, he approached Steu.

"Sad day, no? How are the Prudens doing?"

Steu shrugged. "As well as can be expected. Quite a shock to us all."

His eyes flared. "The question is, where have you been? Have you seen Cam? Someone told me you two left. What are you up to? What is Cam doing? I'm surprised he's not here." He waited a beat but Mik said nothing so he went on.

"Seriously, I heard you two were hustled down to Denver on a special train. So tell me, what gives?"

"Long story, Steu. Long story." Mik gathered his thoughts. Steu, he decided, was loyal to the road if any one was. He needed to know the story. He knew how to keep his mouth shut. It was time to tell him.

Mik. "Let's have a seat." He started, "You know that couple..."

About an hour later, they were still on the back porch of the ranch house.

"So, to recap. Cam should be on the way to Hot Sulphur Springs to file the right of way deed. I have a decoy briefcase here. Joe is, well, I don't know where he is. Nor the Dale Smertz character, and his sidekick Ella."

Steu nodded. He was too busy digesting the story to say anything.

Mik added a postscript. "I think Joe will hold them off for a few hours. I imagine that one way or another, those three are at sword's point over in Boulder."

The encounter in Boulder wasn't as hostile as a sword's point confrontation, but it was not a warm reunion of old friends.

Joe worked out an idea of just how to approach the duo. He swung his legs off the bed and sat up. He was ready to go put his plan into action. Just then there was a no nonsense knock on his door. He went to open it when he heard Dale on the other side. The voice was distinctive. He wasn't yelling, quite. But he was sure talking louder than in a polite parlor voice.

"Mister Eggers. We know you are in there. We need to talk, you and Ella and me. Our plans for the road, to do what we discussed, we need to talk." Joe noted that he had been careful not to mention any specifics. No place or company names, no mention of a dam or of railroad rights of way. Even in the James you never knew who might be listening.

Ella jumped in. "We need your expertise and advice. We need you to help us spike their plans."

Maybe you need to spike their plans, but that is the last thing I want, thought Joe.

"One moment" he answered. Calmly waiting for thirty or forty seconds to regain at least some initiative, he walked over and cracked the door.

Dale shoved the door open and forced his way in, pushed by Ella. Joe was taken aback by her sudden aggressiveness.

Dale snarled, "I know you were in Denver yesterday. What were you doing? You were with Myron Mast. What did you talk about? Did you tell him? Why did you spend the night there? If you rolled over and told them, I'll, I'll..."

"You'll what?" asked an angry Joe. He saw red.

"You and your 'friend' here are always making threats. Why don't you go out and actually do something? So far all I've seen you do is to follow me, a fellow UP man, around. And ask me suspicious questions. A lot of good that does. For the love of God, I am tired of your useless, stupid shenanigans."

Ella jumped in. "We're not talking about us but about you and what you are doing. Don't you change the subject!"

Dale nodded. He too was a little surprised at her sudden assertiveness. She continued.

"What did you tell Mast? Dale tells me he has a briefcase he is guarding like life itself. What is in it? You have been talking with Moffat employees while we have been out on the proposed route. How do we know you have been working for us on our side, not for something or somebody else?"

She paused for a moment, gathering her thoughts. "You call our efforts shenanigans. Well, what we have done, you don't know. We have been working hard to sow doubt and distrust, all along the line and in work camps. And! And, it was us, me! who came up with the best idea yet to stop them.

But you, all you can do is traipse around and talk to some Moffat employees about who knows what. That is all we want to know, what are you saying out there?"

Eggers glared at her then turned his eye on Dale.

"You clowns are busy trying to play troublemaker, as if anyone pays attention. You have been too busy playing spy to actually talk to people. If you had, you would have found out some things. Like I have."

They watched, saying nothing. Dale made a "come on" motion with his hand.

Joe made them wait, then threw out the bait. Again, he stretched the truth to suit his aims.

"Mast heard of some sort of plans to block access to the Gore Canyon. He was hazy about just what but seemed concerned. He ran me down to ask about the rumor. He wouldn't tell me what he knew or where he heard it or anything." He paused for effect.

"Reading between the lines I think that company dick, Steven or Steuben or something, got onto it somehow." Here Joe flat out lied. He had to sow mistrust, make them doubt themselves.

"I found out from another source that he can get copies of telegrams sent from Denver. Have you been sending information to New York about your quote unquote plan? Maybe he got a copy of something, or at least got to read it."

He paused, trying to see what impact his talk was having.

"Anyway, I told Mast I knew nothing. Nothing about the Gore Canyon and nothing about blocking it. All I did was talk to him. You ought to try it some time. Actually, I was able to wheedle more information out of him than he from me. Get him talking about the road and you can learn a lot."

Joe made a show of pausing to concentrate, to remember. "Come to think of it, Mast did have a briefcase. And he did hold it close. Maybe it held some important information or papers. I don't know. I never got a look inside it. And I sure couldn't just ask, 'say what do you have in that case you guard so closely?', now could I?"

Dale stepped up and got close, facing Joe inches away. "So you didn't tell Mast or anyone else anything?"

"That is what I am saying. In fact if anything, it is you divulging information to them. I suspect that your telegram got read before it left town. And they likely know about you. And your sidekick there." He glanced at Ella as he said this.

He had an inspiration, one which surely should get rid of the two troublemakers.

"If I were you, I'd think about moving on. Mr. Harriman sent us out here to do a job. He didn't send you out here to follow me. And he certainly didn't want you to allow your messages to be read by those you are spying on. He expects better of his people."

The couple exchanged looks and the conversation lagged. Then Ella spoke up.

"If we find out you are lying, we will be back."

Dale added, "And we will find you."

Joe fired back. "More big talk."

They left. Joe grinned as the door closed. Perfect. He had a story to tell Mr. H about the duo. Now he saw a way to leave the company cleanly. He could resign and not be under a cloud. He felt free, and knew that it was time to start the transition to his new life in Colorado.

Good riddance to Ella and Dale. He was glad to shed them. Those two buffoons were likely now going to chase after the company bull, Steu. The guy probably knew nothing about outgoing wires. Whether he did or not, he would take no guff. In fact he was the type to relish a confrontation. Guys like him loved to meet up with a couple of trouble-makers hired by the competition.

And, Joe realized, they would probably also try to find Mik. It would take them time to find and talk to all those folks. By then it would be too late for them. Soon, Mik's big friend would be done with whatever important job he had. The Dale and Ella duo would be disgraced. If they were smart they would get out of town before then. But that wasn't his problem.

Joe laid back down, hands behind his head, enjoying the success. Already he was thinking of ways to meet Mr. Moffat.

As Eggers enjoyed his victory, Dale and Ella left the hotel. At the same time, in Eldorado Springs, the funeral was done and the mourning was winding down. At least it was for the non family members. Not so easy for the family. They had many pieces of their lives to pick up yet.

Steu and Mik went in to pay a short visit to the Pruden family. The family sat in the living room. Mik wondered at the parents' strength.

"Mr. Pruden, Mrs. Pruden, I am so sorry. I didn't get to know Seth real well but he seemed a nice young man. No doubt he will be missed."

Charlie looked at him with deep, numbed eyes. "Thank you. It is beyond words."

Jenny Pruden had pain filled words, reliving the past days. "Oh my God, how can I stand it. They brought my boy home dead."

Steu and others made their condolences and offered what help they could. The thought of a young life, gone, added extra sorrow. Gathering to see off a loved one who had enjoyed seventy or eighty years of life was reason enough to grieve. Having to get together to remember one who got to live and enjoy not even two decades was worse. So short a life seemed somehow unfair and even cruel.

Every person has strengths and weaknesses, skills, blind spots and special insights. A person may be a user, a drifter, a worker, a leader. The gods in their wisdom put every person's skills to use somehow. To those of us here on the ground, to regular people, some of the skills used seem put to unproductive ends. That is not for us to say: in the long run a mean or sordid act today may have generous and beneficial results a week or a year or decades later. Sad to say, the reverse is true as well. Generously intended acts can have unpleasant, unintended consequences. Some things don't make sense in this life. Perhaps those who have crossed the river understand it all.

Mik and Wentz felt well for having paid respects. They were ready to go back to work and intended to go up the hill. The thing was, neither was entirely sure if the camp was at the new or old location.

Steu called in a favor and got Mik a horse to ride. They headed up to camp at a walk, side by side.

Steu was sad but put aside the Prudens' anguish. He had done all he could, having said good bye to Seth Pruden. He was back on the job, thinking railroad and security. "So if Cam is up filing the deed, these characters… What do they call themselves?"

"Dale Smertz, Dale and Ella."

"So if Cam has successfully filed the deed, this combo of Dale and Ella are out of business. For now at least. Is that how you read it?"

"Yeah. The thing is, they may not know it yet. So they may try to go after him to stop him. Or at least throw a wrench in the works to buy time."

Steu asked, "What about you? They saw you with Eggers, right? Do you think they will come after you? Try to see what you know, or something?"

"Could be. I'll have to keep an eye out."

"You know where I am. Let me know if you sense trouble."

He looked closely at his friend. "You aren't armed. Do you need a sidearm?"

Mik considered that. He really didn't want to carry a gun. Still, he wasn't sure just how loco this Dale character or his flighty friend might be. "I hope it doesn't come to that but I'd better have something."

"Stop by my tent, I'll get you set up with a good one."

The old camp was pretty much abandoned. A few workers picked up loose items and saw to cleanup and so forth. Mik and Steu had to follow the trail about two miles up the grade to the new location.

"Cam will be pleased that this move went off without any big problems," observed Mik.

"Yeah, I hope he makes it back tomorrow. That would mean his job with the deed is done. He'll be as glad as I am that the Gore Canyon sideshow is over. Now we can get back to the important stuff. Pushing track up the canyon."

Mik stopped by Steu's tent for a sidearm, then went and found a tent to sleep in. He couldn't bring himself to return to the dreary, sad boarding house tonight. The Prudens needed some alone time. They didn't need him hanging around. More important to Mik, he had some thinking to do.

He missed Sula. He missed his friends and cell phones and cold beer and TV and cars and everything. He wondered how had he managed to land in the midst of the wrangling over railroad development? How did he end up having a central role to play in the progress of Mr. Moffat's road?

Was it time to bail out of this bizarre adventure? The road was progressing. There was potential personal danger lurking in the form of a tall man and a woman dressed as a man. There could well be, probably were, other hazardous unknowns on the horizon.

Where was that spot he came in from? It was way down the road from here, far from the new camp...Sleep overtook the worries and he dreamt of his wife. It was a lonely dream because she was far away in a place he could see but couldn't quite reach. He saw and heard her but she couldn't hear him calling.

With morning, decisions were made. In Boulder, a couple decided how they would try to run down a threat. Across town, a man decided he would move his base of operations. At the new camp by tunnel six, the visitor from another time decided that it was not time to try to leave. Not quite yet.

Ella shook her head, hair flying. She wouldn't understand if someone had told her, but her hair cascaded elegantly around, like in a TV ad for shampoo. The sensation of long hair sent her thoughts off on a tangent. Maybe it was time to start dressing as a woman again? Men's clothing was boring and baggy. At first she liked the stares she got in public, but that was getting old. She would make that change soon, in the next day or two. Bur first, another issue. Ella yanked her mind back to the immediate problem.

"I don't trust that Joe Eggers, Dale. We need to contact New York somehow and see what they say. He said he was a 'fellow UP' man but I'm not so sure. He may be something else."

"No, we don't want to involve New York. We can't tell them that. They'd know then that we are out of control. We can't admit that we don't know who and what is happening out here. Besides, even if he is UP, the last thing they want is to referee a tussle among company people in the field. Better we figure it out and settle it ourselves. So, the thing to do is, I—we—need to nose around a bit." He thought for a moment, holding her attention.

"One thing we need to do for sure. We need to check on telegrams. Find out if its true that Wentz and the Denver Northwestern are reading our telegrams. Maybe so, maybe not. Either way, we need to know. I don't see how but we need to find out. If they are reading our mail we need to find another way to communicate. Fast. And tell New York."

"Well, alright, but I still think we ought to find out the story on Joe Eggers. He doesn't ring true."

Dale continued, almost as if she hadn't spoken.

"If not, well, we'll have to figure things out. Then we'll have to figure out why Eggers told us we were being snooped."

He paused, frowned, and continued. So much to do! "I think the main thing is, we need to find that Myron Mast. Didn't someone say he went by Mik? Doesn't matter. We need to find out what he knows. Maybe we ought to try to get to Wentz too."

She shrugged. "But where do we do that? Last you saw he was in Marshall. He could be in Denver, here in Boulder, anywhere."

"He's a railroad man isn't he? If I were to bet I'd say he went back to the construction camp on the road. Let's head up there. I want to have a talk with him, just a couple of folks, a nice friendly talk."

"And if he doesn't want to talk? What then?"

Dale answered the question by looking her in the eye as he picked up a revolver and put it in his pocket. "Let's go see what this Mik character knows."

In a way, Joe was sorry to leave Boulder. He glanced around, especially up at the cliffs west of town as he checked out of the James Hotel that morning. On a whim, he asked about them. The clerk was happy to tell him.

"Yes sir. Those cliffs look kind of like a row of laundry irons leaned up against the mountain, business side out. They are spectacular, aren't they? We call them 'The Flatirons.'"

It was time, Joe had decided, to move up. His plan was to take the Presidential Suite in the Station Hotel in Denver. He liked the location and the clerk seemed personable. He smiled a lot, like he was trying not to laugh out loud. Joe liked that attitude. And he figured he may as well let someone else pay his bills while he could. For at least a while he could cover the rooms with his expense account from Harriman's office. After that got cut off he would figure something else out.

A real plus, the main reason, was that the Station Hotel was close to the headquarters of the Denver Northwestern and Pacific. He felt he was already practically a trusted investor and advisor to the officers of that road. Joe wanted to build on that, to get close and involved in the company.

Mik woke up in tent he had appropriated, unsettled by his dreams, not sure for a moment where he was. It came to him pretty quickly. He arose, washed and shaved with a basin of cold water. That experience certainly didn't raise his spirits. The breakfast tent was nearly empty. He joined Steu who was savoring a second cup of coffee.

He wanted the security man to know his plans for the day. "If things went well for Cam he'll be back today. I think

I had better go down to Denver to check. There may be some follow up or loose ends to tie together."

Steu met his eyes, saying nothing. Mik continued.

"If he ran into problems I may need to go over to Hot Sulphur. Or if he is back in town, I want to see him, find out how things went. And I want to sit in when he and Mr. Sumner meet. We all want to be sure the i's are dotted and t's crossed. So I'll be heading out this morning." He paused, adding almost apologetically, "I just wanted someone to know where I am. I'll phone or wire from Denver if anything is up."

Wentz nodded. "Alright. You know you can cut straight down from here to town. You don't need to go back through tunnel four and down that way."

"I wondered about that. Thanks." With that, Mik headed to Eldorado Springs, caught a ride to Marshall, and the train to Denver. He did take the briefcase with him. It was empty but he wanted to leave it at the main office. Someone could use it. If he chanced to meet Dale on the way, it would be good to be seen hugging it still. Mik was relieved but also annoyed and dismayed to see Joe was on the same train.

"Hello Mik. I wondered where you were."

Mik ignored the implied question. Joe continued, "And I see you still have the briefcase."

Mik had his own questions, not implied but asked outright. "Yes. Tell me, what of Mr. Dale Smertz? Did you stall him in Boulder? And his friend Ella? Where are they now? Great God, man, don't tell me they got away."

Joe wanted to tread lightly. He felt obligated to let his companion know that the duo might be looking, maybe even gunning for him. The man was clearly a trusted part of the Denver Northwestern organization and he didn't want to antagonize him. That might hurt his chances to invest. For that matter, and this was an afterthought, he kind of liked Mik and didn't want to him hurt.

On the other hand, he didn't want to let slip to Mik that he had all but sicced the pair on him. No one needed to know that he did it to remove himself from the suspicion of Mr. Harriman. These thoughts passed through his head in a flash, and the pause in conversation was hardly noticeable. He responded.

"They do not know that we know their plans for a dam. I expect they will thrash around and try to find out what we do know. Now, they seem to know who you are and who Wentz is. They may well try to talk to one of you." He tried to read Mik's expression, who gave away nothing with a bland nod.

He continued, trying to put on a positive spin. "Hopefully by the time they figure things out it will be too late to act."

Change the subject, thought Joe. He hadn't really answered Mik's questions.

"Say, I'm moving to Denver. Want to be closer to the railroad since I'll be investing in it." He hoped for an opening to wangle an invitation to accompany Mik. Wherever he was headed it probably had to do with his friend's job and the railroad.

Mik didn't take the bait.

"Oh really, well I wish you the best on that." He still did not fully, one hundred percent trust this man. No way he would tell him where he was headed. The man didn't know who Cam was and Mik meant to keep it that way. He was not going to let this Joe character know he was going to a meeting with Cam, Mr. Sumner, and maybe even Mr. Moffat. He certainly wouldn't invite the man along.

The conversation lagged, then they bantered. By tacit agreement they stuck to general railroad talk. Soon they found themselves at Union Station. Joe went to check on his baggage and confirm his hotel booking. Mik took the opportunity to leave. He was out the door and gone before Joe returned.

The meeting with Cam and Mr. Sumner was brief. Moffat did not attend. Sumner, usually a two syllable man, was positively talkative.

"Braun, we all are relieved and gratified to have the deed filed. Because of it, the Gore Canyon route is clear for the road. You did good work. You took on a potentially dangerous situation which could have ended badly. And you successfully carried out your instructions. Again, good work."

He glanced at Mik. "Both of you. It was good thinking to split up. To confuse and delay your possible pursuers."

He looked back at the big foreman. "Cam, I am increasing your salary by $5 per week. And if you want a supervising office job it is yours."

The foreman thought for not more than five seconds.

"No, Mr. Sumner, thank you. I am quite happy to be outdoors, out on the road. I love pushing tunnels through and track up the grade. It just isn't in me to push paper. But, I am certainly grateful for the raise, can't tell you enough. It will help me and my family tremendously. But, no thank you to the indoors job."

He looked at Mik. "I think we need to head back. I have to see how the move went." His face changed, becoming sharper and more focused. "I have been thinking about a new technique for drilling and blasting. I think we will try it out in tunnel seven…" Hands were shaken all around and the two men took their leave. Mik left the briefcase there.

Joe Eggers was still arranging his rooms at the hotel and did not see them enter Union Station.

As the train approached Marshall, they stood, ready to get off as the train. It slowed and stopped. Mik got off first, and spoke.

"I know how to get direct to the new camp. Its a shorter route, let's do that."

"No, I want to go through the old campsite. I want to see it with my own eyes. Need to be dead sure that there are no loose ends. Then I am ready to turn and concentrate on the grade for the new stretch. When I get to that, I want no distractions. Let's go up the old way to tunnel four and across."

Earlier that day, Dale and Ella had done the same, going up the old route to the old camp location. From there they carefully followed the grade towards the new camp.

Ella nattered, "I told you they were moving camp. Nothing to see here. Let's just go to the new camp, maybe we'll see Wentz, or Mast, or learn something useful." They walked quietly north, alert to anyone they might meet.

Dale muttered, "Wentz. Damn company dick. I'd like to meet him in an alley with a club like his brethren have used on me."

In the new camp things were settling down. Proof of this was that people were back to watching and reporting, not just moving boxes and setting up tents. Steu had gotten word of two people coming up the grade from the old camp. He was glad that the training to pass the word of any strangers in the area had stuck.

Time to go check the report out, he thought. "Hey, Johanssen," he nudged an assistant. "Let's go see what gives with these two people. Give them a proper greeting."

XV

DALE WAS AHEAD OF HIS PARTNER AS THEY WORKED THEIR WAY along the rough railroad grade towards the new camp. They walked silently, almost stealthily. He was upset and still muttering about that damned company bull Steuben Wentz. And how he would love the opportunity to whale on him. Just once! He and Ella came around a corner.

To his surprise, there stood the company dick himself. With him was another man.

They were momentarily surprised by the encounter. Dale couldn't think what to do. Ella kept her wits. She smirked and said, just loud enough for her companion but no one else to hear,

"Well, Dale, here's your chance. Be quick and you can grab his club!"

While walking up, Dale had worked up a head of steam. He resented and disliked cops and security men in general. And he remembered a few rough encounters with guards like Steu. He really resented Steu and all he stood for. That resentment plus worry fueled his efforts to figure out how much the man knew. Would he somehow know they were coming up to the camp? Would they see him? Did he know who they worked for? Did he know anything about Joe Eggers? How about their proposed dam in Gore Canyon? Could he really read any telegram he wanted to, coming into or going out of Denver? Had he and Mast talked?

Imagination is a funny thing, a place in the mind where anything can happen. Things often look really good there. When reality calls, what looks good in imagination often turns out to be so-so at best. Sometimes it is not good at all. The prospect of a conflict with Steu seemed a fine thing to Dale when it was in his fantasies. Bring it on!

A confrontation was not so desirable when he and Ella in fact walked into one. Dale was completely wrongfooted. His bravado cracked and fell to pieces when he actually saw Steu standing astride the path. The security man's arms were crossed, his eyes hard, and his body language confidently and serenely said "This is my railroad!"

To boot, there was another security man with him. Both wore sidearms and for good measure the other guy carried a shotgun. He too looked Dale in the eye as he racked the gun, closing it up and making it a weapon not a big open hinge. The mechanical rasp of the metal on metal indicated that a shell was in the firing chamber. The gesture punctuated by the sound had its intended, intimidating effect.

After a nanosecond's doubt and confusion, Dale tried to take the initiative. After all, he told himself, he had a loaded revolver in his pocket. He took half a step towards the two men and looked Steu in the eye. He was tall and was used to looking down into peoples' eyes. Not today—it was straight across. To grab the initiative, he talked trash.

"Wentz, your boss is in it deep. No way he can make this project work. I hear that soon the road will hit a barrier up in the mountains. Moffat will have to fold his tent. You and all his other underlings will be out of a job. If anyone will have you, you'll have to go back to being a yard bull. You'll be looking for hobos in railroad cars. Checking sidings after midnight."

Unimpressed, Steu let him talk. He was curious what he would say. He kept Dale fixed with a steely glare, pinned like a butterfly.

Dale pressed on. "Yes, the Denver Northwestern and Pacific will die before it ever gets going. But you know that. Hell, we know that you are reading our telegrams and messages. You know how bad things really are. Tell me, when do you think the collapse will happen? Are you ready to go back to work for someone else?"

Ella jumped in. "Your men are being mistreated and worked too hard. They're made to drill, and blast, and do other dangerous, difficult jobs. And the poor animals on the worksite! They are not fed right and are overworked. All for a project doomed to fail. Have you no conscience? We ought to bring in a union. For workers' rights! That would protect the men. And we need—they need—animal cruelty inspectors as well."

Steu didn't know what to make of Dale's accusation about reading their mail, or their telegrams. He wasn't sure what the accusation was really getting at. He figured the guy was just fishing. Common tactic, throw out something outlandish to see the reaction and to see what the other guy knows. Fair enough, he had played that game hundreds of times.

But Ella was a wild card, again. Had she not jumped in he would have fenced with Smertz for a while. It was kind of fun in a way, both sides posturing, learning what they could, hiding what they didn't want known. When he was satisfied or tired of the game, Steu simply would have kicked them out, genially but firmly.

But the talk about a union was a different matter.

Far as Steu was concerned, this was poison. Unions were nothing but trouble. They riled up workers, stopped work, ran up expenses, and generally caused problems. He was ready to mix things up any time. Not a problem. But a union? He and the road didn't need the distractions which came with talk of forming a union.

If you had asked most any manager of most any railroad, they would have said this: A man could run his company any way he wanted and a bunch of union organizers had no say. If a man wanted to hire somebody and pay them for work done, that was his business. It was between the man hired and the company owner, only. There was no need for someone from back east to tell people what they could and couldn't do. The very idea made no sense, none at all.

Steu wanted to stomp on that union talk like on a bug. And animal cruelty inspectors? Who the hell had heard of such a silly thing? The owners and users of animals knew exactly how to feed and care for a beast. They knew how to treat it right to get the most work and longest life. No soft handed office dwelling "inspector" had any business anywhere around a railroad job. That idea, too, needed to be stopped cold.

He hardened his stare even more, putting on his best bad cop, intimidating look. His tone of voice was intended to overawe and coerce.

"You are trespassing on railroad property, private property. Further, you are interfering in a private business. You have no say, nothing to do, with the railroad's operations. You are to leave now. Do not come onto company property again. Do you understand?"

He looked back and forth between Dale and Ella but got no response, just a hostile glare from each. He went on.

"If you do not leave, you will pay the price. You will be met with arrest or if need be, force. Our guards" here he glanced at his assistant Johanssen—"have shotguns. They don't carry them for fun. Our men have been known to use them if they are threatened or if their warnings are ignored."

Dale tried to match up. "Big talk. Soon your road will be drowned in the Colorado River and you'll be looking for work."

Steu took a step forward, hand on his sidearm. "You are lucky that I am in a good mood today. I will not press charges. In fact I will let you walk away. Turn around. Go back down the grade to the first exit, past tunnel four, by the old camp we just moved. Then leave the railroad grade and go down the hill. From there I don't care where you go. Let me be clear. This is the last time I want to see you on or even near company property. Do you understand?"

Johanssen's shotgun swung up from where he had it pointed at the ground. Now it was aimed in the general direction of the two trespassers. He flicked the safety off with an exaggerated motion, staring at Dale.

Time for posturing was over. Discretion won over valor. Dale Smertz and Ella, agents of the Union Pacific Railroad, backed down. Without a word, at the same time, they turned and started walking. Steu called after them. "Get off the grade first chance you get. Johanssen here will be watching to help you get off the mountain."

Johanssen smiled wickedly and started to amble down the track, keeping the duo in sight. He cradled the shotgun lovingly.

Steu too smiled and loudly, for effect, added a chaser. "Remember, Johanssen, if you fire that shotgun I need a written report, in triplicate. So think twice before you do it!"

Ella and Dale silently walked down the grade. Each was thinking about the confrontation. Dale tried to put a good face on their defeat. He grinned.

"Did you see him blink when I said he was reading our telegrams? I think I hit a nerve. They'll think twice before they do that again!" His grin faded. He knew that was a load of manure. He was actually thinking exactly what Ella blurted out.

"If they are reading our messages they know all about us. About the dam. And the workers we have contacted. And the ranchers and others we talked to along the route. If they know all of that, what good are we?" She frowned, and continued.

"We are doing Mr. Harriman no benefit. If anything the opposite, we are harming the UP." They both scowled. They didn't want to acknowledge it. Each had a soul searing moment of clarity, no fun at all. An unblinking realization that they could look honestly at for only a brief time before shying away.

Ella was frustrated and disappointed. She hadn't dared attack Steu. Nor could she say anything to the creep following them with the shotgun. Instead she flailed at her partner.

"Big man, Dale. Some big man. You were talking about wanting to meet that guy with a club. When you got the chance you sure made me proud, yessir. He ran you off with your tail between your legs! Big talk, no walk."

"Shutup. I ain't going up against two revolvers and a shotgun with just one revolver and a mouthy woman. Maybe you're not smart enough to see that but I sure am."

She instantly regretted her outburst.

"Yeah, they did have us outgunned. You're right. I shouldn't have said what I did, sorry." She stopped him and looked him in the eye, searching for some certainty. Then she asked the big question.

"The thing is, what are we going to do now? They know us. They know who we've talked to out here. They know who we work for and who we report to. Sooner or later New York will know that too. We are useless here now. Worse than useless, we are a liability. Of no use to the Union Pacific at all. Our reputations are shot, gone, ruined."

The silence as they realized their predicament lasted maybe a minute. Then she went on.

"Think about it Dale, if New York finds out we allowed a leak, they won't be happy. Maybe we didn't allow a leak, maybe it was already there. Even so, we didn't check before we put confidential business over the wire. We should have. We're being paid to think of such things."

She shook her head in disgust and sorrow. The inevitable conclusion came to her. "Maybe we'd better disappear. Go to California or Texas or somewhere. Somewhere Mr. Harriman won't look for us."

As they walked, the loaded shotgun at their backs pressed on their spirits. Options and possibilities were gone over. Several plans and alternatives were discussed. They were all based on Steu reading their telegrams and reporting them to his bosses. The assumption was false, but that never did occur to them. In their minds, things had gone to hell and they needed to skedaddle. In their minds they were already on their way out of town.

Mik and Cam stopped by Prudens. Cam wanted a change of clothes and to make his condolences. He had missed much while delivering and filing the deed.

Both were relieved to see the family trying to get back in the routine. Charlie was working with a hired man in the fields, haying. The rhythm of the scythe and the rake took all their attention, and the routine was comforting. Jennie and Odessa were washing and cooking, very much their normal slate of tasks.

Cam asked after Ted and found out he had left to go out on a job. It was up on the top of Berthoud Pass of all places. There he would lead a survey team for a water diversion ditch coming in from the west side. After laying it out he would oversee its construction. It was good to see that the family was starting to recover and rebuild after the shock. Seth's sudden passing would leave a hole and a scar but they had to go on.

Each man talked briefly with the family. There was work to be done on the railroad so they didn't dawdle.

They started up the road towards tunnel four. They were on foot so Cam could inspect the route closely and thoroughly. He was happy to be back near his project. Mik filled him in on the past days. Then he turned to the immediate concern. "I wonder if Dale and Ella know you filed the deed."

Cam chuckled and shrugged at the same time.

"If they don't yet they will find out soon enough. Doesn't matter. We're good, the future of our road is secure. Nothing they can do about it. You know, there are drifters and troublemakers hanging around every railroad. Even if they leave some other rascal will soon show up. I guess it is just part of the business." He paused.

"I am just glad to be back on the ground, pushing grade and laying track. I would be happy if I never had to deliver another paper again." Cam earnestly looked the roadside and surrounding country over, making sure his railroad was progressing well.

Mik shrugged. "I'm sure you are. Still, those two bother me. They are a loose end. Joe thought they might be laying for me today. And maybe you too if they are really on the ball. So I guess we want to keep an eye out."

Timing is everything in life, the saying goes.

Just as Mik spoke, who should come around a turn in the trail but Ella and Dale. They were paying no attention. Talking, the two were intent on some important matter or decision. Two hikers came up the hill, two down, and none expected the encounter. They came face to face and stopped.

Dale, thinking quickly, asked a question. He had nothing to lose and might learn something. "Mik, what did Eggers tell you about us? Our plans?"

For Mik, this cemented the thought that Eggers was likely just a friend of convenience. It was convenient for him, that is. Truth be told, he was out for himself alone. Be that as it may, Mik couldn't resist a dig.

"Plans? What, are you a big shot businessman now?"

He kind of smirked but got no rise from either. So he continued. "Eggers has said nothing much. He is always talking about investing in Mister Moffat's road. But talk is cheap. If any money has been offered I am certainly not aware of it."

Mik let that sink in. Then he added, "He did say that you told him that you two were agents for the competition. For Harriman's Union Pacific."

Ella, unable to listen any more, chimed in. "Yes, but what about our plans? Did he talk about them?"

Cam did not know who these folks were. He said nothing at first, merely observed. From their look and Mik's reactions, he decided that they were the infamous Dale and Ella. The pair he had heard so much about. They didn't look like they were "laying" for Mik. They looked like harmless, helpless eccentrics, not like someone who could and would do you harm.

Regardless, he saw where they were going with their questions. He decided to jump in, get to the heart of the matter. He wanted to shut them up and see them off. He had had it with these people. They were getting in the way of his scraping grade and laying track.

"Do you mean the plan for a dam in the Gore Canyon? To stop the Denver Northwestern & Pacific Railway? To force it to go up and over the Park Range and Rabbit Ears Range? To cause it more expense and time? To choke off its access to points west?"

He looked back and forth from the man to the woman for a moment. They were surprised that he knew the plan and the thinking behind it. Who was this guy anyway?

Then Cam delivered his coup.

"Our railway owns deeded, filed right of way through that canyon. No one will stop us from laying rail all the way to where we want to go. We saw you guys and your "plan" coming from a ways off. It never was really much of an obstacle. But whatever it was, it has been eliminated. Dissolved. Avoided. Erased. Whatever you want to say, it is not a barrier to the Moffat Road."

Dale was incredulous. "You didn't read our telegrams to New York? You already knew?"

"A company from out east was organized to build a dam there. We got our deed recorded before they got their construction permit. End of story."

Dale and Ella looked at each other, and grinned. They could stay on the company payroll and do what they did best.

Now they could go on making trouble for trusts and corporations, agitating their workers, and trying to help animals. And they would still get paid for it! They didn't have to run off to another state and start over! Ella could even start the new wardrobe she wanted, and dress as a woman this time!

Neither Mik nor Cam saw a threat from the duo. Neither wanted to to waste any more time on them. Mik spoke up.

"So you two are done here."

Cam nodded, and looked between Dale and Ella. In the distance he saw Johanssen standing, cradling his shotgun, staring at the pair.

"You two will be moving on then. Stay off my railroad."

The gangly man and mannishly dressed woman nodded. Ella couldn't resist a parting shot aimed at Cam.

"You should treat your animals and men better. You wait, unions and animal inspectors will prevail. The forty hour work week will be adopted. And your sort will be in the dustbin!" Even as she was saying this, she and Dale started down the hill, a spring in their step.

Mik looked around, getting his bearings. "Cam, you go ahead. I'll follow in a minute."

Cam nodded, rolling his eyes at El's outburst. Then he waved at Johanssen, motioning him to wait up. He strode up the trail, eager to get back to work. He couldn't wait to meet new problems and push track up the canyon. The man was back in his element. The two men didn't look twice at the pair heading down or at Mik standing on the trail. They started up towards the new camp, talking and laughing.

Mik stood and thought, looking around, his heart full. Much as he missed Sula, he had unexpected feelings and emotions for friends known and made here. And he still wondered what had happened to poor Myron Mast. But, enough.

It was time. The decision was made and the opportunity was here and now. Out came the smart phone he had turned off shortly after arriving. He pulled up the pictures he had taken at the exact spot he had come into this world.

Mik walked to where it should be and stepped through.

XVI

Epilogue

This is a work of fiction. Characters and situations are imaginary and any resemblance to any person living or dead is unintended and coincidental. Dialogue is reconstructed from known facts and is augmented to fill out the story line. That said, there are a few exceptions to this disclaimer.

Charlie and Jennie Pruden, Ted and Odessa Moore, and Seth Pruden were real, living persons. Charlie and Jennie are the author's great grandparents; Ted and Odessa, his grandparents. Seth is a great uncle he never met.

Certain other characters in this book lived at the time. David Moffat, Horace Sumner, and Edward H. Harriman were players on the regional and national railroad stages. Moffat and Sumner were prime owner and chief engineer, respectively, of the Denver Northwestern & Pacific Railway. Harriman ran the Union Pacific and controlled a number of other railroads. He and many others used the not uncommon practice of hiring people to make problems for competitors and throw barriers in their way.

The New Century Power and Light Company was domiciled in New Jersey. This company actually attempted to obtain permits to build a dam, pipeline, and power plant in the Gore Canyon in 1903. There were other claimants and complications up and down the line of the Moffat Road. Most of those were easily handled or eliminated. This utility company out of the east presented a critical hurdle for Moffat and his people.

A deed of right of way ownership was in fact delivered and filed amid secrecy.

Mr. Sumner's son accomplished that task. He had the honor, or perhaps he drew the short straw. We don't know. The details of that assignment are lost to history. In any case it was he who made the trip. He took the deed quietly and as quickly as possible from Denver to the office of the Grand County Clerk in Hot Sulphur Springs Colorado. There he caused said clerk to file and record the deed. His so doing ensured the road's right of way through Gore Canyon with all that followed.

Charlie and Jennie Pruden along with Ted and Odessa Pruden Moore did live at the Pruden Ranch near Eldorado Springs. The house still stands as of this writing in 2014. The two Prudens were real entrepreneurs. They ran a room and board operation on their working ranch. They also had a contract to provide meat, dairy, and vegetables to the crews building the railroad across Eldorado Mountain. Charlie was a Justice of the Peace, the US Postmaster in Eldorado Springs, and had real estate interests.

Their son Seth Pruden lived for nineteen years. He was found by the side of the trail. The young man died alone there while on his way to work on the Moffat Road. He rests in a small cemetery up the hill from the ranch house.

Ted Moore was the surveyor and construction foreman for the Second Creek Ditch which can be seen on the west side of Berthoud Pass to this day. He lived in the ranch house until the late 1960's.

In the early years the Moffat Road made fast, visible progress. Crews laid usable track at a good rate. They worked up to the eastern side of the continental divide in 1904, to the town of Mammoth, now called Tolland. From there the line was built up and over to what is now the ski area at Winter Park. From there it went down to the town of Fraser, the Gore Canyon, and beyond.

This mountain stretch of the road climbed Rollins Pass. The rails more or less followed a Native American route overlaid by a later stagecoach track. The route ascended the summit of the continent and carried one of the highest operating steam railroads in the world. The road was designed and protected to operate year round which meant snowplows and avalanche sheds. The covered-in station and company town at the top was dubbed Corona. The Rollins Pass road was an engineering and railroading feat in itself. It was intended to be a quick fix while a tunnel was bored under the mountain.

Financing and construction issues delayed the building of the tunnel. It was finally opened in 1927. David Moffat spent his personal fortune on the road and died broke. He didn't live to see the opening of the tunnel which bears his name. The Denver, Northwestern and Pacific Railway Company didn't survive but the road and the big tunnel live on.

On Eldorado Mountain, apple trees have long grown here and there along the sides of the old access roads.

About the Author

STAN MOORE IS AN AVID READER, HISTORIAN, AND OUTDOORSman. A third generation Coloradan, he is a Vietnam veteran. When not reading up on today's and tomorrow's past, he is traveling, or more likely is outdoors. Exploring the mountains and canyons of Colorado and the Southwest are among his favorite activities. Moore very much enjoys family, wife, children and their spouses, grandchildren, and friends. He makes his home near Denver with his long suffering spouse and the two cats who let them stay there.

CPSIA information can be obtained
at www.ICGtesting.com
Printed in the USA
FFOW04n1632141114
8766FF